VOLUME 561

JANUARY 1999

THE ANNALS

of The American Academy *of* Political
and Social Science

ALAN W. HESTON, *Editor*
NEIL A. WEINER, *Assistant Editor*

EMOTIONAL LABOR IN
THE SERVICE ECONOMY

Special Editors of this Volume

RONNIE J. STEINBERG
Vanderbilt University
Nashville
Tennessee

DEBORAH M. FIGART
Richard Stockton College
Pomona
New Jersey

 SAGE Periodicals Press *THOUSAND OAKS LONDON NEW DELHI*

Origin and Purpose. The Academy was organized December 14, 1889, to promote the progress of political and social science, especially through publications and meetings. The Academy does not take sides in controverted questions, but seeks to gather and present reliable information to assist the public in forming an intelligent and accurate judgment.

Meetings. The Academy occasionally holds a meeting in the spring extending over two days.

Publications. THE ANNALS of the American Academy of Political and Social Science is the bimonthly publication of The Academy. Each issue contains articles on some prominent social or political problem, written at the invitation of the editors. Also, monographs are published from time to time, numbers of which are distributed to pertinent professional organizations. These volumes constitute important reference works on the topics with which they deal, and they are extensively cited by authorities throughout the United States and abroad. The papers presented at the meetings of The Academy are included in THE ANNALS.

Membership. Each member of The Academy receives THE ANNALS and may attend the meetings of The Academy. Membership is open only to individuals. Annual dues: $59.00 for the regular paperbound edition (clothbound, $86.00). Add $12.00 per year for membership outside the U.S.A. Members may also purchase single issues of THE ANNALS for $12.00 each (cloth-bound, $16.00). Add $2.00 for shipping and handling on all pre-paid orders.

Subscriptions. THE ANNALS of the American Academy of Political and Social Science (ISSN 0002-7162) is published six times annually—in January, March, May, July, September, and November. Institutions may subscribe to THE ANNALS at the annual rate: $281.00 (clothbound, $332.00). Add $12.00 per year for subscriptions outside the U.S.A. Institutional rates for single issues: $49.00 each (clothbound, $57.00).

Periodicals postage paid at Thousand Oaks, California, and additional offices.

Single issues of THE ANNALS may be obtained by individuals who are not members of The Academy for $19.00 each (clothbound, $29.00). Add $2.00 for shipping and handling on all prepaid orders. Single issues of THE ANNALS have proven to be excellent supplementary texts for classroom use. Direct inquiries regarding adoptions to THE ANNALS c/o Sage Publications (address below).

All correspondence concerning membership in The Academy, dues renewals, inquiries about membership status, and/or purchase of single issues of THE ANNALS should be sent to THE ANNALS c /o Sage Publications, Inc., 2455 Teller Road, Thousand Oaks, CA 91320. Telephone: (805) 499-0721; FAX/Order line: (805) 499-0871. *Please note that orders under $30 must be prepaid.* Sage affiliates in London and India will assist institutional subscribers abroad with regard to orders, claims, and inquiries for both subscriptions and single issues.

Printed on recycled, acid-free paper

THE ANNALS

© 1999 by The American Academy of Political and Social Science

Editorial Office: 3937 Chestnut Street, Philadelphia, PA 19104.

For information about membership* (individuals only) and subscriptions (institutions), address:

SAGE PUBLICATIONS, INC.
2455 Teller Road
Thousand Oaks, CA 91320

From India and South Asia, write to:
SAGE PUBLICATIONS INDIA Pvt. Ltd
P.O. Box 4215
New Delhi 110 048
INDIA

From the UK, Europe, the Middle East and Africa, write to:
SAGE PUBLICATIONS LTD
6 Bonhill Street
London EC2A 4PU
UNITED KINGDOM

SAGE Production Staff: ERIC LAW, LISA CUEVAS, DORIS HUS, and ROSE TYLAK
*Please note that members of The Academy receive THE ANNALS with their membership.
Library of Congress Catalog Card Number 98-60539
International Standard Serial Number ISSN 0002-7162
International Standard Book Number ISBN 0-7619-1733-0 (Vol. 561, 1999 paper)
International Standard Book Number ISBN 0-7619-1732-2 (Vol. 561, 1999 cloth)
Manufactured in the United States of America. First printing, January 1999.

The articles appearing in THE ANNALS are indexed in *Academic Index, Book Review Index, Combined Retrospective Index Sets, Current Contents, General Periodicals Index, Public Affairs Information Service Bulletin, Pro-Views,* and *Social Sciences Index.* They are also abstracted and indexed in *ABC Pol Sci, America: History and Life, Automatic Subject Citation Alert, Book Review Digest, Family Resources Database, Higher Education Abstracts, Historical Abstracts, Human Resources Abstracts, International Political Science Abstracts, Journal of Economic Literature, Managing Abstracts, Periodica Islamica, Sage Urban Studies Abstracts, Social Planning / Policy & Development Abstracts, Social Sciences Citation Index, Social Work Research & Abstracts, Sociological Abstracts, United States Political Science Documents,* and/or *Work Related Abstracts, Westlaw,* and are available on microfilm from University Microfilms, Ann Arbor, Michigan.

Information about membership rates, institutional subscriptions, and back issue prices may be found on the facing page.

Advertising. Current rates and specifications may be obtained by writing to THE ANNALS Advertising and Promotion Manager at the Thousand Oaks office (address above).

Claims. Claims for undelivered copies must be made no later than twelve months following month of publication. The publisher will supply missing copies when losses have been sustained in transit and when the reserve stock will permit.

Change of Address. Six weeks' advance notice must be given when notifying of change of address to ensure proper identification. Please specify name of journal. **POSTMASTER:** Send address changes to: THE ANNALS of the American Academy of Political and Social Science, c/o Sage Publications, Inc., 2455 Teller Road, Thousand Oaks, CA 91320.

THE ANNALS

of The American Academy of Political and Social Science

ALAN W. HESTON, *Editor*
NEIL A. WEINER, *Assistant Editor*

--------------- FORTHCOMING ---------------

See page 2 for information on Academy membership and
purchase of single volumes of **The Annals.**

CONTENTS

BOOK DEPARTMENT CONTENTS

INTERNATIONAL RELATIONS AND POLITICS

AFRICA, ASIA, AND LATIN AMERICA

EUROPE

UNITED STATES

SOCIOLOGY

ECONOMICS

ANNALS, *AAPSS*, **561**, January 1999

Emotional Labor Since
The Managed Heart

By RONNIE J. STEINBERG and DEBORAH M. FIGART

ABSTRACT: The phrase "emotional labor" was coined by sociologist Arlie Hochschild in 1983 in her classic book, *The Managed Heart*. Jobs requiring emotional labor typically necessitate contact with other people external to or within the organization, usually involving face-to-face or voice-to-voice contact, especially in service work. In this article, the authors summarize Hochschild's pathbreaking work and assess the state of the current multi- and interdisciplinary literature on emotional labor. They distinguish between two interrelated areas of research on emotional labor. The first area involves predominantly, though not exclusively, qualitative case studies of employees at workplaces in the service sector. A second set of studies, primarily quantitative, investigates the link between emotional labor at home, in different jobs, or in nurturing activities (a specific form of emotional labor) and its consequences for individual employees' job satisfaction, productivity, and pay.

Ronnie J. Steinberg is professor of sociology and director of the Women's Studies Program at Vanderbilt University. She is the author of Wages and Hours: Labor and Reform in Twentieth Century America *and editor of* Equal Employment Policy for Women *and* Job Training for Women. *She has authored or coauthored more than 35 articles on feminist reforms, employment policies, and gender-based labor market inequality. She edits the series* Women in the Political Economy, *for Temple University Press.*

Deborah M. Figart is associate professor of economics at Richard Stockton College. She is coauthor of Contesting the Market: Pay Equity and the Politics of Economic Restructuring. *She has written more than 30 articles on employment, wages, and work time and is a founding member of the International Association for Feminist Economics.*

THE job of flight attendant requires its incumbents to be "nicer than natural," while the job of bill collector involves being "nastier than natural," according to sociologist Arlie Hochschild. Hochschild, in her classic book, *The Managed Heart* (1983), called these occupations the "toe and heel" of the growing service sector, coining the phrase "emotional labor" to describe the work involved in being "nasty" or "nice." Most service jobs fall between these two extremes.[1]

Emotional labor emphasizes the relational rather than the task-based aspect of work found primarily but not exclusively in the service economy. It is labor-intensive work; it is skilled, effort-intensive, and productive labor. It creates value, affects productivity, and generates profit. It is why frontline service workers and paraprofessionals have been referred to by Cameron Macdonald and Carmen Sirianni (1996) as the "emotional proletariat" (3).

Consider a set of instructions drawn from an employee handbook distributed by a gourmet deli, which also serves a variety of specialty coffees. Two of the items in the company's mission statement make clear how important customer satisfaction is to the company's fiscal success. First, the company strives "to be a progressively balanced company that focuses on integrity and profitability by placing people and product first." Second, it works to "achieve a high level of excellence." A third objective is "to ensure that the 'guest' is wholeheartedly pampered so that the experience always exceeds the customer's satisfaction level."

The statement continues:

Our . . . company is a pleasant gathering spot where one can be sure to meet and greet neighbors and friends. We offer much more than just great food. [We] . . . challenge a way of life.

Remember . . . a positive attitude is a basic ingredient. . . . If you are not having fun, you can be sure the people around you won't be smiling either (customers or coworkers). . . . You control your attitude. . . . [Your] . . . attitude can make the difference in someone's entire day. . . . A friendly, positive, upbeat attitude will give you and the Company . . . [an advantage].

Customer courtesy begins and ends with you. Each and every employee, regardless of position, must demonstrate concern for total customer satisfaction. . . . Always. . . .

Under no circumstances should a customer ever wonder if you are having a bad day. Your troubles should be masked with a smile. Tension can be seen and received negatively resulting in an unhappy dining experience, or what is called *frustrated food*. . . . Once an unhappy or dissatisfied customer walks out the door, they are gone forever!

When . . . faced with a dissatisfied, upset or irate customer, do what it takes to change the situation into a positive experience . . . *no matter who or what is at fault!* (italics in original)

The employer advertises regularly that it is hiring "smiling faces," a phrase seen more and more frequently on billboards of fast-food national chains as well. The wages of employees to whom this company's explicit instructions are directed begin at $6.00 an hour, and employees can work their way up to $8.00 an hour. If they work full-time at 40 hours, year-round, they can earn as much as $12,000 to $16,000 before taxes. Yet the human relations skills, communication skills, and emotional effort necessary for this frontline work is considerable. By the employer's own admission, these dimensions of job content are critical to their profitability and even the survival of the company. Nonetheless, employees are not remunerated for these skills and job demands.

Viewing emotional labor more generally, Arlie Hochschild (1983) points to the need for an employee to "induce or suppress feeling in order to sustain the outward countenance that produces the proper state of mind in others" (7). In addition to performing mental and physical labor, Hochschild emphasizes how employees are required to manage or shape their own feelings to create, in their interaction with others, displays that affect others in desired ways.[2] Thus, while focusing on employee skills and effort, Hochschild's definition of emotional labor involved both the emotions of the employee performing the labor and the emotions of others to whom these emotions are addressed. Since the range of emotions most often captured in research on emotional labor is stereotypically associated with femininity, emotional labor has typically been identified with historically female jobs, although it is also performed by police officers, by managers, and by professionals with clients or the public. In this introductory article, we develop more fully the contours of the concept of emotional labor as characterized by Hochschild and others, after which we review

and assess the state of the current multi- and interdisciplinary literature that examines this form of work.

IDENTIFYING EMOTIONAL LABOR IN PAID EMPLOYMENT

Emotional labor is performed through face-to-face or voice-to-voice contact. Initially, Hochschild pointed to facial and bodily displays that were observable. Later scholars, however, broadened these mechanisms to include spoken word, tone of voice, and other "efforts that are expressed through behavior" (Wharton and Erickson 1993, 458; see also Rafaeli and Sutton 1987, 1989). Although some work activities involving emotional labor may intersect with sexuality at the workplace, most of them do not. For example, Barbara Gutek (1985) notes that secretaries, receptionists, and waitresses are expected, as part of the normal performance of their jobs, to be friendly and to look attractive. Some men interpret these behaviors, usually inappropriately, as sexual or romantic attraction, affecting both workers and their organizations. Moreover, at the extreme, such reactions may result in female employees' being sexually harassed. Emotional labor, though, is not the display of sexuality at the workplace, although smiling, touching, and flirting may be an implicit part of job content for certain occupations under some circumstances.

While Hochschild and scholars following her approach emphasize the work that is involved in performing emotional labor, Paula England and George Farkas represent another group of researchers on emotional labor. This second group proposes an alternative definition that underscores the effect of that emotional labor on others (1986). For them, emotional labor involves "efforts made to understand others, to have empathy with their situation, to feel their feelings as a part of one's own" (England and Farkas 1986, 91). In a similar vein, introducing the concept to a primarily British audience, sociologist Nicky James (1989) defines emotional labor as "the labour involved in dealing with other people's feelings, a core component of which is the regulation of emotions" (15). In other words, the purpose of emotional labor is to make customers feel good (in the case of retail sales) or feel bad (in the case of prison guards or police officers). In the labor of detectives and criminal interrogators, the object is not only to make suspects and alleged criminals feel bad but to have them confess (Stenross and Kleinman 1989; Rafaeli and Sutton 1991).

Emotional labor is not only differentiated on the basis of whether the employee's or the client's feelings are the focus of attention but also on the basis of the degree of authenticity of the employee's emotion. Here the concern is less the work that is being performed than the effect of emotional labor on the employees who perform it. Hochschild, for instance, differentiates between surface acting and deep acting (Hochschild 1979, 1983). In surface acting, the employee feigns emotion, so that the displayed emotion differs from what the employee actually feels. Deep acting, by contrast, focuses on inner feelings and tries to invoke the actual displayed feelings or emotions, as a method actor does when portraying a role.

Service workers may, for example, be trained to greet customers in a certain way, to smile, make eye contact, thank customers, and close a transaction with "Have a nice day" (see, for example, Leidner 1991, 1993; Sutton and Rafaeli 1988; Sutton 1991; Hall 1993). Other employees such as insurance sales agents learn very specific and detailed scripts for handling the patterned responses they are likely to receive as they knock on people's doors (Leidner 1991). Indeed, those who study emotional labor from this vantage point have uncovered management-defined norms, or "display rules," and management-controlled, routinized, and scripted performances. Some of these scripts are so detailed that they tie the specific response to each of the ways a customer might reply to a particular pitch. Hochschild notes that, in her case study of flight attendants, applicants are actually selected for their presumed capacity for performing emotional labor. Even after a careful hiring procedure, flight attendants receive training to enhance these qualities.

Even the authentic expression of emotion is work. According to Blake Ashforth and Ronald Humphrey (1993), it includes "spontaneous and genuine" emotion that can be displayed with little prompting (94): for example, a nurse's deeply felt concern for patients and those emotionally close to their patients, expressed as efforts to console, comfort, or empathize with them (see also O'Brien 1994).

A third way to differentiate the use of the concept of emotional labor is in terms of whether the effort is executed internally within the workplace or externally to clients, customers, or the public. Initially, studies of emotional labor focused exclusively on employees dealing with clients, customers, or the public outside the organization. Amy Wharton and Rebecca Erickson (1993) use the phrase "external boundary spanning" to refer to a worker's interactions with individuals outside the organization. More recent research has acknowledged that emotional labor is also performed within organizations when, for instance, the job holder is involved in managing the emotions of supervisors, subordinates, and coworkers, as in a paralegal's or a secretary's interactions with his or her supervisor or a manager's relationship with his or her assistant (Kunda 1992; Pierce 1995). Some social scientists suggest that managing emotions across hierarchical divisions within work organizations is better distinguished as emotional work (Lively 1998).

In this volume, Gideon Kunda and John Van Maanen examine the emotional labor performed by managers vis-à-vis their supervisors at a time of economic restructuring. These managers express full commitment to their firm while internally feeling insecure about their future job prospects within that firm (Kunda 1992; see also Pierce 1995). Using Wharton and Erickson's categories (1993), then, "internal boundary spanning," or what others call emotional work, encompasses not only an employee's

managing of subordinates or superiors (that is, influencing the feelings of others) but also an employee's feigning emotional responses he or she does not have. This categorization becomes problematic, however, in the characterization of the work of an employee who represents the department horizontally by interaction with other employees in other departments within the organization. Is the unit the department or the organization? Are the employee's skills, effort, and responsibilities utilized in representing her or his department an explicit requirement of the job, or are they something implicitly expected but which, if made explicit, would probably be denied by its beneficiaries?

RESEARCH ISSUES IN EMOTIONAL LABOR

The scholarly focus on emotional labor encompasses several research questions. Initially, research examined the effect of providing emotional labor on an employee's well-being, with special emphasis on the negative consequences for employees of burnout, fatigue, and emotional inauthenticity. To perform emotional labor, and in contrast with mental and physical work, employees must give something of themselves to others with whom they have no ongoing personal, noninstrumental relationship. Although sometimes they may form what would be considered authentic, caring relationships with clients or coworkers, this is not necessarily a requirement of the job. Whether or not they do care, they must pretend to care, in a way that involves what Van Maanen and Kunda (1989) call "self-investment" (54), suppressing or managing their own feelings or emotions. Even when such employees act authentically and spontaneously, to care about, manage, and absorb the emotional reactions of many others on a daily basis can, it is believed, have potentially negative consequences. Yet, ironically, the empirical picture has been far more mixed than scholars hypothesized. As Amy Wharton and her colleagues have found, emotional labor does not have a uniformly negative impact on job satisfaction (Wharton 1993; Wharton and Erickson 1995; see also Morris and Feldman 1996).

A second area of research on emotional labor explores both theoretically and empirically its contours as a dimension of organizational behavior. In recognizing that emotional labor is skilled labor in a variety of work settings, this research has sought to understand the relationship between emotional displays and organizational effectiveness. In the service sector, for example, attention to the customer has meant that managers are concerned about the impact of frontline service workers on measures such as product quality, sales volume, profit, and customer satisfaction. This body of scholarship also examines unremunerated, but nonetheless required, emotional labor up and down the job hierarchy and in the home. Such labor, called emotional work as well, facilitates smooth working relations where one employee (typically the subordinate) expresses and absorbs emotions, which results in fewer expressed workplace tensions.

A third area of inquiry in which emotional labor has been introduced is in the examination of compensation practices. Special attention is paid to the invisibility of emotional labor as a job requirement and the consequent lack of remuneration for the competent performance of those skills and the exertion of considerable effort. This research encompasses both job content that is required for the competent performance of the job (such as the work of registered nurses in hospitals) and emotional work that is not essential to the normal performance of the work but is expected by supervisors from the employee (as in the case of female paraprofessionals). In neither case is the employee compensated for the emotional labor performed. Indeed, in one study of compensation practices, Jacobs and Steinberg (1990) found that registered nurses actually lost money (net of other job characteristics) because they worked with difficult patients or clients.

In sum, jobs with emotional labor have several defining characteristics and may be analyzed along several dimensions. First, they require contact with other people external to or within the organization, usually involving face-to-face or voice-to-voice interaction, especially in service work. Emotional labor also requires a worker to produce an emotional state in another person while at the same time managing one's own emotions. The expression of emotional labor may be authentic, but it need not be so. It also may be expressed to clients and customers but is not limited to those who seek the services provided. Emotional labor expressed among coworkers as well as with supervisors and subordinates is an invisible, yet expected, component of job performance. Moreover, while emotional labor is reactive, it is not just reactive. Through selection, training, and supervision of employees and through the development of social scripts, employers are able to exercise a degree of control over the emotional labor of employees, thus affecting productivity and profit.

SITUATING THE LITERATURE ON EMOTIONAL LABOR

The scholarly attention to emotional labor grows out of the merger of two parallel research traditions, one on the sociology of emotions and the second on the social construction of skill in compensation practices. On one hand, the analysis of emotional labor emerges from the more general study of the sociology of emotion. Peggy Thoits (1989) and Arlie Hochschild (1990) have provided excellent summaries of the emergence of this area of inquiry. This focus on emotions from a sociological perspective recognizes that human beings not only are rational economic actors but also act on the basis of emotional attachments or affective commitments (Thoits 1989, 317). As Hochschild (1990) put it, "We make the simple assertion that what we feel is fully as important to the outcome of social affairs as what we think or do" (117).[3]

The concept of emotional labor has also been articulated by those focusing on the social construction of skill, especially gendered definitions of skill. Feminist explorations of the social construction of skill emerged out of a concern with the pay inequities identified by the comparable-worth or pay-equity movement. This literature also flourished in response to research on the labor process, most notably in relation to the deskilling hypothesis forwarded in Harry Braverman's exemplary book, *Labor and Monopoly Capital* (1974).

Braverman hypothesized a tendency for monopoly capitalism to lower the skill content of jobs. Initially, research on historically female jobs, and especially on clerical work, accepted the deskilling hypothesis by suggesting that the introduction of new technology reduced the skill necessary to perform the job (Feldberg and Glenn 1979). This hypothesis was debated for some years, until feminists recast the issue to suggest that the very concept of what constitutes skill is gendered (Phillips and Taylor 1986; Steinberg 1990; Gaskell 1991; Wajcman 1991). Hegemonic notions of skill have relied on increasingly outdated assumptions about work based on nineteenth- and early-twentieth-century craft and manufacturing work. Yet the expansion of the service sector has intensified the necessity of expanding the definitions of skill to include emotional labor.

As developed in relation to gender-based wage discrimination, critiques of off-the-shelf job evaluation systems, developed in the 1940s and 1950s, noted the unacknowledged and uncompensated skills differentially found in historically female work. The range of these skills included not only technical skill but also human relations and communication skills, aspects of which fall within the contours of emotional labor (Steinberg and Walter 1992). Research in comparable worth has also uncovered the significance of effort and responsibility in compensation outcomes. As Steinberg points out in her contribution to the present volume, the measurement of what sociologists call emotional labor includes not only skill components but also emotional effort, aspects of supervisory responsibility as well as responsibility for client well-being.

In our review of the body of research on emotional labor, we distinguish between two interrelated types of inquiry that address these three broad questions. The first and most common route involves case studies of employees at workplaces in the service sector, research that is predominantly, though not exclusively, qualitative in its methodology. These studies examine the contours of emotional labor, its impact on employee satisfaction or well-being, or its effect on productivity or profits. In most of these studies, a major issue has been the gendered character of this work. A second focus of investigation links emotional labor at home and at work or in different jobs with caring work or nurturing. This research tends to be quantitative, and much of it assesses the impact of nurturing on job satisfaction or on pay.

CASE STUDIES OF EMOTIONAL LABOR ON THE JOB

Case studies of emotional labor have appeared primarily in sociology and management journals.[4] In sociology, the emphasis has been on documenting the content of emotional labor and, to a large extent, its gendered aspects. Studies have also examined the impact of emotional labor on incumbents' job satisfaction and on negative psychological effects of performing the work. For organizational behavior scholars, the motivation has been to call attention to the importance of managing emotion effectively in order to improve employee recruitment and training, increase product quality, and raise profitability.

The qualitative studies examined jobs with the most obvious emotional labor content, most notably those positions in the service sector that deal with the public. These include relatively low-paid service workers who must help customers, such as supermarket and convenience store cashiers (Sutton and Rafaeli 1988; Rafaeli 1989), fast-food service workers at McDonald's (Leidner 1991, 1993), waiters and waitresses (Hall 1993; Paules 1996), hair stylists (Parkinson 1996), and even ride operators at Disneyland (Van Maanen and Kunda 1989). Emotional labor is also extensive within many female-dominated professions and in professional occupations involving considerable work in helping and caring for others, such as paralegals, flight attendants, nurses (Pierce 1995; Hochschild 1983; Smith 1988; James 1989;

O'Brien 1994). Other researchers have studied traditionally male or male-concentrated jobs such as engineers (Van Maanen and Kunda 1989), detectives or criminal interrogators (Stenross and Kleinman 1989; Rafaeli and Sutton 1991; Sutton 1991), and door-to-door insurance agents (Leidner 1991).

A few examples from sociological research confirm the gendered dimension of labor. In notable studies of the role of gendered scripts in performing emotional labor, Elaine Hall (1993) and Robin Leidner (1991, 1993) focused on the good service scripts of restaurant employers who reproduce traditional gender relations by constructing different scripts for male and female servers and also through the use of rules about demeanor and appearance. For example, management encouraged and trained women to smile, defer, and flirt with (male) customers, carefully monitoring body language, displays of emotion, and personalities. According to Hall, this organizational behavior structured the interaction of women servers as sexual objects. While Leidner's account (in this volume and elsewhere) of scripting among fast-food workers indicates that the scripts are relatively simple, they are still designed to offer consistent and positive service that will draw the customer back to the company to purchase other meals.

The gender-differentiated delivery of emotional labor is also echoed by Jennifer Pierce in her study of paralegals (1995; this volume). Women paralegals were expected to give (male) trial lawyers tremendous support through deference and care-

taking while managing their own anger and the anger of attorneys. Male paralegals, by contrast, were not expected to be nurturing, were treated by trial attorneys as if they were preparing for law school, and were often included in the lawyers' social gatherings. Annual performance reviews and job ratings, especially for female paralegals, entailed implicit evaluation of emotional labor job content, evaluating the paralegal's relationship to clients as well as her "attitude" in working with the legal staff (Pierce 1995, 88). Pierce recounts anecdotal evidence that supports her contention that gender ideology may influence these performance evaluations and thus the compensation these women receive for their work. Indeed, the employee's attitude as assessed in annual performance evaluations may be a neutral, acceptable proxy for employer expectations about appropriate emotional labor. Such assessments may also be gendered (Burton 1991; Martin this volume).

The gendered aspects of emotional labor can also affect job satisfaction, both whether workers enjoy their jobs and whether the tasks confirm their sense of gender identity. In a study of police detectives and sheriff interrogators interviewed by Stenross and Kleinman (1989), detectives viewed themselves as "crime solvers," maintaining that this more cerebral aspect of the job constituted "real detective work" (441). By implication, the emotional labor involved in servicing the community was less "real." Contrary to what the researchers expected, detectives disliked their interactions with the victims who were their clients, even though they were on the same side. Instead, detectives reported that they enjoyed their encounters ("matching wits") with alleged criminals. While these detectives could exert control in their aggressive questioning of suspects, they may well have been uncomfortable with the hand-holding and nurturing of those victimized by crime. Thus they defined their work in terms of its more masculine characteristics and expressed dislike for the feminine work of caring. In another example of how emotional labor contributes to the construction of gender identity at work, Leidner (1991) finds that insurance salesmen reconcile the content of their jobs with their sense of their own masculinity by viewing the transaction as a contest of wills requiring aggressive determination. They are less likely to acknowledge that selling insurance also requires a veneer of friendliness, empathy, and politeness.

Not all researchers are sensitive to the gendered meanings underlying emotional labor and to their consequences for workers. Consider O'Brien's study (1994) of the nursing profession in Great Britain. O'Brien believes that nurses' emotional labor is key to realizing the British health service's agenda to promote heart health. Even though he recognized that the nurses' tasks were imperative to organizational objectives, he did not examine whether they were paid for their emotional labor. In fact, O'Brien claimed that many of the skills possessed by nurses derived "not from the qualities of being a *nurse* but from the qualities of being

a *woman*" (399)—a statement that clearly rendered nurses' skills and the effort associated with such work as invisible by naturalizing and essentializing them.

The contribution of emotional labor to organizational goals has also been the focus of several articles in management journals. In the case studies by Anat Rafaeli, Robert Sutton, John Van Maanen, and Gideon Kunda, management's informal and formal norms about the emotional labor required by their jobs and those they supervise have been made visible. These authors argue that the expression of emotion at work ought to be taken seriously since it affects customer behavior, job satisfaction, sales, and labor productivity. Further, understanding the role that emotion plays can help organizations recruit properly socialized employees, as in the happy-faced Disneyland ride operators (Van Maanen and Kunda 1989), the socially comfortable flight attendants able to make airline passengers feel at home on an airplane (Hochschild 1983), or the aggressive interrogators or bill collectors able to strip away emotional defenses (Rafaeli and Sutton 1989; Sutton 1991; Rafaeli and Sutton 1991).

Implicit in these studies, as well, is the influence of cultural norms on selecting the appropriate person to perform different jobs. Gender is implicated within these social norms, which vary by culture. In the United States, for example, where service organizations emphasize emotional displays of friendliness, women are more likely to be hired to work in these organizations because it is believed that, on average, they smile and display more warmth than men do. Yet in Muslim culture, such displays are restricted by employees because they would provoke a sexual response (Rafaeli 1989; Rafaeli and Sutton 1989).

QUANTITATIVE RESEARCH ON EMOTIONAL DEMANDS

The empirical focus solely on occupational case studies has been criticized because it "obscures variability in work role emotional demands" (Wharton and Erickson 1993, 457-58). Such case studies also fall short in demonstrating that there is a connection between emotional labor and job satisfaction or worker burnout. Attempting to correct for these shortcomings, Wharton (1993) sampled employees in a bank and a hospital to evaluate the consequences of performing emotional labor. The effect of emotional labor was captured by comparing the coefficients across two regression equations on the variable jobs with emotional labor content and the variable jobs presumably without emotional labor content. Wharton found that workers employed in jobs identified as having significant amounts of emotional labor were no more likely than others to experience emotional exhaustion. Thus, if employees in work involving emotional labor suffer from emotional exhaustion, it may not be due to the emotional demands of their job. Instead, Wharton found that a worker's level of job autonomy and involvement with his or her job af-

fected whether employees experienced emotional exhaustion.

In general, exploratory research that has attempted to measure emotional labor does so by treating it as a dichotomous or dummy variable. For example, one study of convenience store clerks coded emotional labor as the presence or absence of displays of positive behaviors. The four actions measured as evidence of emotional labor were greeting, thanking, smiling, and eye contact (Sutton and Rafaeli 1988). These variables were then aggregated to create an index of positive emotion in a multiple regression analysis of the effect of emotional labor on store sales. In contrast to what was expected, store sales were not directly related to displays of positive emotional connection. Further analysis suggested that the presence of long lines in busy stores were indicators of sales and, in these situations, sales clerks did not have time to engage in emotional labor in each transaction.

Another stream of quantitative research has evaluated the impact of emotion management at work on earnings either at the level of the individual firm or utilizing national data sets. Because, to date, much of the kind of emotional labor performed for pay has been perceived to be consistent with an essentialist conception of nurturing and mothering work done in the home, feminist sociologists have pointed out that such work is undervalued, if it is even recognized (James 1989; Steinberg 1990).

In the comparable-worth study for the state of New York, Steinberg et al.

(1985) found that several of 112 questions on the job-content questionnaire clustered around two factors associated with emotional labor: "contact with difficult clients" and "communication with the public." In wage models, both of these factors were significantly related to the gender (female) composition of the job, and "communication with the public" produced a negative effect on earnings. "Contact with difficult clients" had no statistically significant effect, positive or negative, on wages.

Utilizing multiple regression analysis, a select set of studies led by Paula England and Barbara Kilbourne using national data sets tests the effect of nurturant social skills on wages. Determinants of earnings by detailed job category are the independent variables, including controls for characteristics of jobs taken from the *Dictionary of Occupational Titles* (see England et al. 1994; Kilbourne et al. 1994). The authors used a nurture dummy variable for those job characteristics where incumbents spend a major share of working hours providing face-to-face service to clients and customers. The conclusions emerging from this work are that nurturance is more likely found to be performed in historically female jobs and that occupations involving nurturance skills lower wages of both women and men, ceteris paribus. Although these empirical studies accept a somewhat crude measure of emotional labor as provided by the *Dictionary of Occupational Titles*, they both recognize the prevalence of emotional labor as part of job content and acknowledge the role of emotional labor in compensation.

OVERVIEW OF THE
PRESENT COLLECTION

Each of the contributors to this issue of *The Annals* has conducted significant, original research on emotional labor in the United States, Canada, or Europe. In this *Annals* issue, they evaluate emotion work in the home and emotional labor in paid employment. They examine this form of work through the lenses of organizational behavior, sociology, and economics. The articles mirror the methodology of prior research to date, a blend of theory with case studies, participant-observation, and quantitative empirical analyses. The range of jobs covered in this research on paid and unpaid labor in the service economy include professionals, managers, college and university professors, paralegals, police officers, fast-food workers, child care workers, and mothers.

We begin this volume with three articles that explore the relationship between the concept of emotional labor and ideas about caring and nurturance at home and in the workplace. In her article, British feminist economist Susan Himmelweit pulls together concepts from home and paid work. She evaluates the gendered separation of (paid) labor from caring. The former is rewarded while the latter is not. Sociologist Paula England and economist Nancy Folbre continue to examine caring that is unpaid at home but paid when it is performed for a wage. They compare caring labor to related concepts and review the empirical evidence of the monetary penalty for holding a job that involves caring work. They conclude by assessing theoretical explanations for the devaluation of caring.

The final article in this section is written by Marjorie DeVault, whose 1991 study, *Feeding the Family*, offers an original account of the invisible work that goes into accomplishing successful family meals. In her piece in the present volume, she broadens our vision both of what a family looks like and of the range of invisible emotional labor that is performed in families. She focuses on unpaid caring activities performed in personal life. She accentuates emotional work that has been relatively neglected in the literature: advocacy of children by female single-headed households; survival or identity work for people of color; and "passing" and resistance work for lesbian and gay parents.

The second group of articles comprises case studies of emotional labor in specific jobs, major occupational titles, or sectors of the economy. Gideon Kunda and John Van Maanen contextualize the emotional labor that managers and professionals must do to create an image of loyalty and commitment to the firm. Even at a time of globalization and economic restructuring, and when the model of lifetime job security in exchange for managerial loyalty has broken down, managers and professionals must express loyalty, however unreciprocated.

Looking at a different class of workers, Robin Leidner discusses emotional labor in the service sector. She focuses on low- to midlevel frontline service workers: clerical workers, insurance agents, fast-food servers, salespeople, and waitresses. These workers often have highly routinized scripts that they must follow, extending managerial control to aspects of workers' selves formerly not subject to employer intervention. Leidner had anticipated finding a great deal of employee resistance, but she found less than she had expected. She suggests that, in interactive service work, the conflict between labor and management shifted to a three-way tug-of-war between workers, management, and clients, with workers and management sharing the same objectives toward clients. Clients often were manipulated into buying products or services they did not necessarily need. Scripted emotional labor can assist employees in enforcing their will over others. Thus, while there are costs to employees in performing employer-controlled, scripted behavior and in manipulating others, there are also the practical and psychological benefits of distancing oneself from these emotional performances.

Marcia Bellas offers new insights into the emotional labor involved in academic work. Her article provides an accompaniment to her earlier work on remuneration of employees in academia and the wage discrimination suffered by female professors. Using the three categories of teaching, research, and service, she illustrates the emotional labor associated with the work in each of these categories performed by university professors. She especially focuses on teaching, both inside and outside the classroom, to illustrate the range of emotional labor expected of professors by their students and how teaching commitments and behaviors often vary by gender.

In her article, Susan Martin graphically depicts the critical forms of emotional labor in police work. There is a wide gap between the work police officers actually do and the public image of their work. This discrepancy serves to maintain the belief that the police are tough and masculine because they fight criminals. With aggressive crime fighting seen as the real work of police, their role in the provision of services and caretaking activities is downplayed. Through the lens of police work, we can see as well that both the actual and the perceived emotional content of the job vary by the sex of the incumbent, as female officers violate, on a daily basis, the assumption that only men can fight crime. Despite an organizational and occupational culture that privileges stereotypically masculine activities, effective police work involves both the "command presence," to borrow Susan Martin's phrase, that is the basis for decisive action and good communication, listening, and empathy skills.

Based upon fieldwork in two large firms, Jennifer Pierce evaluates "emotional labor among paralegals." Her study demonstrates that the gendered stratification of law firms reproduces gender relations through the emotional requirements for the paralegal position. Male and female paralegals perform, and are expected to execute, different forms of emotional labor. Neither are remunerated for their emotional labor.

The third section of this *Annals* issue contains three articles that seek to measure emotional labor on the job, the consequences of performing emotional labor, and the valuation of emotional demands as part of job content. In the first article, Ronnie Steinberg describes a gender-neutral job evaluation system she developed in conjunction with a court-ordered decision of the Ontario, Canada, Pay Equity Tribunal to resolve a wage discrimination conflict involving registered nurses working for the municipality of Haldimand-Norfolk. Pay equity, a reform that seeks to correct for wage discrimination in historically female jobs, emerged in the late 1970s. Studies to identify gender bias in compensation practices that resulted in lower wages for incumbents of historically female jobs discovered that emotional labor required in the normal performance of a job was treated as invisible and thus not remunerated. The gender-neutral job evaluation system and the job content questionnaire that describes work according to 17 broad dimensions of work include the measurement and evaluation of emotional labor as a significant component of 4 of these broad dimensions. While the system was tested during deliberations to resolve the conflict, and the results of the job evaluation exercise could have been implemented, the bargaining parties chose, instead, to resolve the conflict through a negotiated settlement, in which average pay equity wage adjustments fell short of the adjustments that would have been made as a result of the measurement of emotional labor and other invisible work found disproportionately in historically female jobs.

The evaluation system and questionnaire represent a preliminary attempt to measure emotional labor fully and con- cretely, awaiting modification and refinement.

Amy Wharton, whose research on the impact of emotional labor on job satisfaction remains at the cutting edge, summarizes the importance of the repercussions of emotional labor in her article. She highlights findings on both the economic and noneconomic costs and rewards in the workplace and at home, drawn from the qualitative and quantitative research literature. She concludes that although there are negative psychosocial consequences under certain circumstances, jobs requiring emotional demands also have a positive effect on workers' well-being.

The final article, by volume editors Ronnie Steinberg and Deborah Figart, demonstrates that many of the same emotional skills, demands, and responsibilities found in paid employment are found not only in female jobs but also in male jobs. Steinberg and Figart develop two indexes to measure the emotional labor and emotional demands associated with the work of registered nurses, police officers, and managers. Their findings are consistent with their assertion that emotional labor is not unique to historically female work, even though we privilege it in female work because of our imposition of gender stereotypes.

CONCLUDING THOUGHTS

Research on emotional labor has blossomed in the 15 years since the publication of *The Managed Heart*. While the definition first proposed by Arlie Hochschild has stood the test of time, many others represented in this volume have grounded and shaped our understanding of what it means—to employees and service recipients, as well as to organizational dynamics and firm profitability—to "induce or suppress feeling" or to produce "the proper state of mind in others." Not only are the contours of emotional labor more complex than can be captured by reference only to whole jobs, but reactions to the performance of emotional labor by employees also varies, as does resistance to manipulation by clients and customers. While emotional labor can be used toward beneficial ends, it can also be used to undercut legitimate client anger or to manipulate unnecessary purchases. Thus neither its use nor its moral consequences can be reduced to easily generalized conclusions.

As emotional labor, and especially caring work, moves from the household to the labor market, the distinction between the public and private spheres, so central to the process of industrialization, is blurred. As emotional labor is made more visible in paid work, it becomes increasingly visible as a critical aspect of unpaid work in the home. As the family is fed, so it is nurtured, as Marjorie DeVault shows in her astute description of the dozens of actions that go unnoticed but are critical to the construction of the family itself. As our society moves toward ever greater diversity in the types of living arrangements that are labeled as family, emotion work expands to legitimate these forms of intimate connections—forms that violate hegemonic conceptions of family life. Similarly, as we move emotional labor from the family and into the workplace, it is required not only in meeting product and service objectives but also in building effective and acceptable working relationships.

The increased visibility of emotional labor in the workplace and in the home raises many ethical and practical issues. While it is clear that manipulation of other people for personal ends was not invented with the articulation of the prevalence of emotional labor, the many layers of manipulation—of self and others—embedded in emotional labor are greatly clarified. Ethical issues surrounding emotional labor have been raised by Hochschild and others. But few have gone beyond these initial remarks to reflect deeply about the moral, and even social, consequences of our ever more sophisticated tools for inauthentic authenticity.

Nor have many confronted the issue of pay for the performance of emotional labor, involving, as it does, skills, responsibilities, and effort. Which types of jobs should receive compensation for the emotional labor they perform? An easy choice would be the registered nurses who work in a variety of specialties for the municipality of Haldimand-Norfolk. So, too, would be university professors, police officers, waitresses, insurance agents, flight attendants, and others whose work directly meets primary organizational directives. But should insecure managers who convey loyalty be remunerated for the skills and effort involved in conveying that orientation? Should female paralegals be paid for all of the emotional labor they perform for the lawyer or lawyers with whom they work? What about emotional labor performed in the home—should such work be compensated? Should housework studies begin measuring the time involved to perform emotional labor? What effect would modifying the allocation of household work studies to encompass emotional labor have on the findings that the gap between men's and women's work in the home is declining? These and related questions have received little attention. As we take stock of what we know about emotional labor, we hope to stimulate a serious debate about these issues.

As our economy moves increasingly toward the provision of services and as the public-private distinction further blurs, the skills, effort, and responsibilities associated with emotional labor will become more central to our understanding of what it means to work. We hope this collection of articles contributes to a broader understanding of emotional labor: what it is, what is involved in its performance, who does it, its effects on those who perform it and to whom it is directed, its gendered and hierarchical character, and its significance to competent and collegial work performance. We hope, as well, that this volume stimulates further inquiries into the contours and consequences of emotional labor for individuals, for relationships, for workplaces, and for the larger culture that shapes us all.

Notes

1. Hochschild (1983, 153, 235) calculated that about one-third of all workers and one-half of women workers executed some type of emotional labor in the labor market.

2. For Hochschild (1990), the phrase "emotion work" refers to the emotion management we do in private life, whereas "emotional labor" is the emotion management we do for a wage (118). DeVault (this issue) evaluates emotion work.

3. An emotion involves an appraisal of a situational context, a change in a physiological bodily sensation, the display of gestures, and a cultural label applied to one or more of the foregoing (Thoits 1989, 318). For Thoits, emotions are distinguished from feelings, affects, moods, or sentiments (318). A feeling is a more diffuse or mild emotion (Hochschild 1990, 118-19).

4. Many additional studies of stress and professional burnout among certain types of workers have been authored by psychologists.

References

Ashforth, Blake E. and Ronald H. Humphrey. 1993. Emotional Labor in Service Roles: The Influence of Identity. *Academy of Management Review* 18(1):18-115.

Braverman, Harry. 1974. *Labor and Monopoly Capital*. New York: Monthly Review Press.

Burton, Clare. 1991. *The Promise and the Price: The Struggle for Equal Opportunity in Women's Employment*. North Sydney, Australia: Allen & Unwin.

DeVault, Marjorie. 1991. *Feeding the Family: The Social Organization of Caring as Gendered Work*. Chicago: University of Chicago Press.

England, Paula and George Farkas. 1986. *Households, Employment, and Gender: A Social, Economic, and Demographic View*. New York: Aldine.

England, Paula, Melissa S. Herbert, Barbara Stanek Kilbourne, Lori L. Reid, and Lori McCready Megdal. 1994. The Gendered Valuation of Occupations and Skills: Earnings in 1980 Census Occupations. *Social Forces* 73(1):65-99.

Feldberg, Roslyn L. and Evelyn Nakano Glenn. 1979. Male and Female: Job Versus Gender Models in the Sociology of Work. *Social Problems* 26(5):524-38.

Gaskell, Jane. 1991. What Counts as Skill? Reflections on Pay Equity. In *Just Wages: A Feminist Assessment of Pay Equity*, ed. Judy Fudge and Patricia McDermott. Toronto: University of Toronto Press.

Gutek, Barbara A. 1985. *Sex and the Workplace: The Impact of Sexual Behavior and Harassment on Women, Men, and Organizations*. San Francisco: Jossey-Bass.

Hall, Elaine J. 1993. Smiling, Deferring, and Flirting: Doing Gender by Giving "Good Service." *Work and Occupations* 20(4):452-71.

Hochschild, Arlie Russell. 1979. Emotion Work, Feeling Rules, and Social Structure. *American Journal of Sociology* 85(3):551-75.

———. 1983. *The Managed Heart: Commercialization of Human Feeling*. Berkeley: University of California Press.

———. 1990. Ideology and Emotion Management: A Perspective and Path for Future Research. In *Research Agendas in the Sociology of Emotion*, ed. Theodore D. Kemper. Albany: State University of New York Press.

Jacobs, Jerry A. and Ronnie J. Steinberg. 1990. Compensating Differentials and the Male-Female Wage Gap: Evidence from the New York State Comparable Worth Study. *Social Forces* 69(2):439-68.

James, Nicky. 1989. Emotional Labour: Skill and Work in the Social Regulation of Feelings. *Sociological Review* 37(1):15-42.

Kilbourne, Barbara Stanck, George Farkas, Kurt Beron, Dorothea Weir, and Paula England. 1994. Returns to

Skill, Compensating Differentials, and Gender Bias: Effects of Occupational Characteristics on the Wages of White Women and Men. *American Journal of Sociology* 100(3):689-719.

Kunda, Gideon. 1992. *Engineering Culture: Control and Commitment in a High-Tech Corporation*. Philadelphia: Temple University Press.

Leidner, Robin. 1991. Selling Hamburgers and Selling Insurance: Gender, Work, and Identity in Interactive Service Jobs. *Gender & Society* 5(2):154-77.

———. 1993. *Fast Food, Fast Talk: Service Work and the Routinization of Everyday Life*. Berkeley: University of California Press.

Lively, Kathryn. 1998. Discussant comments for the panel on emotional labor, annual conference of the Eastern Sociological Society, 16 Mar.

Macdonald, Cameron Lynne and Carmen Sirianni, eds. 1996. *Working in the Service Society*. Philadelphia: Temple University Press.

Morris, J. Andrew and Daniel C. Feldman. 1996. The Dimensions, Antecedents, and Consequences of Emotional Labor. *Academy of Management Review* 21(4):986-1010.

O'Brien, Martin. 1994. The Managed Heart Revisited: Health and Social Control. *Sociological Review* 42(3):393-413.

Parkinson, Brian. 1996. *Changing Moods: The Psychology of Mood and Mood Regulation*. New York: Addison Wesley Longman.

Paules, Greta Foff. 1996. Resisting the Symbolism Among Waitresses. In *Working in the Service Society*, ed. Cameron Lynne Macdonald and Carmen Sirianni. Philadelphia: Temple University Press.

Phillips, Anne and Barbara Taylor. 1986. Sex and Skill. In *Waged Work: A Reader*, ed. Feminist Review. London: Virago.

Pierce, Jennifer L. 1995. *Gender Trials: Emotional Lives in Contemporary Law Firms*. Berkeley: University of California Press.

Rafaeli, Anat. 1989. When Cashiers Meet Customers: An Analysis of the Role of Supermarket Cashiers. *Academy of Management Journal* 32(2): 245-73.

Rafaeli, Anat and Robert Sutton. 1987. Expression of Emotion as Part of the Work Role. *Academy of Management Review* 12(1):23-37.

———. 1989. The Expression of Emotion in Organizational Life. In *Research in Organizational Behavior*, ed. Barry M. Staw and L. L. Cummings. Vol. 11. Greenwich, CT: JAI Press.

———. 1991. Emotional Contrast Strategies as Means of Social Influence: Lessons from Criminal Interrogators and Bill Collectors. *Academy of Management Journal* 34(4):749-75.

Smith, Pam. 1988. The Emotional Labor of Nursing. *Nursing Times* 84:50-51.

Steinberg, Ronnie J. 1990. Social Construction of Skill: Gender, Power, and Comparable Worth. *Work and Occupations* 17(4):449-82.

Steinberg, Ronnie J., Lois Haignere, Carol Possin, Donald Treiman, and Cynthia H. Chertos. 1985. *New York State Comparable Worth Study*. Albany, NY: Center for Women in Government.

Steinberg, Ronnie J. and W. Lawrence Walter. 1992. Making Women's Work Visible: The Case of Nursing—First Steps in the Design of a Gender-Neutral Job Comparison System. In *Exploring the Quincentenniel: The Policy Challenges of Gender, Diversity, and International Exchange*. Washington, DC: Institute for Women's Policy Research.

Stenross, Barbara and Sherryl Kleinman. 1989. The Highs and Lows of Emotional Labor: Detectives' Encounters with Criminals and Victims.

Journal of Contemporary Ethnography 17(4):435-52.

Sutton, Robert I. 1991. Maintaining Norms About Expressed Emotions: The Case of Bill Collectors. *Administrative Science Quarterly* 36(June): 245-68.

Sutton, Robert I. and Anat Rafaeli. 1988. Untangling the Relationship Between Displayed Emotions and Organizational Sales: The Case of Convenience Stores. *Academy of Management Journal* 31(3):461-87.

Thoits, Peggy A. 1989. The Sociology of Emotions. *Annual Review of Sociology* 15:317-42.

Van Maanen, John and Gideon Kunda. 1989. "Real Feelings": Emotional Expressions and Organizational Culture. In *Research in Organizational Behavior*, ed. Barry M. Staw and L. L. Cummings. Vol. 11. Greenwich, CT: JAI Press.

Wajcman, Judy. 1991. Patriarchy, Technology, and Conceptions of Skill. *Work and Occupations* 18(1):29-45.

Wharton, Amy S. 1993. The Affective Consequences of Service Work: Managing Emotions on the Job. *Work and Occupations* 20(2):205-32.

Wharton, Amy S. and Rebecca J. Erickson. 1993. Managing Emotions on the Job and at Home: Understanding the Consequences of Multiple Emotional Roles. *Academy of Management Review* 18(3):457-86.

———. 1995. The Consequences of Caring: Exploring the Link Between Women's Job and Family Emotion Work. *Sociological Quarterly* 36(2): 273-96.

Caring Labor

By SUSAN HIMMELWEIT

ABSTRACT: Caring has two different aspects: the motivation of caring for other people and the activity of caring for them. Furthermore, good-quality care depends on the developing relationship between a carer and the person cared for. In paid employment, however, relationships are usually assumed to be reduced to an exchange transaction and motivation to be simply monetary, provoking concern about whether paying for care diminishes its quality and authenticity. Similar issues have arisen in the context of emotional labor more generally. Much emotional labor, however, is of a transitory nature in which no long-term relationship is set up between worker and customer. This article argues that because of the relationship that tends to develop, paid caring may not be so different from unpaid caring. Rather, caring occupations should be seen as part of a whole class of occupations that are not fully commodified, in which workers have motivations that are not purely monetary and also care about the results of their work.

Susan Himmelweit is senior lecturer in economics at the Open University. She has previously taught women's studies at the University of Sydney and worked on women's employment issues for the Greater London Council. She has published widely in feminist economics, particularly focusing on issues to do with unpaid domestic labor, reproduction, and caring. She is on the board of directors of the International Association for Feminist Economics and an associate editor of its journal Feminist Economics.

T HE idea of caring labor involves a strange concatenation of terms, pulling together concepts from both sides of the institutional divide between home and work. Industrialization consolidated that divide by creating the workplace as a physical and social institution with its own norms and practices, distinct from those of the home. These norms did not include meeting the care needs of the young, the old, and the sick, nor even those of workers; all these were to be met outside paid labor time in the home, or its extension, the community.

This institutional separation was, of course, also a gendered one: stereotypically, that ideal employee unbothered by his own or others' needs during working time was male, and the "angel in the house" who tended to those needs was female. He did the labor, she did the caring. A defining characteristic of labor[1] is that it is done only for an extrinsic reward, whether that reward be pay for an employee, the price at which a self-employed producer can sell his product, or the use of the product itself for a subsistence producer. Caring, on the other hand, is not necessarily rewarded in any explicit way. Why people care cannot then be understood within the same rationality as labor. Instead, caring for others is typically explained as a natural human, but more frequently female, proclivity. Women care for others because it is in their nature to do so. Men labor because it is second nature to them, almost natural but needing certain social conditions to induce it. In particular, they do not labor for no reward.

In such a dichotomized picture, which places home, care, and women on one side and the workplace, paid labor, and men on the other, there is no room for caring labor. Labor is an activity done for an extrinsic reward; caring is frequently unrewarded. But this is not because caring does not involve work; much time and energy are spent on activities, in the workplace as well as at home, by men as well as women, that may or may not be rewarded, whose purpose is directly to cater to the welfare needs of others. Rather, it is the dichotomized picture that needs adjusting to remove the distorting dualism that leaves no room for care to cross the boundary into the workplace, or for work to be recognized in the caring activities that go on in the home.

In this article, I want to show how that dualism can be challenged. To do this, I shall first explore one of its poles, an abstract, highly idealized notion of caring as an unpaid domestic activity that is built on certain assumptions about the motivation and identity of carers and the type of relationship they form with the people for whom they care. Implicit, and sometimes explicit, in this discussion will be an equally abstract notion of the other pole of the dualism, paid employment, where no relationship is assumed but the simple exchange transaction by which a worker's ability to labor is purchased, and nothing further of her personhood is required or given. I shall then move on to considering whether and how the characteristics of caring change when caring becomes a form of paid work and what differences these changes make to the givers and recipients of care. In the following section, I shall consider what distinguishes such caring labor from other types of emotional labor before trying to resolve the puzzle of why the performance of emotional labor is usually taken to be a cost to the worker, whereas workers performing caring work frequently see it as a desirable aspect of their employment. In the concluding section, I shall explore some implications of my analysis for conceptions of work and labor more generally.

DIFFERENCES BETWEEN UNPAID DOMESTIC CARING AND PAID WORK

Caring is a difficult concept to pin down because it means two different things: both caring for and caring about another person. The first is the activity of catering directly to another person's needs, both physical and emotional; the second is the desire for the other's well-being that motivates the activity. A carer will not succeed in delivering good care unless she appears to the person being cared for (the caree) to be motivated by genuine concern for his well-being. One significant aspect of his well-being and the success of her caring, then, is his belief that he is being cared for by someone who cares about him.

This is not true of most paid work, nor indeed of all unpaid domestic work. There are many paid services and some domestic activities where motivation has no intrinsic importance to the activity itself. When a room is cleaned, its cleanliness can be assessed independently of the motivation of the person who cleaned it. She may have done the cleaning for

pay, for love, for fear of the consequences of not doing it, or even to enjoy the clean room herself, but the room will be in a similar state and the task of cleaning it will have been much the same whatever her motivation.

In the way it is assigned, however, unpaid domestic caring is more like other unpaid domestic activities and quite unlike paid labor. In general, people find themselves caring not because they consciously choose to do so but because of social norms that both legitimate the needs of certain people, such as young children's need for supervision, and give them a call on the time and energy of others in particular relationships to them. Typically, such norms assign responsibility for caring on the basis of an existing, usually kin or marital, frequently gendered, relationship such as that of parent to child or wife to husband. Caring responsibilities are not a choice in that sense, though negotiations may take place between people in appropriate relationships as to who specifically bears such responsibilities and how they are to be carried out.

Relationships matter not only in the allocation of caring; the process of caring is itself the development of a relationship. The care a carer provides is basically inseparable from the relationship that is being developed with the person she is caring for. Through that developing relationship, the carer also learns skills appropriate to caring for that particular caree. Other people may be able to care for that person, too, but in doing so they will be developing their own, different relationship. Similarly, a carer will have a different relationship with each of her carees. Caring activities cannot therefore be entirely bundled up into interchangeable tasks to be given to interchangeable people, because it matters who is doing what for whom. Further, a carer's identity and motivation are created and developed by her relationship with her caree. Even when caring is initiated in response to wider social expectations, as time goes on the relationship will develop its own specific obligations and dependencies. This characteristic of a developing relationship is another difference between caring and many other unpaid domestic tasks, and although such relationships may in practice develop during paid labor, the notion of paid labor certainly does not require this to be the case.

Caring often has two meanings, physical care and the more relational side on which I have concentrated so far, and the two usually go on simultaneously. It may in fact be impossible fully to care in the relational sense without also doing some of the physical work. Relationships cannot be developed in a vacuum; something has to be going on—whether it is the feeding of a young baby, helping an older child with homework, or pushing the wheelchair of an elderly parent—around which the relationship can develop. If people needed only physical care, then caring would be relatively simple and not easily distinguished from other types of domestic labor. However, when people need only emotional care, as a physically capable adult may do, then we tend to talk about this more as a need for friendship in the hope that it will be provided for in an equal relation-

ship with another adult rather than in an asymmetrical carer-caree relationship. In practice, what is talked about as care seems usually to include both physical and emotional activities.

Whether such an activity should count as care or a personal service depends largely on the type of relationship involved. Kari Waerness distinguishes between care and providing help and services to healthy adults, who could perform the activities themselves. She uses the term "caregiving work" to refer to "services, help and support given . . . to persons who according to generally accepted social norms, are dependent, i.e. persons who cannot take care of themselves" (Waerness 1984, 71). She considers that "care" might also be an appropriate term when healthy adults provide for each other's emotional and personal needs on an equal reciprocal basis—this is what I referred to as "friendship" earlier. However, there is frequently an imbalance, and, even in apparently symmetrical relationships, women are expected to and do provide more of such support than men. Where this is the case, Waerness considers that such excess care is more appropriately seen as a form of personal service.

Thus whether "caring" is an appropriate term for an activity depends in another way on the relationship involved: "care" should be reserved for relationships in which the recipients are dependents who cannot provide for their own needs, though more broadly it could be extended to include reciprocal relationships of true equality. No such distinction would make sense for paid work, where the market allocates a worker's product impersonally so that who the recipient is should not matter; the only requirement of a customer is the ability and willingness to pay. Gendered inequality in the domestic division of labor more generally frequently turns much caring into another form of servicing, though domestic labor done for children and others who genuinely cannot provide for themselves is just an aspect of their physical care.

In this section, I have examined some of the ways in which unpaid caring ideally differs from both paid labor and other unpaid domestic work. In doing so, I have emphasized a number of ways in which care in its unpaid domestic form is defined by the relationship between carer and caree. First, a carer's motivations and a caree's beliefs about those motivations are part of what being cared for means; the caree has to feel cared about in order for the care to be successful. Second, the responsibility for care for particular individuals tends to be assigned by social norms on the basis of specific, gendered, kin relationships. Third, the process of caring is itself the development of a particular caring relationship, so that the identity of both carer and caree matters. Finally, if care is not to be just a form of personal service, the relationship between caree and carer must be either one of dependence, in which the caree is not currently able to reciprocate by giving as well as receiving care, or a mutually caring one in which such reciprocation takes place on an equal basis.

PAID CARING

Over the past half century, the amount of time spent by women on unpaid domestic work has fallen. Although the proportion of that time spent on caring activities has risen, there has also been a concomitant growth in caring activities provided through the market (Gardiner 1997; Gershuny and Robinson 1988). In particular, paid child care is a burgeoning industry in most advanced capitalist countries, and the elderly, whether in institutions or in their own homes, are increasingly being looked after by paid workers. This means that the proportion of the labor force that is employed in jobs that involve caring labor is rising.

Implicit in the idealized abstract description of unpaid caring of the previous section was a contrasting equally abstract notion of paid employment. According to this notion, the motivation of a paid laborer is irrelevant to her performance, and, since she has no intrinsic interest in her work, her only motive for working is money. Workers choose jobs from the labor market, rather than being allocated to them through any existing relationship. Further, because jobs are relatively interchangeable and no relationships develop in the course of taking a job, workers will be ready to move at any time to a job with better pay. (Compensating differentials for the pleasantness or otherwise of working conditions and different types of work could be taken into account—but these just reflect how a worker likes to spend his time, not any intrinsic belief in the value of the work itself.)

The products of paid work are also allocated impersonally by the market, so that customers buy interchangeable products produced by interchangeable workers. Workers therefore have only a market relationship to the consumers of their work, and no deeper relationship can develop in the course of their work. Consumers are just customers, and since the only obligation set up is that of paying for services received, not reciprocating them, issues of dependency or inequality do not arise.

If all paid work conformed to this account, paid caring would be impossible. No meaningful relationship could develop between carer and caree/customer. Paid carers would not care about the welfare of those they were employed to care for, only about their own pay and working conditions. Carers would be allocated to carees on a market basis alone, changing jobs whenever market conditions provided better alternatives. The carees of paid carers would also feel and behave differently; instead of the gratitude of a dependent, as customers, they, or those who paid for their care, would expect to bargain about the terms and conditions of the care they purchased.

Much sociological research, however, shows that paid care is nothing like that. In terms very similar to those I used in the previous section, Challis and Davies (1986) talk of finding a developing relationship between paid carers and the elderly people they were employed to look after.[2] Paid carers were found to feel a strong sense of responsibility for the welfare of their clients and often undertook tasks beyond those specified

in their original contract. Further, because of strong attachments to their clients, helpers often did not like to change clients even when new clients were offered who would be more convenient for them. Finally, these strong attachments sometimes resulted in carers asking their own families to help with their clients: asking husbands to do odd jobs in their clients' homes, or preferring their own daughter rather than a paid substitute when they themselves could not cover their usual arrangements.

Challis and Davies interpret this as additional "informal care," that is, unpaid domestic care, being given as the relationship between client and paid carer develops. Other writers, notably those influenced by Scandinavian practices, where paid care for both children and old people has been common for many years, question whether this is a helpful way to see this phenomenon. Rather, they would argue, there is no reason to assume that personal attachments cannot develop in market relationships. It is not so much that we are adding an element of the unpaid to the paid but that paid relationships themselves can include strong feelings and personal attachments (Ungerson 1990, 21). Such writers criticize the former attitude as justifying the poor pay of care workers on the grounds that they are doing two jobs, a paid one and an unpaid one. Rather, caring, whether unpaid or paid, can and does consist of both labor and love (Nelson 1998). The main distinction in this view between unpaid and paid caring is in how particularistically it is allocated— whether on the basis of an existing relationship or to an initially unknown client—and this does not determine the relationship that subsequently develops (Waerness 1984, 74).

Hazel Qureshi (1990) analyzes some of the effects that the payment of carers has on the relationship between carer and caree and finds many of these are positive.[3] One effect is to give an elderly or disabled caree less anxiety about dependence and being a burden on the carer. Payment can be seen as in lieu of the reciprocal care that carees would like but are unable to offer, thus equalizing the relationship. This equalizing is even, as is often the case, where payment is by a third party: another family member, a voluntary agency, or the state. Carees also often appreciated paid help with more intimate physical tasks, such as bathing or toileting, as letting them retain their personal dignity with their family; women in particular were not used to having family members provide such intimate help. Further, recognizing the demands on their relatives' time, carees often preferred to be able to spend such time as they did have with their family free of such physical demands.

Many old people, however, did prefer care by relatives to paid care because they saw this as providing more of a personalized commitment. This idea, as well as cost cutting, lies behind the policy of successive U.K. governments of developing "care in the community," which often just means unpaid care by female relatives, in place of paid or institutional care, whose motivation is seen as less personal. However, care that is brought about through a sense of obligation or because "there is no one else" may not be appropriately motivated either. Qureshi (1990) found that, for women particularly, it could prove difficult to resist the pressure to care unpaid for their elderly relatives. Not all this pressure came from their own consciences either; social expectations of appropriate caring behavior resulted in active demands that daughters make themselves available, even when professionals were also involved in caring for their elderly parents. Neither paying nor not paying for care guarantees the right sort of caring motivation, though in either case, more desirable motivations can and frequently do develop in the course of the caring relationship (Qureshi 1990).

This may explain why carers are so poorly paid, or at least why, once in their jobs, improvements in their pay and working conditions are not forthcoming. Because carers tend to be motivated by a genuine concern for their clients' well-being, caring becomes to some extent its own reward, and to that extent carers' wages can be set lower than those of workers with objectively comparable skills (Folbre and Weisskopf 1998). Further, because they care, carers are not as prepared to jeopardize their relationship with those for whom they care in pursuit of their own self-interest as other workers may be to undermine the product of their more alienated labors; this difference may make paid carers more vulnerable to exploitation.

Some paid carers may have chosen their job because they like the particular work involved; others may see themselves as having a career in caring; and many will be doing it because it is work that fits in with their other unpaid caring commitments. Nonetheless, even when caring is a chosen career, the choice is unlikely to have been motivated purely by its extrinsic rewards. Rather, if a carer feels she made a choice, it will be for reasons that touch on the type of work itself.

Paid carers may have skills that unpaid carers do not; someone with a career in caring will have more incentive and opportunity to develop skills and obtain qualifications than someone who sees herself temporarily in a caring role. Because the work involves the development of a relationship, caring labor provides limited scope for routinization and control by the worker (or her employer) or for economies of scale to be reaped through professionalizing caring. In addition, the skills needed in caring are not in general the codifiable skills of a formal training scheme. Rather, many of the skills that a carer needs are tacit, difficult to codify, and generally picked up in the course of developing a particular caring relationship with a particular caree. Kari Waerness (1987) talks of a different rationality that applies to caring, based more on personal experience and knowledge than on the application of abstract principles; this does not exclude the possibility that formal training is important but emphasizes the relational aspect of caring.

EMOTIONAL LABOR

Besides caring labor, there are other growing sectors of employment in which workers' motivation matters. As technology has gradually replaced both workers' physical and mental skills, employment is being concentrated in those jobs for which machines have not yet been developed, jobs that require workers to have emotions as well as muscle and brain. The academic literature on emotional labor is recognition of this phenomenon. However, there are at least two somewhat different definitions of emotional work to be found in this literature. One talks about the "labor involved in dealing with other people's feelings" (James 1989, 21). The other talks of the management of the worker's own feelings, as in Arlie Hochschild's definition of emotional labor as "the management of feeling to create a publicly observable facial and bodily display" (Hochschild 1983, 7). Not all emotional labor is caring labor, but caring labor is a type of emotional labor—and the second of the preceding definitions captures why this is the case much better than the first.

The first definition, which refers only to other people's feelings, does not sufficiently distinguish a category of work or labor process. Indeed, in terms of neoclassical economic theory, all work is ultimately concerned with the enhancement of consumers' feelings, for people buy goods and services only in order to experience the increase in utility that their consumption brings. This first definition takes emotion (other people's) as the raw material on which emotional work is done, but it does not say anything about emotion in the labor process itself.

Work that is emotional labor in the second sense, of requiring a worker to act on her own feelings, will almost always be emotional labor in the first sense, too. That effort of management over one's own feelings will usually be made in order to create a desired emotional state in others, and Hochschild's definition does specify that the aim of emotional work is to create a public display, thus implying that it is work whose effectivity is measured by its consequences for others.

Because of the double characteristic of caring—that it is both motivation and activity—caring labor is emotional labor in both senses. It requires that the worker has a caring motivation and that her activity transmits to the caree the experience of being cared for, in an emotional as well as a physical sense. Both of these aspects may require effort on the part of the carer. Sometimes the motivation comes easily, and at other times it has to be worked on; a developing relationship often seems to help sustain this, as we have seen. Similarly, the amount of effort needed to ensure that the caree feels cared for will vary. For some old people, continual reassurance is not enough; many two-year-olds, on the other hand, appear to have little difficulty accepting that they are the center of their carer's world.

However, much of the emotional labor discussed in the literature, such as that done by flight attendants, prostitutes, or bar maids, or even the negative emotional labor required of debt collectors, is of a transitory nature in which the interaction with any particular person is limited in time. Indeed, one of the reasons such work is often consid-ered emotionally wearing is because it is so one-sided and temporary, so that no meaningful relationship can develop—though jobs vary in the extent to which performing emotional labor is a cost or a benefit to workers (Wharton 1993). Caring, however, specifically involves the development of a relationship, not the emotional servicing of people who remain strangers. This is why paid carers are usually allocated on a continuing basis to particular carees and often show a marked preference for maintaining such relationships, even in the face of some personal inconvenience.

This may explain why, although both the transitory type of emotional labor and caring labor can be wearing, many paid carers find their work rewarding and frequently do more than they are contracted to do. Specific techniques, such as those described by Hochschild (1983) in the training of flight attendants, may be needed to engender the appropriate emotions when emotional labor is performed for strangers. However, where a continuing relationship is set up, as is usually the case for caring labor, its own development may be all that is needed to generate the appropriate emotional ties.

Both carers and most other emotional workers are usually employed by a third party. In the carer's case, this means she has two different types of long-term relationships to negotiate, and there may be conflict between the two. One way of resolving this conflict, as we have seen, is to let the developing relationship with the caree override the contractual relationship with the employer. This, of course, is how self-exploitation by the carer can result. Employers, not surprisingly, seem content to save money by letting this happen. In the more transitory forms of emotional labor, the relationship between employee and employer is a more lasting one than the relationship between employee and customer. The employee therefore has no particular incentive to let the latter override her contractual relationship, but she may find her employer's demands in conflict with her own sense of self (Hochschild 1983).

CARING WORK OR CARING LABOR?

In this article, I have argued that caring labor is a form of emotional labor because it requires both the emotion of caring about and the activity of caring for another person. However, not all emotional labor is caring labor because the latter involves the development of a particular sort of relationship. Although caring relationships are traditionally associated with domestic unpaid activities, we have seen that such relationships may also exist in somewhat different forms under conditions of paid employment. In practice, it seems that the relationships developed through paid and unpaid care differ less than talk in terms of the rigid dichotomies of "public and private," "paid and unpaid," and "market and nonmarket" would suggest.

I have found Margaret Radin's notion of "incomplete commodification" (1996) useful for understanding why this should be the case and refuting the idea that caring and paid labor are incompatible poles of a dualism. She argues that not everything that is sold is completely commodified and that market understandings and nonmarket understandings of the same situation can coexist. In particular, this can happen for employment, because what people hope to take from work is not just pay and cannot be fully understood in monetary terms. In recognition of this, Radin draws a distinction between work and labor in which work always contains a noncommodified element, while labor is the fully commodified version—the opposite pole to unpaid domestic caring in the dualistic view with which this article started.

According to this distinction, although "labor" remains incompatible with a caring motivation, "work" can take on many of the relational characteristics of caring. For

laborers are sellers: fully motivated by money, exhausting the value of their activity in the measure of its exchange value. Laborers experience their labor as separate from their real lives and selves. Workers take money but are also at the same time givers. Money does not fully motivate them to work, nor does it exhaust the value of their activity. Work is understood not as separate from life and self, but rather as part of the worker and indeed constitutive of her. Nor is work understood as separate from relations with other people. (Radin 1996, 105)

Radin lists some of the occupations in which she would expect to find this type of identification of people with their work. "Nurses and people who care for children, the elderly, the retarded, the handicapped" appear in this list, but flight attendants, prostitutes, bar maids, and those who do the more transitory types of emotional labor do not, nor do debt collectors. Of course, individuals doing these jobs may identify with their work and get some satisfaction from it, but that identification is not expected, nor perhaps does it matter to performance. However, Radin also lists many other types of occupations, not related to emotional labor, where the nonmarket aspect of work can be important, such as fire fighting, writing, or, indeed, any skilled trade. Her list includes anybody who takes pride in his or her work and does a good job for that reason, anyone, that is, who cares about the results of his or her work.

This suggests that the adverse reaction to emotional labor, both of workers themselves and of commentators on it, is the result of the full commodification of emotion, that is, the requirement that emotion be a product of labor, not an outcome of work. This is a deeper form of alienation than the commodification of the traditional labor power of muscle and brain. In emotional labor, an even more personal aspect of workers' identity, their emotional integrity, is sold as a constituent part of their labor power. Workers cede control of their labor power for a period when they sell it to their employer; if that labor power includes emotions, emotional control and integrity are also given up.

However, when emotions are part of the noncommodified aspect of incompletely commodified work, the same problem does not arise. Indeed, as Radin (1996) notes, work is what we would all like our jobs to be, not just labor. "That there should be the opportunity for work to be personal in this sense does seem to be part of our conception of human flourishing—which is why those who see increasing depersonalization deplore it. Complete commodification of work—pure labor—does violence to our notion of what it is to be a well-developed person" (107).

Caring, therefore, may avoid the alienation of much other emotional labor because, even when caring is paid, it tends to be incompletely commodified. This is because caring involves the development of sustained relationships between carer and caree, and these cannot easily be commodified. Of course, there are no guarantees in this; paid or unpaid carers may not always succeed in developing such relationships. If they do not, maintaining appropriate emotional engagement may be as hard and as wearing as in the more transitory forms of emotional labor.

Further, there are many other types of paid work in which workers care about the outcome of their work, some of which are well paid. Recognizing this should help allay fears that if people are paid to care for someone, they will fail to care about them. The caring aspect of many types of paid work remains because of an incomplete commodification of labor power. Much of the quality of our lives would be lost if the imposition of inappropriate forms of market rationality turned such work into mere labor.

Notes

1. "Laborers are sellers, fully motivated by money, exhausting the value of their activity in the measure of its exchange value" (Radin 1996, 105). This quotation represents one pole of a distinction Radin makes between work and labor, to which I shall return later in this article.

2. The study by Challis and Davies (1986) was of a Kent (England) Community Care scheme in which paid, and sometimes unpaid, helpers were recruited to care for elderly people who would otherwise have needed residential care.

3. Qureshi (1990) considers the results of two studies: the first is the Kent Community Care study of mostly paid carers referred to previously; the second is of the informal care provided by friends, relatives, and neighbors to elderly people in Sheffield, England.

References

Challis, David and Bleddyn Davies. 1986. *Case Management in Community Care*. Aldershot: Gower.

Folbre, Nancy and Tom Weisskopf. 1998. Did Father Know Best? Families, Markets and the Supply of Caring Labor. In *Economics, Values and Organizations*, ed. Avner Ben-Ner and Louis Putterman. New York: Cambridge University Press.

Gardiner, Jean. 1997. *Gender, Care and Economics*. New York: Macmillan.

Gershuny, Jonathan and J. P. Robinson. 1988. Historical Changes in the Household Division of Labor. *Demography* 25(4):537-52.

Hochschild, Arlie Russell. 1983. *The Managed Heart: Commercialization of Human Feeling*. Berkeley: University of California Press.

James, Nicky. 1989. Emotional Labour: Skill and Work in the Social Regulation of Feelings. *Sociological Review* 37(1):15-42.

Nelson, Julie. 1998. For Love or Money—or Both? Paper presented at Out of the Margin 2, June, Amsterdam.

Qureshi, Hazel. 1990. Boundaries Between Formal and Informal Care-Giving Work. In *Gender and Caring: Work and Welfare in Britain and Scandinavia*, ed. Clare Ungerson. Hemel Hempstead: Harvester Wheatsheaf.

Radin, Margaret J. 1996. *Contested Commodities*. Cambridge, MA: Harvard University Press.

Ungerson, Clare. 1990. The Language of Care. In *Gender and Caring: Work and Welfare in Britain and Scandinavia*, ed. Clare Ungerson. Hemel Hempstead: Harvester Wheatsheaf.

Waerness, Kari. 1984. Caring as Women's Work in the Welfare State. In *Patriarchy in a Welfare Society*, ed. Harriet Holter. Oslo: Unversitetsforlaget.

———. 1987. On the Rationality of Caring. In *Women and the State*, ed. Anne Showstack Sassoon. London: Hutchinson.

Wharton, Amy S. 1993. The Affective Consequences of Service Work: Managing Emotions on the Job. *Work and Occupations* 20(2):205-32.

ANNALS, *AAPSS*, **561**, January 1999

The Cost of Caring

By PAULA ENGLAND and NANCY FOLBRE

ABSTRACT: Caring work involves providing a face-to-face service to recipients in jobs such as child care, teaching, therapy, and nursing. Such jobs offer low pay relative to their requirements for education and skill. What explains the penalty for doing caring work? Because caring labor is associated with women, cultural sexism militates against recognizing the value of the work. Also, the intrinsic reward people receive from helping others may allow employers to fill the jobs for lower pay. Caring labor creates public goods—widespread benefits that accrue even to those who pay nothing. For example, if children learn skills and discipline from teachers, the children's future employers benefit, with no market mechanism to make the pay given to care workers reflect these benefits. Even when the public or not-for-profit sectors do step in to hire people to provide such services for those too poor to pay, the pay is limited by how much decision makers really care about the poor. Finally, the fact that people feel queasy about putting a price on something as sacred as care limits the pay offered—as paradoxical as it is to pay less for something when it is seen as infinitely valuable!

Paula England is professor of sociology at the University of Arizona and author of Comparable Worth: Theories and Evidence *(1992) as well as many articles on gender and labor markets. From 1993 to 1996, she served as editor of the* American Sociological Review.

Nancy Folbre is professor of economics at the University of Massachusetts–Amherst and author of Who Pays for the Kids? *(1994). An associate editor of* Feminist Economics, *she is also cochair of a research network on the family and the economy, funded by the MacArthur Foundation.*

WORK that involves caring pays less than other kinds of work. This is true even after statistical adjustments for other job characteristics known to affect pay, such as educational requirements, physical demands, and union membership. This penalty for caring explains part of the sex gap in pay, since more women than men do caring work. To explore this topic, we start by explaining what we mean by caring work. Next, we review the empirical evidence showing that occupations that involve this type of work are penalized by lower pay. Finally, we explore several possible explanations for this care penalty.

WHAT IS CARING WORK?

Although caring work can be either paid or unpaid, we focus on paid caring work in this article. We employ a simple behavioral definition that roughly matches what has been operationalized in the research we will review here: caring work includes any occupation in which the worker provides a service to someone with whom he or she is in personal (usually face-to-face) contact.[1] The work is called "caring" on the assumption that the worker responds to a need or desire that is directly expressed by the recipient.[2] Caring work includes such jobs as child care, teaching, physical and psychological therapy provision, nursing, doctoring, and the work of sales clerks and wait persons, to name a few. Such work spans most of the range of occupational prestige and educational requirements. The jobs are disproportionately female, but there are some predominantly male jobs among them.

Caring work does not include manufacture of a physical product, such as assembly work in a factory, because here the worker is not in personal contact with those who gain from the work (the consumers buying the product). Nor does it include service work where there is some contact between worker and client, but this contact is incidental to the service. For example, carpenters have contact with their customers, but this interaction is incidental to getting the house built, so we do not call it caring labor.

This definition does not require that the worker be motivated by care for those helped in the job.[3] However, those who choose to do caring work often feel some affection, altruism, or obligation toward the people they care for (for a typology of caring motives, see Folbre and Weisskopf 1998). Any job will attract people who obtain satisfaction from the work itself. Also, caring motives may be developed through doing caring work because social roles often shape the personality and preferences of the people in them. The processes of selection into the job and socialization on the job make it likely that individuals in caring occupations are concerned about the welfare of their customers and clients.[4] Therefore, they probably do not conform to the traditional model of rational economic man, who is concerned only about his own earnings and leisure.

EVIDENCE OF
THE CARE PENALTY

A great deal of caring work is done at home for family members without any pay. Women do much of this. Unpaid work, by definition, carries a pecuniary penalty: one forgoes the potential earnings from working the same hours in a paid job. In addition, because pay is affected by how much job experience one has, women who leave employment to rear children suffer wage penalties for years after they reenter the job market (Waldfogel 1997). Mothers who work part-time while their children are young also pay a penalty since part-time experience has a lower return than full-time experience (England, Christopher, and Reid forthcoming). Being employed fewer years also affects mothers' pension and Social Security benefits. These effects are particularly consequential if a caregiver lacks the financial support of a spouse or other partner specializing in market work.

The focus of our concern here, however, is the disadvantage of working in a paid caring occupation, which seems to resemble the disadvantage of providing unpaid care. To determine whether caring work carries a wage penalty, one needs to perform an analysis that compares the pay in caring work to pay in other jobs, after making statistical adjustments for other pay-relevant differences. These adjustments entail the introduction of control variables into a regression analysis predicting mean or median earnings in jobs from job characteris-

tics, including the required qualifications of the workers.

Human capital theory suggests that skills of all kinds will have positive returns. Skills cost something to acquire, and a wage premium may be necessary to induce a sufficient supply of workers to invest in acquiring them. Another possible explanation for skill premiums is that they are normatively harmonious with American meritocratic ideology and often institutionalized in organizations' pay structures. In any case, it is clear that jobs requiring the cognitive skills we associate with formal education pay more than those that do not (England and McLaughlin 1979; England, Chassie, and McCormick 1982; Steinberg et al. 1986; Parcel and Mueller 1989; Parcel 1989; England 1992; Kilbourne et al. 1994; England et al. 1994; Farkas et al. 1997). The effects of requirements for physical skill, such as manual dexterity, and requirements for heavy lifting are less clear (England and McLaughlin 1979; England, Chassie, and McCormick 1982; Sorensen 1989; and Parcel 1989 find negative or no effects, but England 1992 and Kilbourne et al. 1994 find premiums).

The neoclassical economic perspective on earnings includes a theory of compensating differentials that calls attention to differences between jobs in how many people like or dislike the work itself. These nonpecuniary amenities or disamenities will affect how many people are willing to work in a job. Theoretically, employers will have to increase the wage to compensate for nonpecuniary disamenities of jobs, and they will be able to pay less than they otherwise would in jobs with nonpecuniary amenities. Most of the relevant studies have focused on physical hazards or physically onerous working conditions, probably because researchers find a certain face validity in assuming that most workers would prefer to avoid such conditions if they have an option of an otherwise equivalent job with the same wage.[5] Studies looking for wage premiums in such jobs are conflicting. Smith's review (1979) of many studies noted that less than half show the predicted positive effects on wages for characteristics such as physical repetitiveness, lack of freedom, and job insecurity. Among later studies, two found wage premiums for hazardous work for male but not female workers (Barry 1985; Filer 1985), one found premiums for both sexes (Duncan and Holmlund 1983), and two found no premium for either sex (Kilbourne et al. 1994; England 1992). England (1992) found evidence of premiums for nonphysical disamenities: repetitiveness of the job, and having to engage in tasks against one's conscience. Jacobs and Steinberg (1990) examined the pay for New York State government jobs, finding only 1 of 14 onerous job characteristics to have a significant positive effect on pay (working with sick patients). Several had negative effects (cleaning others' dirt, loud noise, strenuous physical activity, repetition, and being told what to do). Thus the evidence is mixed but generally nonsupportive of the proposition that characteristics we would expect most workers to find undesirable have wage premiums.

Some industries have been found to offer higher wages than others.[6] Various theories, from dual economy theory to efficiency wage theory, have been offered to explain these differentials across industries. (For reviews, see Farkas and England 1994.) Thus studies assessing whether caring work has a penalty have generally controlled for which industries the caring occupations are in (where the public sector is treated as one industry). Another necessary control is how extensive unionization is in the occupation or industry, since unionized jobs generally pay more than comparable nonunionized jobs (Freeman and Medoff 1984).

Whether men or women typically do the work has been found to affect wages. That is, jobs filled largely by females pay less than is commensurate with their skills, onerous working conditions, union status, and the industries in which they occur.[7]

Studies investigating whether there is a penalty for doing caring work should control for as many of the factors discussed previously as possible. The studies reviewed next have generally controlled for other skill demands of the occupation, educational requirements, the percentage of workers who are female, unionization, industry, and some measures of amenities and disamenities. While most of the investigators did not use the term "caring work," most of their operationalizations capture something close to face-to-face service work.

England (1992, chap. 3) created a dummy variable for caring work (using the term "nurturant work"), by making a judgment from each detailed census occupational title as to whether a primary task in the job was giving a face-to-face service to clients or customers of the organization for which one worked. This dummy variable closely corresponds with our behavioral definition of caring work as face-to-face service work discussed earlier.[8] Controlling for many other occupational characteristics, the study found that both men and women earned less if they worked in a caring occupation in 1980. England et al. (1994) also found a negative return (wage penalty) for working in a caring occupation using another measure. This measure was constructed from a survey of undergraduates asking them to rank jobs according to "how much they involve helping people, encouraging the development of people, or taking care of people." Kilbourne et al. (1994) developed a scale to measure nurturant skill from the dummy variable developed by England (1992) previously described, plus other measures from the *Dictionary of Occupational Titles* (U.S. Department of Labor 1977) involving dealing with people, and demands for talking and hearing. Other things being equal, working in an occupation scoring higher on this scale reduced earnings for both men and women. In an analysis of the New York State civil service jobs, Steinberg et al. (1986) found that a number of scales that tapped caring social skills had negative returns. These included communication with the public and group facilitation, both of which relate to caring work (152).

We know of no studies that have included a measure of a concept resembling caring work in an earnings regression and not found a negative effect. Thus the evidence is strong that there is a pecuniary penalty for working in a caring occupation. The fact that the studies reviewed control for many variables allows us to dismiss some possible explanations of this result. But we are left with a puzzle: why are caring occupations paid less?

EXPLANATIONS FOR
THE CARE PENALTY

This question probably does not have a simple answer. We outline five possible explanations that could provide a framework for future research.

Gender bias

Caring labor may pay less because we associate caring skills and functions with women and their mothering role, which are culturally devalued (Kilbourne et al. 1994; England et al. 1994; England 1992; Steinberg 1990). If sexist cultural norms affect employers' valuations, then predominantly female jobs will pay less than sex-integrated jobs or those filled by males, and caring work will pay badly because many caring jobs are filled by women. The studies previously reviewed found a penalty for doing caring labor even net of the job's sex composition. This notion of devaluation by association could also explain a penalty for doing work involving a skill or function associated with women, even when not all the jobs to which this applies are filled by women.

When we talk about the devaluation of jobs because they involve a function or skill associated with women, what more specific mechanisms do we envision? One mechanism may be cognitive error: decision makers are more apt to recognize the contribution of jobs done by men or involving skills culturally coded as male. They simply do not perceive the true importance of skills culturally coded as female. Another mechanism may be social norms that dictate that male skills deserve greater compensation. Once such biases affect wage setting, institutional inertia may keep the differences in force over time.

Intrinsic rewards

Low wages in caring work could result from the intrinsic rewards of care for others. The neoclassical economic theory of compensating differentials implies that jobs with nonwage characteristics that the marginal worker finds onerous must offer higher wages. The same theoretical logic implies that jobs entailing intrinsically satisfying work can, all else being equal, offer a lower wage.

Does the amenity of doing caring work help explain why it pays less?[9] The argument is consistent with but not necessarily implied by our claim that caring work disproportionately attracts people with caring motives. The process of learning a skill often goes hand in hand with developing a preference for exercising that skill

(England and Folbre 1997), so that by selecting people with the skills for a job, employers unwittingly select more of those who would take the job for lower pay than others. But every job disproportionately attracts people who find the job requirements an amenity. For example, intellectually demanding work attracts those who enjoy using their mind, yet cognitive requirements have a positive, not negative, return.

Compensating differentials could explain the low wage of caring labor only if there were, in a sense, an oversupply of individuals who wanted to enter a caring occupation, so that the last worker hired would be willing to do the job for less than otherwise equivalent jobs. This is a possibility, but we cannot directly observe the tastes of the last (or marginal) worker hired. The claim that intrinsic rewards may help explain the care penalty is theoretically plausible but empirically unsubstantiated.[10]

Another problem concerns the cultural construction of intrinsic rewards. If women consider caring work an amenity only because they have been socialized to believe that such work is more appropriate or more feminine, this amenity may be considerably attenuated by changes in social norms. Also, a worker who initially derives some nonpecuniary benefits from her job may find that these decline over time but that the costs of changing occupations are prohibitively high. In this instance, the amenity obviously does not continue to provide compensation for low pay.

Public goods and free riders

Some goods or services provide widespread benefits that are difficult to price because nonpayers cannot be excluded from enjoying them. Such public goods include many forms of public infrastructure, such as roads, bridges, and military defense, and many aspects of our physical environment, such as our climate, water, and air. Human capital, in the form of education, has traditionally been considered a public good. One could also think of social capital, including levels of honesty and trust that are necessary to the efficient functioning of a market economy, as public goods (Coleman 1990; Putnam 1993, 1995).

Many people share in the benefits when children are brought up to be responsible, skilled, and loving adults who treat each other with courtesy and respect. Employers profit from access to skilled, disciplined, and cooperative workers. The elderly benefit from the Social Security taxes paid by the younger generation. Fellow citizens gain from having law-abiding rather than predatory neighbors.

Care work helps create these forms of human and social capital. There is, however, no practical way for those who do this work to charge a price that reflects the value of their contributions. Mothers cannot demand a fee from employers who hire their adult children and benefit from their children's discipline. They cannot send a bill to their children's spouses for the extra qualities provided because of their many years of good parenting. When child care workers or elementary teachers do a good job, their students internalize an eagerness to learn and willingness to cooperate that later teachers and employers benefit from. When nurses do a good job, patients' families and employers benefit. Anyone who treats another person in a kind and helpful way creates a small benefit that is likely to be passed along. The beneficiaries of caring labor, who extend beyond the actual recipients of the care, are thus free riders on the labor of those who do caring labor.

In addition to being diffuse, the benefits of caring work are more difficult to measure than the quality of physical products such as cars, or standardized services, such as data entry. Neither child care service providers nor parents can easily assess the effects of care quality on children's cognitive and social development. Neither standardized test scores nor conventional measures of physical health adequately capture our success in enhancing human capabilities. Social scientists find it extraordinarily difficult to measure the kinds of "neighborhood effects" that lead to "collective efficacy" (Sampson, Raudenbush, and Earls 1997).

Neoclassical economic theory concedes that the forces of supply and demand alone cannot ensure adequate production of public goods. Government funding of schools is justified by the argument that we collectively benefit from a better-educated citizenry. A case for public support of child rearing and public subsidies for the wages of workers in caring occupations could be framed in similar terms (Folbre 1994a, 1994b). The fact that economists remain largely uninterested in this issue reflects their tendency to assume that care is a natural activity that does not deserve or require remuneration.

Poor clients

Caring labor often involves helping those who lack the resources to pay for their own care: the young, the ill, the poor. In the public and non-profit sectors of the economy, levels of pay for workers in caring occupations are largely determined by political forces. The amount of money allocated for programs such as Head Start, Medicaid, child care, compensatory education, and other social safety net programs depends critically on how much voters, charitable givers, and state decision makers really care about those who will receive the services. In the United States today, a widespread ideology of individualism blames the poor for their own problems and makes redistribution suspect. The low pay offered to state workers serving low-income populations puts downward pressure on the pay for all caring occupations.

Sacred cows

The belief that love and care are demeaned by commodification may, ironically, lead to low pay for caring labor. Many people seem to think that caring motives are so sacred that it is offensive to talk about their exchange value. At issue is what can be commodified, where we should draw the lines around what may be exchanged for gain (Radin 1996). Laws against slavery reflect a social norm that human beings should not be allowed to own one another. Laws against prostitution reflect a belief that sexual intimacy should not be bought and sold. Rules that adoptive parents may not pay for a baby from a birth mother (but only for expenses) can be interpreted as a taboo against purchase of children.

Similar concerns come into play when we discuss the commodification of care for others, particularly family members. We see love as sacred—and caring most effective—when it is done for intrinsic rather than extrinsic reasons. The principle that money cannot buy love may have the unintended and perverse consequence of perpetuating low pay for face-to-face service work.

CONCLUSION

Children need care for their initial development, and all of us are ill or otherwise in need of special assistance at times. Some minimal level of care is necessary even for healthy adults. Therefore, the research reviewed in this article, showing that occupations involving face-to-face services to others are paid less than others, is disturbing. We see a need for a national dialogue on how we recognize caring labor as work and support those who make these contributions to the public good.

We also encourage research that can help us arbitrate competing explanations of the care penalty. This entails refining the links between conceptual and operational definitions of caring. Our behavioral definition of caring labor as face-to-face service work had the advantage of corresponding with the way the concept has been operationalized in past empirical research. This definition misses something, however. Among those jobs involving face-to-face service work, there is considerable variation in how important it is to the well-being of the recipient that the caregiver really care about him or her. Customers may be happier if a sales clerk, flight attendant, or waitress treats them with genuine kindness and concern, but they are not dependent upon such forms of care.

The situation is quite different when the recipient of a service is very young, ill, or infirm. It matters a great deal whether a child care worker or nurse or home health worker cares about his or her client, because a worker's motives affect the likelihood of abuse and the overall quality of care. Dependents often do not have the resources or power to fire a caregiver they do not like and hire another. Third parties who do have this power (for example, parents of a child, adult children of an elder, or the state) cannot continually monitor the caregiver's performance.

It would be useful to rank caring occupations along a continuum defined by the impact that caring motives may have on the quality of services provided. Comparative ethnographies of occupations at different points on this continuum could tell us a great deal. How exactly do workers' feelings and attitudes affect the client's well-being? Are workers with caring motives successfully matched with jobs in which these motives matter? What kinds of institutional features and work organization foster the cultivation of genuinely caring motives among workers? The public-good aspect of caring labor

means that levels of service and pay for caregivers may depend upon collective action. It would be useful to study the roles that unions, worker initiatives, and state regulation play in defending standards of care and higher pay for those doing caring work.

As Arlie Hochschild (1983) has emphasized, workers themselves may feel burdened by the requirements of emotional labor. How do these feelings compare across jobs in different places on the care quality continuum? Do workers talk about the need to display affections they do not genuinely feel? Do they experience the opportunity to provide care as a positive or a negative feature of their job? Are they frustrated when their job environment minimizes their opportunities to develop personal relationships with their clients or patients? Do workers in occupations higher on this continuum experience more or less burnout? Thoughtful qualitative research could shed light on these issues.

There is also a pressing need for quantitative research on determinants of the size of the care penalty. Does caring work pay more when provided to a relatively affluent clientele? Does it pay more when provided to a clientele more able to measure its benefits? Statistical analyses that go beyond an analysis of occupational characteristics to look at industrial structure and the composition of consumer demand could shed some light on these factors.

It is also important to go beyond an analysis of the causes of the care penalty to consider its consequences. Apart from the obvious negative financial impact on many women workers, there is a risk that the well-being of children, the sick, and the elderly is compromised by high levels of worker turnover and stress resulting from low pay for caring labor. The norms and more explicit forms of discrimination that once restricted women to caring occupations are weakening. In a culture that encourages self-interested calculation, the number of women who choose to enter caring occupations will probably decline. Continued commodification may both raise the price and lower the quality of important care services.

On the other hand, simple resistance to commodification is no solution, and we should be suspicious of any argument that decent pay demeans a noble calling. The notion that women should provide care out of the goodness of their hearts has traditionally reinforced low pay for caring occupations. We should reward care work fairly in both the market and the home. Doing so may require significant changes in the way we remunerate all types of work.

Notes

1. Some services provided through written or telephone communication might be personal enough to qualify as caring work, even though they are not face-to-face.

2. The service is something that someone has decided the recipient should have. But sometimes others may view the worker as engaged in social control rather than care of the client. In principle, we would not want to call the former caring work, but it is hard to operationalize the distinction.

3. Elsewhere, one of us has stressed the role of motives in defining caring work (Folbre

and Weisskopf 1998), which Susan Himmelweit (this volume) also emphasizes. Since motives are not observable, however, we are relying on a simpler criterion of service provision with personal contact here.

4. Our concept of caring work differs from Hochschild's notion (1983) of emotional labor. For her, emotional work involves changing the emotions of the person who is served and requires the worker to display emotions that are often not genuine. We agree that both of these may occur in caring work, but we do not include them as part of our definition. As a matter of emphasis, we are more inclined to see authentic caring motives where Hochschild focuses on the alienation of having to "fake" emotions for pay. Nonetheless, the face-to-face service occupations that meet our behavioral definition of caring work are largely the same occupations Hochschild lists in her appendix as involving emotional work.

5. Of course, individuals will differ in what job characteristics they consider positive and negative and how much the wage needs to be increased or could be decreased to keep them in the job. According to neoclassical theory, it is the "marginal" worker whose tastes determine the penalty or premium that will just "compensate" for the nonpecuniary amenity or disamenity (England 1992, 69-72).

6. An industry is defined by the product or service that the organization sells or provides, and an occupation is defined by the function the worker performs. Thus one can be a secretary, janitor, or manager—three occupations—in the automobile, mining, grocery, or hospital industries.

7. Sorensen 1994, tab. 2.1, reviews many studies. See also Steinberg et al. 1986; England et al. 1988; Baron and Newman 1989; Parcel 1989; Kilbourne et al. 1994; England et al. 1994; Macpherson and Hirsch 1995; England, Reid, and Kilbourne 1996. All find negative effects of percentage female; two studies finding no effects of percentage female are Filer 1989 and Tam 1997.

8. One difference between the two definitions is that England's dummy variable (1992) required that the recipient of the service be a client or customer of the organization. Jobs requiring service to another employee of the organization (for example, secretaries to managers, paralegals to lawyers) were not coded as

caring work. If this restriction had not been made, coding would have required deciding whether managers provided services to those they supervised. Under some styles of management, this may have occurred, but England's preference (1992) was to keep a cleaner distinction between authority and caring work. Using a separate measure of whether jobs entailed supervisory authority showed authority to have a positive return.

9. The thesis that caring work pays less because it is more satisfying (at least to the marginal worker) contrasts sharply with Hochschild's claim (1983) that emotional labor is more onerous for virtually all workers than physical or mental labor because it involves acting, suppressing feelings, and a virtual denial of the self. (She has little to say about the relative pay of emotional labor, however.)

10. Most research on compensating differentials, such as that reviewed previously, relies on circular reasoning. It assumes we know whether the marginal worker likes or dislikes a characteristic (say, danger of loss of life, because virtually everyone views this negatively), then uses this information to test the theory. Alternatively, it assumes that compensating differentials are the only source of otherwise unexplained differences and uses empirical findings on what job characteristics carry penalties or premiums to discern what the marginal worker considers an amenity or disamenity.

References

Baron, James and Andrew Newman. 1989. Pay the Man: Effects of Demographic Composition on Prescribed Wage Rates in the California Civil Service. In *Pay Equity: Empirical Inquiries*, ed. Robert Michael, Heidi Hartmann, and Brigid O'Farrell. Washington, DC: National Academy Press.

Barry, Janis. 1985. Women Production Workers—Low Pay and Hazardous Work. *American Economic Review* 75:262-65.

Coleman, James S. 1990. *Foundations of Social Theory*. Cambridge, MA: Harvard University Press.

Duncan, Greg J. and Bertil Holmlund. 1983. Was Adam Smith Right After All? Another Test of the Theory of Compensating Wage Differentials. *Journal of Labor Economics* 1:366-79.

England, Paula. 1992. *Comparable Worth: Theories and Evidence*. New York: Aldine.

England, Paula, Marilyn Chassie, and Linda McCormick. 1982. Skill Demands and Earnings in Female and Male Occupations. *Sociology and Social Research* 66:147-68.

England, Paula, Karen Christopher, and Lori L. Reid. Forthcoming. How Do Intersections of Race/Ethnicity and Gender Affect Pay Among Young Cohorts of African Americans, European Americans, and Latino/as? In *Race, Gender, and Economic Inequality: African American and Latina Women in the Labor Market*, ed. Irene Browne. New York: Russell Sage Foundation.

England, Paula, George Farkas, Barbara Kilbourne, and Thomas Dou. 1988. Explaining Occupational Sex Segregation and Wages: Findings from a Model with Fixed Effects. *American Sociological Review* 53(4):544-58.

England, Paula and Nancy Folbre. 1997. Reconceptualizing Human Capital. Paper presented at the annual meeting of the American Sociological Association.

England, Paula, Melissa S. Herbert, Barbara Stanek Kilbourne, Lori L. Reid, and Lori McCready Megdal. 1994. The Gendered Valuation of Occupations and Skills: Earnings in 1980 Census Occupations. *Social Forces* 73(1):65-99.

England, Paula and Steven McLaughlin. 1979. Sex Segregation of Jobs and Male-Female Income Differentials. In

Discrimination in Organizations, ed. R. Alvarez, K. Lutterman, and Associates. San Francisco: Jossey-Bass.

England, Paula, Lori Reid, and Barbara Stanek Kilbourne. 1996. The Effect of the Sex Composition of Jobs on Starting Wages in an Organization: Findings from the NLSY. *Demography* 33(4):511-21.

Farkas, George and Paula England. 1994. *Industries, Firms, and Jobs.* New York: Aldine.

Farkas, George, Paula England, Keven Vicknair, and Barbara Stanek Kilbourne. 1997. Cognitive Skill, Skill Demands of Jobs, and Earnings Among Young European-American, African-American, and Mexican-American Workers. *Social Forces* 75:913-38.

Filer, Randall. 1985. Male-Female Wage Differences: The Importance of Compensating Differentials. *Industrial and Labor Relations Review* 38: 426-37.

―――. 1989. Occupational Segregation, Compensating Differentials and Comparable Worth. In *Pay Equity: Empirical Inquiries,* ed. Robert Michael, Heidi Hartmann, and Brigid O'Farrell. Washington, DC: National Academy Press.

Folbre, Nancy. 1994a. Children as Public Goods. *American Economic Review* 84:86-90.

―――. 1994b. *Who Pays for the Kids? Gender and the Structures of Constraint.* New York: Routledge.

Folbre, Nancy and Thomas Weisskopf. 1998. Did Father Know Best? Families, Markets and the Supply of Caring Labor. In *Economics, Values and Organization,* ed. Avner Ben-Ner and Louis Putterman. New York: Cambridge University Press.

Freeman, Richard B. and James Medoff. 1984. *What Do Unions Do?* New York: Basic Books.

Hochschild, Arlie Russell. 1983. *The Managed Heart: Commercialization of Human Feeling.* Berkeley: University of California Press.

Jacobs, Jerry A. and Ronnie J. Steinberg. 1990. Compensating Differentials and the Male-Female Wage Gap: Evidence from the New York State Comparable Worth Study. *Social Forces* 69:439-68.

Kilbourne, Barbara Stanek, Paula England, George Farkas, K. Beron, and D. Weir. 1994. Returns to Skills, Compensating Differentials, and Gender Bias: Effects of Occupational Characteristics on the Wages of Women and Men. *American Journal of Sociology* 100:689-719.

Macpherson, D. A. and B. T. Hirsch. 1995. Wages and Gender Composition: Why Do Women's Jobs Pay Less? *Journal of Labor Economics* 13:426-71.

Parcel, Toby. 1989. Comparable Worth, Occupational Labor Markets, and Occupational Earnings: Results from the 1980 Census. In *Pay Equity: Empirical Inquiries,* ed. Robert Michael, Heidi Hartmann, and Brigid O'Farrell. Washington, DC: National Academy Press.

Parcel, Toby and Charles W. Mueller. 1989. Temporal Change in Occupational Earnings Attainment, 1970-1980. *American Sociological Review* 54:622-34.

Putnam, Robert. 1993. *Making Democracy Work: Civic Traditions in Modern Italy.* Princeton, NJ: Princeton University Press.

―――. 1995. Bowling Alone: America's Declining Social Capital. *Journal of Democracy* 6:65-78.

Radin, Martha. 1996. *Contested Commodities.* Cambridge, MA: Harvard University Press.

Sampson, Robert J., Stephen W. Raudenbush, and Felton Earls. 1997. Neighborhoods and Violent Crime: A Multilevel Study of Collective Efficacy. *Science,* vol. 16.

Smith, Robert. 1979. Compensating Wage Differentials and Public Policy: A Review. *Industrial and Labor Relations Review* 32:339-52.

Sorensen, Elaine. 1989. Measuring the Pay Disparity Between Typical Female Occupations and Other Jobs: A Bivariate Selectivity Approach. *Industrial and Labor Relations Review* 42:624-39.

———. 1994. *Comparable Worth: Is It a Worthy Policy?* Princeton, NJ: Princeton University Press.

Steinberg, Ronnie J. 1990. Social Construction of Skill: Gender, Power, and Comparable Worth. *Work and Occupations* 17(4):449-82.

Steinberg, Ronnie J., Lois Haignere, C. Possin, C. H. Chertos, and D. Treiman. 1986. *The New York State Pay Equity Study: A Research Report*. Albany: Center for Women in Government, State University of New York Press.

Tam, Tony. 1997. Sex Segregation and Occupational Gender Inequality in the United States: Devaluation or Specialized Training? *American Journal of Sociology* 102:1652-92.

U.S. Department of Labor. 1977. *Dictionary of Occupational Titles*. 4th ed. Washington, DC: Government Printing Office.

Waldfogel, Jane. 1997. The Effect of Children on Women's Wages. *American Sociological Review* 62:209-17.

ANNALS, *AAPSS*, **561**, January 1999

Comfort and Struggle:
Emotion Work in Family Life

By MARJORIE L. DeVAULT

ABSTRACT: Though family life is typically associated with emotion rather than work, the concept of emotion work reveals the effort behind family feeling. Existing literature on family emotion work emphasizes caregiving and interpersonal support—activities associated with the housewife ideal of the industrial age. This article examines not only such caregiving and support activities but also several other forms of emotion work that become visible when we consider families whose lives diverge from this privileged ideal.

Marjorie L. DeVault is associate professor of sociology and a member of the women's studies program at Syracuse University. She has written on women's work (both paid and unpaid), family studies, and qualitative research methods. Her articles on feminist research are concerned with sexism and racism in traditional research methods and strategies for producing more broadly inclusive knowledge of the social world.

F AMILY life is so strongly associated with emotion that phrases such as "family work" may at first seem oxymoronic—most people understand family as a place of feeling. Feminist scholars, however, examine the unacknowledged efforts that produce family life and make wage work possible, and suggest that if families appear to be havens of comfort and personal attention for some, it is usually because women work to make them so.

When, in *The Managed Heart* (1983), Arlie Russell Hochschild introduced the concept of emotion work, she distinguished between the "emotional labor" that employers require in paid jobs and the unpaid efforts of family and personal life, which she referred to as "emotion work." In both cases, she meant to identify an intentional management and display of one's own feelings, usually undertaken in order to influence the feelings of others. My purpose here is to highlight the emotional strand in the varied lives and activities of household groups. I will suggest that some family groups, compared to others, are asked to do more or different work, producing forms of social inequity rendered invisible by the most common ways of thinking about family life. I begin with those forms of emotion work that have most often been discussed as such, and move toward a more expansive formulation.

WHAT IS FAMILY EMOTION WORK?

Consider some examples based on interviews I conducted during the mid-1980s (DeVault 1991). The first example is of a middle-class white woman who lives in the suburbs north of Chicago. She leaves her part-time job to drive her children to their sports activities. She sits with them while they have a macaroni supper and, after homework, bathes them and puts them to bed just as their father arrives home from the city. He checks on them briefly and changes his clothes while she prepares dinner for the two of them.

This woman works to produce comfort for a partner; she does so through long-term strategic choices—by handling most of the children's care—and in more directly emotional ways each evening—by serving a special dinner and joining him to chat about the day. When I asked about her double cooking, she explained, "[My husband] is in a very demanding work situation. It's almost as though a decent meal is a reward for getting through a bad day, a difficult day."

The second example is of a white secretary who hurries home to a smaller house nearby, considering how to use the leftovers from a weekend potluck. She pulls them quickly from the refrigerator and calls her husband to the table; he has half an hour to eat before leaving for his night-shift job. Just before he leaves the house, she proposes a family day on the weekend; she will cook something special if he will take them to the zoo. He grumbles, too rushed to think that far ahead; she takes a few minutes to control her angry frustration and then settles down to play and read with the children, saving the dirty dishes until they have gone to bed.

This woman works to provide a family dinner within the constraints of a difficult schedule, organizing her work so as to spend time with her children. She plans for family recreation and struggles to involve her spouse as an active partner in family activities. "We're going through a slight revolt at my house right now, about who's doing what," she explains, laughing. Less happily, she adds, "Basically, I'm doing it."

The third example concerns a social worker who lives in the city. She gathers with her family: elderly parents and two school-aged children. They are Colombian and eat "Spanish food": mostly soups, or beans and rice. They have discovered recently that her father is diabetic, and the whole family has been helping him change his diet. They now eat more salads than before, more rice, and foods that are not so sweet.

This woman helps her father adjust to his chronic illness. She accompanies him to the doctor, seeks information about diet, and changes her own habits in order to support his efforts. Giving up alcohol has been hard, she explains, and adds, "And coffee. We love coffee because we come from a country that's very rich in coffee. But we aren't drinking it so much now. . . . It's not fair, if we are drinking and drinking coffee every time and he's just watching us; it's terrible. Now we are very familiar with these herbal teas."

Another example concerns a white nurse in a different urban neighborhood. After work, she returns to a comfortable older home. She browses the cupboard, thinking of dinner, but soon her husband arrives from his job, very hungry. They leave a note for their teenaged children and walk down the street to a neighborhood restaurant. Soon, their daughter joins them with her boyfriend.

This mother has worked at giving her children both autonomy and responsibility; as they have grown, family members have negotiated a balance between independence and a sense of family. They enjoy meeting for a meal when they can, but people expect to fend for themselves, and they often use the nearby restaurant. Still, this mother organizes and makes sure the house is stocked with food and other necessities. Overall, she says, "You try to make things mesh together. It doesn't always work. This happens to work." But one can see that it does not "work" fortuitously; it is a routine involving both material and emotional activity that has been negotiated over the years.

These examples point to expressive uses of food that give emotional weight to caretaking activities. Child care has a similarly braided quality, combining physical caretaking with love, nurturance, and emotional guidance. Philosopher Sara Ruddick (1980) has called attention to the dual character of mothering; she argues that dominant conceptions of mothering as simply a matter of feeling miss the intentional, crafted qualities of maternal effort, and she urges readers to see what she called "maternal thought." Brenda Seery (1996), building on this notion, interviewed middle-class white women about the emotional aspect of this work and found that they spoke readily about their attempts to shape children's emotional experiences and development. They discussed conscious efforts to protect their children from hurt and disappointment, to help them manage the problems of everyday life, to spend everyday time with children, and to organize special events and celebrations. Seery points out that inaction is sometimes a strategic effort (as when mothers control anger and frustration or avoid doing or saying things that could hurt their children). She uses the mothers' accounts to identify a multistepped work process that involves knowing about family members' situations, assessing their needs, and then acting strategically.

Other authors have focused on interpersonal support work conducted primarily through talk. For example, Reed Larson and Maryse H. Richards (1994) suggest that conversation is "the medium of mothering." These researchers studied daily activities in 55 two-parent white families with at least one adolescent child. They collected the data on the activities by paging family members randomly and having them note their activities and feelings at the time. Mothers in their study spent more time than fathers engaged in conversation, but found it less pleasurable. The authors argue that these women use talk as the "glue" that holds their families together, making plans, connecting family members, doing emotional caretaking, and responding to emergency needs. For these women, talk is work. Rebecca Erickson and Amy Wharton (Erickson 1993; Wharton and Erickson

1995) also focus on the provision of emotional support. In a survey of women in two-worker marriages, they operationalize emotion work by asking about behaviors such as "initiat[ing] talking things over" and "offer[ing] me encouragement." While their analysis parallels that of Larson and Richards in some ways, it seems more optimistic: they find that women who do more emotion work—and especially those who say that their husbands share that work—report more happiness in marriage. Emotional support is work, they suggest, but it can be a source of satisfaction.

In general, scholars of family life agree that women do the great bulk of housework and child care and that this pattern holds for emotion work as well. British sociologists Jean Duncombe and Dennis Marsden (1955), focusing on the emotion work that maintains the couple relationship itself, maintain that many men overvalue breadwinning and fail to recognize or share emotional contributions to family life. In such situations, adjusting to inequity becomes another kind of emotion work. For example, Hochschild shows that negotiating the household division of labor requires managing not only work but also feelings about it (Hochschild with Machung 1989). She suggests that women and men, both individually and as couples, develop "gender strategies" with emotional components that allow them to live with their work bargains (Hochschild 1990).

These studies highlight the kinds of work associated with a housewife role, one element in the nuclear family ideal that developed with industrialization. Wage work and household life were separated with industrialization, and the family wage bargain between employers and the best-paid industrial workers institutionalized this division: men were to be paid enough to support their wives and children financially, and women were to support these male workers through the maintenance of a comfortable home. This breadwinner-housewife pattern was never a uniform reality, and it seems now to be crumbling rapidly. Even middle-class wives and mothers expect to be wage earners as well, and small living groups of various sorts lay claim to the honorific label "family" with varying degrees of success. But the ideal of the soothing and supportive housewife seems a powerful underpinning for some patterns of emotion work even in households that look quite different from the breadwinner-housewife image. Research on family life is also shaped by this history: most studies are built on a conceptual foundation that Dorothy Smith (1993) labels "SNAF"—the idea of a "standard North American family." Researchers routinely design studies that include only married couples with children, only middle-class, white family groups, only families with relatively minor difficulties. Other household groups are implicitly defined as exceptional, included under the rubric of "diversity." Troubles are studied as instances of poverty, illness, or disability rather than as part of the fabric of family experience.

SOME RELATIVELY NEGLECTED KINDS OF EMOTION WORK

The studies discussed previously, including my own, share the limitations of the SNAF model to varying degrees. Many researchers note these limitations and, often, promise further research with more diverse groups. Such promises, however, do little to expand the scholarly view of family life. In this section, then, I look beyond the standard literature in an attempt to sketch a more broadly inclusive picture. Collecting clues from existing studies, I consider several kinds of family activity that seem to qualify as emotion work, though they are not typically discussed under that rubric.

Advocacy

In many situations, parents mobilize to support their children's encounters with outside institutions—work that often requires forceful assertion, patience, and tact. These efforts become especially visible when children depend heavily on services. For example, consider the following scenario (based on material from Traustadottir 1992). A white, middle-class mother meets with the local school district's Special Education Committee, hoping to obtain additional services for her daughter, a 12-year-old with a developmental disability and some visual impairment. She presents her request and then listens patiently, suppressing her frustration with bureaucratic obstacles and her anger at these strangers' evaluations of her child. Carefully but forcefully, she explains her child's capacities, the kinds of accommodation necessary to allow her daughter fuller participation, and the extra work that she herself will do to ensure that the proposed arrangement will not unduly burden the classroom teacher. When the meeting ends on an inconclusive note, she is deeply disappointed. Driving home, however, she puts aside her frustration and begins to plan her next move.

When children have disabilities, child care expands to include not only specialized caregiving but also the work of monitoring the child's needs and organizing resources to meet those needs. In most families, mothers take primary responsibility for this work. Rannveig Traustadottir (1992) found that middle-class mothers, especially, coordinate numerous professionals; most report that vigorous advocacy is required in order to obtain needed services. Many become skilled lobbyists, sharing strategies in support groups (and some extend these efforts to include action on behalf of other children with disabilities). Though mothers do most of this work, they often enlist fathers to participate in encounters with professionals, since the presence of a man seems to provide a "status shield" (Hochschild 1983) that helps counter the professionals' tendency to discount mothers' views.

This advocacy work is significant in its own right, but it also helps to make visible the more common efforts that many family members undertake to support kin in encounters with institutions. Many parents—again, mostly, though not only, mothers—monitor children's school experiences and make decisions about strategic interventions. Assisting successfully is a challenge that requires time, resources, reflection, and at least a minimal ability (and willingness) to take up the language and frame of reference of school personnel (Smith 1987; Griffith and Smith 1987). Sometimes, parents defend their children against institutional slights; sometimes they decide that nonintervention is more appropriate.

Ironically (though not surprisingly), institutional advocacy often seems most necessary in family situations that make it most difficult. For example, in their book analyzing the high school experiences of Mexican-origin "at-risk" students in Texas, Harriet D. Romo and Toni Falbo (1996) document the systemic obstacles that make graduation difficult for these students. The authors describe many ways that some parents work at keeping children in school: they monitor students' lives, take charge and set limits, listen, and constantly stress the importance of school. But many of these parents work long hours at low-wage jobs, speak little or no English, and do not have cars or telephones. The scope and extent of efforts required to assist students appear in a chapter that recounts the excruciating details of Romo's attempts to re-enroll a student who wished to return to school. Getting through the bureaucratic maze took weeks and required the following, at minimum: frequent access to a telephone and transportation; time for meeting with personnel at several school district offices; tact, patience, and firm authority in dealing with authorities; persistence and faith that the effort was worthwhile; and—perhaps most challenging of all—an ability to sustain the student's motivation to return to a system that certainly looked like it did not want him.

Survival and identity work

Oppression increases the work of maintaining a family and imposes distinctive emotional demands. For example, studies (such as Dill 1980; Rollins 1985) of domestic work, for decades one of the only jobs available for African American women, suggest the following scenario. A middle-aged African American woman walks to the subway each weekday morning and rides to an affluent suburban neighborhood, where she does child care for a white professional couple. In the afternoon, she walks with her young charge to a well-appointed playground and watches him play, hoping that her own children have arrived safely at her sister's house after school. In the evening, she picks up her children; walking home, she quizzes them about school and their homework for the morning. She is proud that she can support her family but wants to make sure that her children can find better jobs.

Bonnie Thornton Dill (1988) points out that those in racial-ethnic groups whose labor has been exploited have been forced to adopt adaptive strategies for sustaining family life; the title of her article, Our Mothers' Grief, alludes to the emotional costs of these efforts. Many parents make extraordinary efforts to support their children's education, hoping they will do better than their parents and managing the mixed emotions that such an aspiration produces. Some take on debt in order to dress their children appropriately for school or provide them with some of the things that other children have. In addition, parents and children engage in painful (and no doubt often unspoken) dialogue about mutual responsibilities and aspirations. For example, one domestic worker interviewed by Dill reported:

They told me, my younger one especially, he said: Mommy, I don't want to go to college at your expense . . . I would not think of you workin' all your days—sometimes you go sick and I don't know how you gonna get back. You put us through school and you gave us a beautiful life. We'll get to college on our own. (1980, 113)

The effort of managing aspiration, opportunity, and the "hidden injuries of class" (Sennett and Cobb 1972) arise for white working-class and poor families as well.

Another task for some is helping family members survive a racist society. Much of this work may be relatively invisible, a matter of dignified persistence. Much of it looks straightforward and ordinary, simply a matter of loving attention to children, partners, and kin. But such loving attention acquires special significance when care and respect outside the family cannot be taken for granted. Family life is important for modeling and learning "survival strategies" (Ladner 1977) and the capacity to "travel" from one cultural "world" to another (Lugones 1987).

As family members share experiences and support, they must sort through various readings of their lives, developing both individual and collective interpretations that involve complex evaluations of strengths and failures; problems and joys; discrimination, resistance, and possibility.

Surviving oppression is not often identified as a distinctive form of work, perhaps because it is so much a part of the fabric of life in communities under siege. Some parents seem to avoid discussing racism, in order to manage their own pain and frustration or because they hope to protect their children by postponing such issues (Van Ausdale 1992). But autobiographical accounts (for example, hooks 1989) often convey the importance of family messages about race and identity. This kind of emotion work is also evident in discussions of mixed, or multiracial, family groups formed through marriage or adoption (Ladner 1977). Some suggest that this work spills over the boundaries of family as it is conventionally conceived, as in Elijah Anderson's account (1990) of "old heads" who serve as community mentors and Patricia Hill Collins's discussion (1990) of "othermothering" in African American communities.

These multiple layers of work also appear in the accounts of poor mothers whose children have disabilities. They were more likely than middle-class mothers to see the work of caring for a disabled child as simply "a part of life." Traustadottir (1991) suggests that they are relatively matter-of-fact about the child's disability because everyday struggles to arrange food and housing are so pressing. She also reports that these mothers advocate for services less frequently than middle-class mothers; indeed, they often resist professional intervention, fearing children could be taken away if parents are seen as unable to provide adequate care.

Passing and resistance

In some families, people must work at social acceptance, strategizing about whether and how to reveal stigmatized identities. For example, Laura Benkov's study (1994) of lesbian parents points to such experiences in encounters with institutions outside the home: A white lesbian mother goes to her school district's kindergarten orientation meeting, alone. Though she and her partner are equally involved in parenting and were "out" at their son's preschool, they feel more cautious now. They felt more in control at the preschool, knowing they could choose another setting if there were problems. After much disheartening discussion, they have made a decision, for the time being, at least: "that [they] won't make his life difficult" by being "out" at the kindergarten. They will test living with this new strategy, hoping to create "room to sort it out."

Gay and lesbian parents and their children face a mix of hostility and acceptance outside their homes that is difficult to predict or prepare for. Even those who are proudly and comfortably forthright in most settings make moment-to-moment decisions about what to reveal, to whom, and how. Such decisions, complex enough for individuals, acquire additional meanings when they involve navigating the emotional terrain of family life. Everyday matters such as the names used to distinguish two mothers may affect relationships both inside and outside the immediate family. In addition, children's desires for honesty and discretion change as they develop in awareness and move through varying social and educational settings. One of the mothers interviewed by Benkov (1994) anticipates her daughter's adolescence with some trepidation: "What I imagine is that she'll take me by surprise the first time, because that's often how kids are. They don't give you a month's notice, but two seconds before their friend walks in the door they might say, 'By the way, don't do any of that weird stuff in front of him'" (197). This mother's comment, on its face, emphasizes the need for improvisation at a moment's notice; however, it also reveals that she has begun the emotional preparation for that moment years in advance.

While such efforts are evident in gay and lesbian family life, we may be less likely to notice similar efforts undertaken by members of other families. But nearly every family that differs from the SNAF ideal probably feels some pressure and at least occasional moments of desire to pass as "normal." Step-parents and children negotiate kinship terms in blended families and consider how to present their relationships to others, much like the gay families discussed previously (Cherlin 1978). Single mothers sometimes hide that status from school officials, fearing it will affect professional evaluations of their children (Griffith 1984). Some adoptive parents seek children who are racially similar in order to diminish the salience of the adoptive relationship (Rothman 1989). Mothers whose children have disabilities work hard at maintaining normal family activities such as dinners or outings together, constantly assessing what is possible and what "normal" might mean (Traustadottir 1995). Parents and children often collude in keeping secrets about family troubles such as alcoholism and abuse (Cottle 1980).

Passing, however, is a controversial strategy for managing these family issues. Some parents join movements advocating fuller inclusion for children with disabilities, implicitly resisting pressures to appear "normal." Similarly, many gay and lesbian parents argue that children are best served by honesty, and their family strategies emphasize building pride and courage. Benkov (1994) reports that such parents seek diverse settings where their children will meet others from gay families, and work at helping children respond to homophobia as it arises. They also develop educational strategies: they talk with children about relationships and social attitudes, contact other parents to discuss issues that arise in their children's friendships, or encourage teachers and administrators to use materials representing gay families in positive ways. These efforts require time and resources, and those that are most assertively public carry social risks as well. Benkov does not specify how they are related to social class, but it seems likely that those parents who intervene most confidently with outsiders and institutions are those with other kinds of social power.

Decisions about passing and resistance arise for nearly everyone: moving back and forth between a family group and more public settings offers potent challenges of collective self-presentation (Goffman 1959). In all family groups, adults and children engage—explicitly or only through interaction—in a collective project of knowing who they are and in presenting various versions of that collective identity to outsiders. This work tends to fade from awareness when the wider culture supports it; families resembling the SNAF ideal see themselves reflected in many cultural representations and easily think of themselves as ordinary. The work is more visible and difficult when family members must struggle to sustain a sense of themselves as worthy.

CONCLUSION

Much social policy and public discourse about family life is based on the SNAF ideal. As a result, institutions are frequently organized as if families can provide infinitely flexible emotional safety nets. Schools are organized around a standard curriculum; when students fall behind, teachers depend on mothers to provide extra help with homework (Smith 1987; Griffith and Smith 1987). Health care providers depend on unpaid caregivers at home; managed care is increasing this "work transfer" to the home, and the stress produced by the recruitment of family members to perform as "amateur nurses" likely saps their ability to provide loving support (Glazer 1990). Policies of deinstitutionalization—while liberating those with disabilities from dehumanizing settings—have relied on community care, and feminist researchers have shown that this means increasing the family and volunteer work undertaken mostly by women (Land 1978; Traustadottir 1992). Welfare reform in the United States provides another case: policies insisting that single mothers enter the labor force too often assume someone is at home to provide maintenance and child care.

Even without sharp definition, the idea of emotion work has served as an extremely useful "sensitizing concept" (Blumer 1969, 148). It has put on the public agenda a range of previously neglected activities and made a matter for debate the questions of how such work is to be done and how to support those doing it. Existing studies of family emotion work, mostly emphasizing the work women do in standard North American families, provide one piece of the picture and also provoke further questions. I have suggested a few avenues for expanding the range of the concept, but there are others, too. Few researchers have investigated how men take up or resist these kinds of efforts (exceptions are Hochschild with Machung 1989; Hochschild 1997), or the distinctive forms of work men themselves might identify in their family lives. Similarly, few scholars have considered how children are recruited into family emotion work, yet children surely attend to emotional needs of other family members, and the emotional strategies that parents devise must often implicate children in collective efforts.

Suggestions for expanding notions of family emotion work run up against the charge of nearly infinite conceptual elasticity, as well as resistance to making so much of family life a matter of work. Often, resistance seems to come from those who benefit from the performance of this work. But those who do family work would likely also want to recognize and honor other ways of understanding family relations, as possible sites of pleasure, play, growth, and connection, for example (see Thorne 1987). The reason to label and examine family emotion work, I would argue, is neither to draw distinctions for their own sake nor to impose some monolithic understanding of the activities of family life. What seems valuable in this way of thinking is its potential to provide fuller, more accurate accounts of how family members work at sustaining themselves as individuals and collectivities. Such full accounts are surely an essential foundation for equitable policy aimed at enhancing the well-being of all citizens.

References

Anderson, Elijah. 1990. *Streetwise: Race, Class, and Change in an Urban Community*. Chicago: University of Chicago Press.

Benkov, Laura. 1994. *Reinventing the Family: The Emerging Story of Lesbian and Gay Parents*. New York: Crown Trade Paperbacks.

Blumer, Herbert. 1969. *Symbolic Interactionism: Perspective and Method*. Englewood Cliffs, NJ: Prentice Hall.

Cherlin, Andrew J. 1978. Remarriage as an Incomplete Institution. *American Journal of Sociology* 84:634-50.

Collins, Patricia Hill. 1990. *Black Feminist Thought: Knowledge, Consciousness, and the Politics of Empowerment*. Boston: Unwin Hyman.

Cottle, Thomas. 1980. *Children's Secrets*. Garden City, NY: Anchor Press.

DeVault, Marjorie L. 1991. *Feeding the Family: The Social Organization of Caring as Gendered Work*. Chicago: University of Chicago Press.

Dill, Bonnie Thornton. 1980. "The Means to Put My Children Through": Child-Rearing Goals and Strategies Among Black Female Domestic Servants. In *The Black Woman*, ed. La Frances Rodgers-Rose. Beverly Hills, CA: Sage.

———. 1988. Our Mothers' Grief: Racial Ethnic Women and the Maintenance of Families. *Journal of Family History* 13:415-31.

Duncombe, Jean and Dennis Marsden. 1995. "Workaholics" and "Whingeing Women": Theorising Intimacy and Emotion Work—the Last Frontier of Gender Inequality. *Sociological Review* 43:150-69.

Erickson, Rebecca J. 1993. Reconceptualizing Family Work: The Effect of Emotion Work on Perceptions of Marital Quality. *Journal of Marriage and the Family* 55:888-900.

Glazer, Nona. 1990. The Home as Workshop: Women as Amateur Nurses and Medical Care Providers. *Gender & Society* 4:479-97.

Goffman, Erving. 1959. *The Presentation of Self in Everyday Life*. Garden City, NY: Doubleday.

Griffith, Alison I. 1984. Ideology, Education and Single Parent Families: The Normative Ordering of Families Through Schooling. Ph.D. diss., University of Toronto.

Griffith, Alison I. and Dorothy E. Smith. 1987. Constructing Cultural Knowledge: Mothering as Discourse. In

Women and Education: A Canadian Perspective, ed. Jane Gaskell and Arlene McLaren. Calgary: Detselig Enterprises.

Hochschild, Arlie Russell. 1983. *The Managed Heart: Commercialization of Human Feeling*. Berkeley: University of California Press.

———. 1990. Ideology and Emotion Management: A Perspective and Path for Future Research. In *Research Agendas in the Sociology of Emotions*, ed. Theodore D. Kemper. Albany: State University of New York Press.

———. 1997. *The Time Bind: When Work Becomes Home and Home Becomes Work*. New York: Metropolitan Books.

Hochschild, Arlie Russell with Anne Machung. 1989. *The Second Shift: Working Parents and the Revolution at Home*. New York: Viking.

hooks, bell. 1989. *Talking Back: Thinking Feminist, Thinking Black*. Boston: South End Press.

Ladner, Joyce A. 1977. *Mixed Families: Adopting Across Racial Boundaries*. New York: Doubleday, Anchor Press.

Land, Hilary. 1978. Who Cares for the Family? *Journal of Social Policy* 7:257-84.

Larson, Reed and Maryse H. Richards. 1994. *Divergent Realities: The Emotional Lives of Mothers, Fathers, and Adolescents*. New York: Basic Books.

Lugones, Maria. 1987. Playfulness, "World"-Travelling, and Loving Perception. *Hypatia* 2:3-19

Rollins, Judith. 1985. *Between Women: Domestics and Their Employers*. Philadelphia: Temple University Press.

Romo, Harriett D. and Toni Falbo. 1996. *Latino High School Graduation: Defying the Odds*. Austin: University of Texas Press.

Rothman, Barbara Katz. 1989. *Recreating Motherhood: Ideology and Technology in a Patriarchal Society*. New York: Norton.

Ruddick, Sara. 1980. Maternal Thinking. *Feminist Studies* 6:342-67.

Seery, Brenda L. 1996. Four Types of Mothering Emotion Work: Distress Management, Ego Work, Relationship Management, and Pleasure/Enjoyment Work. Ph.D. diss., Pennsylvania State University.

Sennett, Richard and Jonathan Cobb. 1972. *The Hidden Injuries of Class*. New York: Knopf.

Smith, Dorothy E. 1987. *The Everyday World as Problematic: A Feminist Sociology*. Boston: Northeastern University Press.

———. 1993. The Standard North American Family: SNAF as an Ideological Code. *Journal of Family Issues* 14:50-65.

Thorne, Barrie. 1987. Re-visioning Women and Social Change: Where Are the Children? *Gender & Society* 1:85-109.

Traustadottir, Rannveig. 1991. Mothers Who Care: Gender, Disability, and Family Life. *Journal of Family Issues* 12:211-28.

———. 1992. Disability Reform and the Role of Women: Community Inclusion and Caring Work. Ph.D. diss., Syracuse University.

———. 1995. A Mother's Work Is Never Done: Constructing a "Normal" Family Life. In *The Variety of Community Experience: Qualitative Studies of Family and Community Life*, ed. Steven J. Taylor, Robert Bogdan, and Zana Marie Lutfiyya. Baltimore, MD: Paul H. Brookes.

Van Ausdale, Debra. 1992. Learning About Race: Racial Socialization Techniques Used by Black, Middle Class Parents. Master's thesis, University of Florida.

Wharton, Amy S. and Rebecca J. Erickson. 1995. The Consequences of Caring: Exploring the Links Between Women's Job and Family Emotion Work. *Sociological Quarterly* 36:273-96.

ANNALS, *AAPSS*, **561**, January 1999

Changing Scripts at Work:
Managers and Professionals

By GIDEON KUNDA and JOHN VAN MAANEN

ABSTRACT: In this article, the authors explore how structural changes in the labor market for professional and managerial employees might be changing the nature of emotional labor required in these occupations. They first draw on ethnographic data in a firm noted for stable long-term employment to illustrate how efforts to create a corporate culture focus on shaping employees' emotional labor toward displays of loyalty and commitment to their employer. This is followed by a speculative analysis of how the current shift toward market-based forms of employment and an entrepreneurial work ethic is changing both the substance and the style of emotional labor.

Gideon Kunda is a senior lecturer in the Department of Labor Studies at Tel Aviv University. His book Engineering Culture *(1992) won the American Sociological Association's Culture Section Book of the Year award in 1994.*

John Van Maanen is the Erwin Schell Professor of Organization Studies in the Sloan School at the Massachusetts Institute of Technology. He has published in the areas of occupational and organizational sociology. His most recent book is Representation in Ethnography *(1995).*

Our sense of being a person can come from being drawn into a wider social unit; our sense of selfhood can arise through the little ways in which we resist the pull. Our status is backed by the solid buildings of the world, while our sense of personal identity often resides in the cracks.

—Erving Goffman (1961, 320)

From any popular business book plucked from the rack of an airport bookstore these days, it would appear that the "solid buildings" of Erving Goffman's crisp analogy are fast melting away. Change, on all fronts, personal, social, and institutional, is the mantra of our times; we are reminded—endlessly and relentlessly—that the only constant is change. To survive, we must come to terms with turbulent environments, thrive on rampant chaos, welcome rapidly changing markets, adjust to high degrees of uncertainty, and celebrate seemingly perpetual technological revolutions. If change is now the norm, lessons learned from the past are suspect. A new age, it seems, requires new solutions.[1]

The discourse centering on change seems particularly pronounced when it comes to understanding the occupational and organizational realities within which the more central participants in corporate life—managerial and professional employees—pass their days. If we are to still trust conventional wisdom and scholarship, these are the people who, as both subjects and agents of control, represent the core of the corporate world. Once referred to as "white-collar" (in an age when categories were clear-cut and dress codes carried homogenizing weight), they are still identifiable by the long hours they work, the responsibilities they shoulder, the Dilbert-like cubes they occupy, and the kinds of special expertise they claim. By all accounts, managers and professionals (particularly engineers) are those who most closely identify with the companies for whom they work.[2] They are the heart and soul of the modern corporation, representing its intellectual capital, organizational memory, and, in business school code, core competencies.

The close identification of managers and professionals with their employing firms rests historically on a bargain or social contract struck when organizations first began to grow rapidly in size, scope, and power: loyalty in return for a career, commitment in return for identity, dedicated performance in return for meaningful work. As part of the deal, companies offered not only good salaries, generous benefits, and, in some cases, equity in the form of stock options but also the presumption—psychological if not legal—of long-term job security.[3] Managers and professionals, in return, were expected to bring to the job not only their cognitive capacities and technical expertise but, more crucially, a willingness to put forth a form of what Hochschild (1983) calls "emotional labor"—a publicly displayed investment and passion for the work they do, the work relations they forge, and the company that employs them.[4] Such emotional labor concerns the way managers and professionals represent agency and responsibility to others in the organization. It can be indexed by the ease or difficulty they have absorbing and making use of the socially acceptable language heard and spoken in a firm as to the kind of employee that gets ahead and, by implication, the kind of employee they are, at least on the surface, to emulate.

This discourse has undergone change over the past decade or so and is the subject of our somewhat breathless analysis. Our remarks rest on the well-founded worry that the historical social contract between large corporations and their central employees is being challenged, if not voided, by waves of reengineering, downsizing, outsourcing, layoffs, renegotiated work contracts, and reneged promises of job security. The center, it seems, no longer holds. Surviving residents of the core of the business firm are beginning to experience conditions once reserved—indeed, thought natural— for their distant neighbors, the hourly workforce of blue, pink, or no collar. Evidence for this new turn is everywhere.[5] A growing number of technical and managerial positions are taken up by contract workers. Promises of guaranteed employment are now increasingly retracted and, at best, replaced with promises of "employability," a fur ball of a term suggesting that in return for hard work in one firm, employees learn skills and gain experience useful to other firms and thus gain some advantage in external job markets. Work roles in firms are stripped away or redefined such that long-tenured employees become independent contractors who must market their services to others inside (or outside) the company. Others pick up the slack created by a thinner corporate entity while continuing to do whatever it was they did before their office mates departed.[6] Such structural changes do not, of course, lessen the physical, cognitive, or emotional demands that go with contemporary work, but they are quite likely to change the way they are felt and expressed. How have the changing conditions and expectations about employment influenced the ways that managers and professionals approach, perform, and talk about their work? How, in particular, is emotional labor in the workplace changing for managers and professionals, and what might we expect in the future?

We address these questions by first linking them to a set of ideas loosely bundled under the heading "organizational culture." We begin by commenting on the emergence of this framework and then provide a brief glimpse from the past of an organization noted for its concerted attempt to elicit and direct emotional labor. This look into the recent past provides a contrast for our closing (and speculative) glance at how recent structural changes may be altering the language, work relations, and performed identities of managerial and professional employees in the organizations of the present and future.[7]

CULTURE IN THE CORPORATION

It was to gain an understanding of the complex and often unique ways organizations developed over time and shaped the work lives of their employees that the term "corporate culture" emerged some 15-20 years ago. Borrowed by a small set of students of organization from their reference disciplines of anthropology and sociology, the culture concept found widespread use and acceptance in both academic and applied domains.[8] Business firms, argued the culture vultures, are best viewed not as rational systems driven simply by concerns for efficiency and profit but as collective systems governed by socially relevant rules and meanings that members draw on to carry out and make sense of their work activities and relations with others. Work organizations, like any other form of human association, are cultural phenomena best understood and managed by taking into explicit account their symbolic character, ritual properties, and embedded—if contested—systems of meaning.

Much of our own research attempts to represent organizations in just this sort of cultural light. Based on ethnographic fieldwork, we have worked on cultural portraits of a variety of organizations including police agencies, amusement parks, and probation departments (see, for example, Kunda 1986; Barley and Kunda 1992; Van Maanen and Kunda 1989; Van Maanen 1986, 1992). The study we will draw on to illustrate our argument (Kunda 1992) offers a critical analysis of self-conscious managerial efforts to design, articulate, and impose an explicit corporate culture in a business organization that was, for a time, enormously successful. The company is High Technologies Corporation ("Tech")—a pseudonym for a leading computer firm of the 1970s and 1980s, celebrated by the business press as a leading exemplar of successful cultural management. Brief illustrations of the practical realities of such cultural management and the emotional labor it prompted at Tech follow. Of importance, however, is that the Tech of today is different from the Tech of yesterday. It has lost both its glitter and its independence. This is a critical matter because it allows us the opportunity to suggest just how the emotional labor expected of professional and managerial employees at Tech—and elsewhere—may also be changing. But let us turn to the ethnographic record first.

HIGH-TECH WORK: THE LABORS OF LOYALTY

High Technologies Corporation gained its reputation not only for its much heralded technical expertise, complex and altogether creative products, and, for its time, market power but also for the social vision that emerged and apparently guided Tech's founders during the firm's formative years. Senior management believed that a corporation wishing to encourage state-of-the-art innovation and the heavy investment of time and effort required on the part of its core employees must offer a working environment that was challenging but safe. A strong rhetoric of autonomy ("be your own boss," "show initiative," "talk back") and security ("lifetime employment," "organizational tenure," "a career, not a job") flourished within the firm. To realize and accompany this discourse, top managers tried in a most self-conscious fashion to design a kind of workplace that would relieve employees of the constraints and frustrations of bureaucracy while encouraging them to take risks, yet foster a sense of community within which employees could feel secure.

Considerable efforts were undertaken in the firm to codify and disseminate a Tech culture. In particular, attempts were made to specify rather precisely the kind of emotional labor required of successful and hence exemplary employees in the firm. Consider, for instance, an excerpt from a widely distributed booklet available to employees outlining the Tech philosophy.

We believe that individual discipline should be self-generated. . . . We promote people according to their performance; not only their technical ability but also their ability to get the job done and to take the responsibility that goes with the job. Ability is measured not only by past results but also by attitude and desire to succeed. (Kunda 1992, 55)

How exactly an employee might display such an attitude and desire was laid out more explicitly in another of the company's more popular internal publications, the *Tech Culture Handbook*.

A lot of people we hire into this company, at least the ones that stick around, have basically the same mindset. Someone who is innovative, enthusiastic, willing to work hard, who isn't hung up on structure, and who has absolutely no concern with educational background. They demand an awful lot from themselves. The harshest critic in the system is yourself and that drives you to do some terribly difficult things. You have to be a self-starter. An individual who takes chances and risks and moves ahead. The expectation is that everyone is going to work hard, not for hard work's sake, but for the fun of it, and enjoy doing what they are doing, and show commitment no matter what it takes. A core of the environment is individual commitment, a lot of integrity, and a very high level of expectations from yourself. Hassle is the price of the organizational structure. For those who don't like it, it's very frustrating. You can wrap those three or four things together (openness, honesty, success, fairness) and you can sum it all up in one word and that is caring. Caring about your job, the people who work for you, yourself. (Kunda 1992, 73)

Such managerial-sponsored codification of required emotional responses was a ubiquitous, familiar, and almost taken-for-granted backdrop to everyday life at Tech (and, at the time, no doubt, elsewhere). Metaphors of "total involvement," "passion," and "addiction to work" framed notions of company loyalty and work commitment. There was more to Tech culture, however, than abstract formulations. The texts of emotional labor were brought to life in many of the ritualized encounters between employees and recognized by all members as an integral and required part of work life. These occasions— group meetings, presentations of various sorts, training sessions, speeches on the part of senior managers, as well as the less formal (but nonetheless public) interactions between managers and professionals of the firm occurring in corridors, parking lots, cafeterias, and cubicles— offered countless opportunities for organizational members to experience, learn, display, and comment on the prescribed emotions that were thought to go with membership. A workshop designed to introduce new engineers to the company's way of life provides an elaborate and extended look back at the frontstage management of emotion and meaning at Tech. The workshop focuses on teaching the participants, in no uncertain terms, exactly what Tech culture is all about and what it demands of them.

Ellen (the trainer) writes the word "culture" on a large flipchart and says:

"The topic today is culture. We have a spectrum of people here from all over the company. Feel free to chime in. 'Culture' has become something of a fad. First, what is 'culture?' What do you think?"

A young engineer slouching in the corner answers: "Fungus. I had a culture for my senior science project. But my dog ate it." Some laugh. Ellen smiles too, but continues undaunted. "We're looking at behavior, at people. What is the characteristic of people at Tech?" She waits, marker in hand, with a warm, inviting looking smile, nodding in anticipation, perhaps indicating the signs of affirmation she is looking for. Her question hangs. No answers. Some coffee sipping. "You feel like you've all been chosen, right?" she says, nodding her head more vigorously and still smiling. Still no replies. The stony silence highlights the incongruity of her demeanor, but she persists. "What else? What are people like at Tech?" Some volunteers speak up, drawn in by discomfort, if nothing else: "Friendly." "Amicable." She writes it all on the flip chart. The tempo picks up: "Individual- and teamwork." "I'm expected to be a good corporate citizen." "Strong customer orientation." "People tend to like Tech no matter

how confused," she says, and adds: "How do you feel?"

Some of the participants raise their hands. She calls on each in turn.

"I like it here. I hope for profit. I respect Sam [i.e., the founder] a lot."

"Where I worked before you'd hope they fail! Here the executives aren't as ruthless as in other companies; they are more humane. I haven't met anyone here I don't respect."

"I flash off on the (electronic mail) and get to people without them wondering why; they are open and willing to share information."

As they speak, Ellen makes encouraging sounds and lists key phrases on the chart: "profit; not ruthless; humane; respect; open; share info; tolerance, supportive." When the sheet is full, she pulls it off the flipchart, pastes it to the wall and says: "This is what makes Tech a different kind of place. People are relaxed and informal. What else?" Someone says: "There is little difference between engineers and managers; it's hard to tell them apart." "Authority Not a Big Deal," she writes in bold letters on the flip chart. Then she adds: "In other places you're incompetent till proved otherwise; here it's the other way around, right?" Not waiting for an answer, she writes, "Confidence in competence," and says: "They know what they are doing, or believe it." "A little too much," the guy sitting next to me whispers to his neighbor.

Ellen turns to the flip chart, writes "We Are A Family," and says: "This is the most important one. We have a no-layoff policy. It's the ultimate backup plan. It would break some people's hearts if we had to do it. We face it as a family: cutting costs, hiring freezes. Every member is asked to contribute."

A young woman from corporate who has been silent so far, bursts out in a concerned, almost angry tone: "I work in corporate. A lot of the stuff is only a myth there. I see the very high up people fight people fighting to the death. . . ." Ellen interrupts her rather brusquely: "Tech isn't wonderful or glowing. It's not. It's human. But it's the best I've seen! I was a nomad before I came here. I'm sorry you haven't seen the rest of the companies so you can appreciate Tech. (Pause.) That is another thing about Tech. People are quick to point out faults, as if they didn't have any."

(Ellen) wins more and more ground with every minute of the meeting.

The emotional intensity of the module's conclusion seems to captivate all the participants as Ellen flips off the viewgraph, puts down the marker, and gives a short talk that sounds off-the-record, very personal, almost motherly: "There is a downside to all of this! There can be a lot of pain in the system! Be careful; keep a balance; don't overdo it, don't live off vending machines for a year. (Laughter.) You'll burn out. I've been there; I lived underground for a year, doing code. Balance your life. Don't say: 'I'll work like crazy for four years, then I'll get married.' I heard this from a kid. But who will he marry? Don't let the company suck you dry; after nine or ten hours your work isn't worth much anyway."

The sudden switch to a subversive sounding message creates the air of rapt attention. All eyes are on her as she walks slowly from the flipchart to the center of the room. After a brief pause, she adds the finishing touch; "What kind of company do you think allows me to be saying these things to you?" Nobody stirs for a few moments, and then a break is called. (Kunda 1992, 109-13)

Events of this sort capture many of the recurring themes associated with the ritual enactment of Tech culture. In particular, the orientation workshop for engineering newcomers illustrates how the substance of managerial codification and, in particular, the rules for appropriate emotional display are brought to employees' attention, how they are taught appropriate responses, how deviants are sanctioned in public, and how such events allow participants to collectively enact what they are taught. It is these ritual performances that give the official version of Tech culture—then and now—the emotional charge needed to bring it to life.

The continued performance of emotional labor has, of course, consequences. Unlike many lower-level workers, for whom similar emotional displays are delimited, highly scripted, awkwardly and self-consciously performed, and, therefore, while perhaps taxing, not really binding, managerial and professional work requires the sort of emotional labor that runs deep.[9] Some may experience and incorporate the emotional displays asked of them as authentic manifestations of their "real feelings" and "true selves." A common statement of identification (and one we think survives a hint of irony) comes from a Tech engineer in 1988.

You know, I like Tech. I don't think of leaving. People might say that the culture swallowed me, but there really is a feeling of loyalty I have. We have a lot of that in the culture. We like working for Tech. It is a positive company. You get really involved. I get a real charge when Tech gets a good press. Or when people I knew from this other company were dumping on Tech, I was offended. I didn't like hearing it. My husband works for Tech and he feels the same way. We spend time with friends talking about work; we're worse than doctors. I guess you can call me a Techie. (Quoted in Kunda 1992, 170)

On other occasions, submerged irony surfaced explicitly among peers in various backstage settings where maintaining an appropriate distance from company rhetoric was a standard requirement of self-presentation.

They are making more out of this culture stuff than it's worth. You have to laugh. It's an instance of self-consciousness. "Look at us enjoying ourselves, being good guys." I never read that stuff, maybe see it in passing. It's the same nauseating stuff they print in Business Week.

I've learned here that you can do your own job, but you have to let the waves flow over you; ignore them or you'll go crazy. There is a lot of shit coming down, people wandering around, consultants, studies; that's the way it is, but they really stuff ten pounds of shit into five-pound bags. I have a Russian immigrant friend who says it reminds him of the USSR; all this shit about Big Brother.

You have to have a thick skin to survive. You must depersonalize; it's a rough environment. Take all this stuff professionally, not personally. I have to keep reminding myself it's a game. I should watch it and enjoy it.

Techies. We're all Techies. The whole goddamn industry. It's a type of individual who is aggressive and involved, looks loyal, puts in a lot of time. But underneath the surface he is self-serving and owes allegiance only to himself.

I'm developing a thick hide. Before I take anyone's advice, or react to yelling and screaming, I think about what their agenda is. (Quoted in Kunda 1992, 180-85)

That managers and engineers held multiple, often contradictory views on what was expected of them was not a problem at Tech as long as they displayed the appropriate sentiments in frontstage settings. Yet, public displays of identification with managerially prescribed views of membership did raise questions of authenticity and generated a good deal of backstage talk. By and large, however, most engineers and managers at Tech consumed the corporate culture imposed on them by adapting to the parts that suited their needs and distancing themselves from other parts. Even as they talked about "trusting the company," "buying in," or "being a Techie," most could also easily construct and communicate to others an image of the firm as powerful, uncaring, and exploitative. The organizational self that emerged was founded on a precarious balance of contradictory images.[10]

Such a response resembles deCerteau's analysis of everyday life (1984)—including, importantly, work life—where resistance to a dominant ideology is expressed not through action but through the formulation of alternative perspectives on the ideology, hence modifying it to suit one's interests. At Tech, managers and professionals escaped the dominant ideology without leaving the organization since only the public conformity mattered within the firm. Such a stance involves a good deal of emotional labor since in addition to whatever technical skills are required to accomplish one's job comes the necessity of also knowing when, where, and how to display fealty, cynicism, enthusiasm, indifference, and passion while carrying the abiding faith that one's performance skills are up to the task.

In our earlier work, we argued that cultural management of the sort outlined here is a form of corporate control representing a sometimes subtle, sometimes overt attempt to define, shape, and monitor not only the work behavior of employees—the traditional object of managerial control—but also the thoughts and, most crucially, the feelings of employees (Van Maanen and Kunda 1989). As suggested, these well-funded and much discussed practices at Tech were intended to broaden and intensify the inherent pleasures of technical work while bringing forth expressions of loyalty and commitment to the company. As one of the trainers in the culture module described earlier said of her charges, "They come to us in love with the technology; it is our job to marry them to the company."

This type of control focusing on expressed and felt emotion complements Edwards's well-known three-part typology of organizational control systems (1979): simple coercive control, technical control of production processes, and bureaucratic control of workplace rules and procedures. Emotional control, on the face of it, seems particularly suited to the requirements of managing a select, well-educated, and technically skilled workforce comprising individuals not thought to respond well to coercive, technical, or bureaucratic forms of control—forms thought by many students of organizations to stifle creativity, undermine initiative, evacuate meaning, and chill enthusiasm. Compared to traditional control mechanisms, cultural control promised much, and, certainly for a time when Tech and similar companies were riding high as models of managerial best practices, cultural control seemed to work and work well.[11]

Like all theories, of course, cultural management had, even in good times, its share of critics. It was, in fact, the very success and proliferation of "the Tech way" that we—and many others—found troubling enough to justify sharp criticism shaped by a concern for the human and moral consequences of such forms of social control. But the most successful, indeed, the most deadly of critics came not from the ranks of disgruntled social observers but from the top ranks of the corporation itself. Increasingly, those charged with the bottom line began to claim that cultural control was simply too costly to sustain in the long run. Thus, as the cultural management style peaked in the late 1980s, the bargain on which it rested and from which it drew its appeal proved much less stable than we assumed.

Tech itself underwent a series of upheavals as our reports were being published. Its founder and original management team were asked to leave by a board of directors concerned with declining financial performance and threats to long-term viability as perceived by stockholders. One of the first steps taken by the new management, as reported widely at the time in the business press, was to get rid of the culture, streamline management, and, most tellingly, end once and for all the costly no-layoff policy by carrying out large-scale downsizing. Thus, at Tech, the promise of security in return for commitment is now history. With its demise came changes in both the substance and style of the emotional labor required of the firm's professional and managerial employees.

BEYOND LOYALTY

One way to summarize recent developments in many U.S. labor markets of the 1990s is to point out that the distinction between core and periphery employees no longer coincides with a straight-ahead contrast between the exempt, or salaried, class and the nonexempt, or contract, class. In our earlier writings, such a mapping was fairly clear and consequential. Contract employees were mostly lower-level, support, hourly workers and regarded by senior management as marginal, treated as "extra-cultural," and subjected to impersonal but direct forms of control (coercive, technical, and bureaucratic). Core employees were those of the middle and upper ranks, salaried with bonus expectations, considered central, and therefore the targets of cultural engineering. Today, however, in many companies like Tech, the periphery has invaded the center. Moreover, current managerial wisdom and practice has it that such companies—in the name of competi-

tiveness, cost consciousness, and profitability—must treat an increasing part of their managerial and professional workforce as transient.[12] Such wisdom and practice are changing the form and substance of emotional labor in the workplace.

The rhetoric of organizational communities and cultures is being replaced—swiftly it seems—by the rhetoric of markets and entrepreneurs. Miller and Rose (1990) call this the "language of enterprise": when given full voice, employees from the bottom to the top are labeled "empowered," urged to take ownership of their jobs, called on to act as their own bosses and to behave as if they are running their own little businesses within the larger concern.[13] In this hypothetical new world, managerial control gives way to market control, and the marketplace decides what kind of emotional labor pays off. Passions are to be put to work on specific tasks and projects and not directed toward the company or social relations. The imagery of love and marriage fades into obscurity, replaced by an imagery of temporary, short-term affairs or one-night stands. Thus, prevailing rhetorics of motive no longer cite the commitment to corporate communities and the orderly career ladders they provide; instead they emphasize the legitimacy of seeking "sexy projects" and "hot technologies" wherever they may be found.

In this environment, managers and professionals are often told by senior managers to think of their work (or business unit) as a product or service to be sold to others within the firm. Communal feelings give way to market calculations, and emotional labor serves to limit, not embrace, commitment and to manage rejection and separation rather than affiliation. Managerial shoptalk concerns flexibility and ways to grow or shrink the workforce on a moment's notice. To be nimble, to be quick are codes for market responsiveness, and good managers in such a world must find ways to restrict the involvement of an increasingly contingent labor force, prevent emotional attachments to the firm, and make sure that employees, when shown the door, will not seek the window instead.

Such hard-headed discourse and the hard-hearted practices it encourages may suit some but not others within a firm. Yet, whatever an individual's stance toward what Wasson (1996) calls "the language of enterprise," emotional labor remains a matter of concern for organizational members of both high and low rank. For employees still considered central or core, the relationship with their employer remains ostensibly the same. Employers may rely on a thinner, presumably more select cadre of managers and professionals, but they still expect an intense continuing relationship with them governed by the rules of exchanging emotional investment for corporate benefits. Members of this cadre know, however, that the growing number of contingent professional and managerial colleagues is not far away. Core employees realize they could become peripheral on short notice.

This has led to certain rhetorical contortions on the part of employers and employees alike. One frequently heard corporate line says to anxious managers and professionals, "Do not expect lengthy careers in this organization but expect to have your skills tested, polished, and acknowledged such that you will continue to be valued in the labor market." This deal offers employability over continued employment, and those subject to such a deal may well experience acute and contradictory pressures. To wit, performance pressures are likely to become more severe, driven by a desire to remain in the core; but the core itself has no firm foundation and swells or contracts according to a market logic beyond individual and often corporate control.

As we write, the core-periphery model is in its heyday. The benefits of the market-based flexibility of labor seem apparent (and wondrous) as the American economy steams ahead while those of its competitors, including those in Asia once held up as examples of the economic value of communal work cultures and long-term attachments, languish. With such success come promoters of the individualized work ethic who find flattened hierarchies and deregulated market relationships between employers and employees advantageous for all. We are witnessing the use of a fragmented, individualized market model to design optimal organizations in both the private and public spheres. Out of the ashes of discredited bureaucracy, stuck with metaphors of obesity and waste, familiar notions again appear, including laissez-faire capitalism and the survival of the fittest.

In this back-to-the-future world, certain kinds of people are thought more likely to prosper than others. Inside the firm, self-starters are crucial, independence is a must, entrepreneurial spirits are venerated. Individuals, small work groups, and business units are asked to market their services to potential customers in the company. All set profit goals. Each is a customer to others who evaluate one another closely as to the quality of goods and services they send and receive. In theory, any activity, from product design to accounting, from building security to training, from manufacturing to sales, can be turned over to outside providers. Organizational accountability for employee welfare is on the slide. It is now up to the individual, not the firm, to create and sustain a product or service useful to the enterprise. Responsibility for the design and development of a career involving continuous employment, learning, progression, upward or lateral mobility shifts away from the employer to the individual.

In many ways, this language of enterprise is a marked departure from the traditional discourse of organizing. The image of the organization as composed of vertical chains linking superiors and subordinates in a web of prescribed authority relations—the hallmark of bureaucracy—has been replaced by a rhetoric emphasizing horizontal flows of information and networks of supplier and customer relations. When push comes to shove, however, hierarchy reasserts itself. Despite some leveling, major corporate decisions such as restructuring, outsourcing, plant closings, and downsizing are not made by the empowered business units or team leaders directly affected by such decisions. These are choices made by people at the top of the corporate hierarchy, even if their role in the company is now somewhat obscured by the currently fashionable language.

For those managers and professionals occupying the lower levels of the corporation, a good deal of emotional labor these days goes into articulating their autonomy and vaulted, take-charge initiative in the face of obvious but unmentionable constraints. Change efforts aimed at encouraging entrepreneurial-like activities throughout a firm give the impression that old forms of control have been jettisoned in favor of free-wheeling marketplace forms. Employees are, of course, cautious, but most know they must often appear in ideologically correct garb and conduct themselves in public as agents of entrepreneurial zeal: productive, enterprising, flexible, self-regulating active—not reactive—corporate actors. Yet, offstage, as in times past, these same employees are quite able to construct themselves rather differently—as relatively powerless subjects buffeted by larger forces, unable to take control of their own destinies or pack their own parachutes.

Nonetheless, emotional labor remains as intense and critical as ever. The loyal subjects of the 1980s may have become the entrepreneurial agents of the 1990s, but they must still take care to manage impressions properly while getting work out the door. However, the entrepreneurial agent, more so than the loyal subject, must also deal with an austerity logic that governs—at least partially—the financial choices made by firms. It is a neoliberal, marketplace logic that treats individuals as the locus of decision making and holds that efficiency, quality, and productivity are best achieved through markets existing both outside and, of increasing importance, inside the organization. If a market does not exist within the firm, it must then be created. Such a logic transforms managers and professionals into responsible agents who are to sell their services to potential customers in and out of the company. Demand is the measure of their worth, and they must build a market for their work or find themselves moved to the periphery or beyond. Survival for entrepreneurial agents depends not only on the usefulness or value of the services they offer but also on their sales skills, communication abilities, and image- building talents, all matters requiring considerable emotional labor but rather different from that associated with loyal subjects.

There are limits to the marketplace model. In particular, the model's viability rests on assumptions upon which its own theoretical underpinnings cast doubt—namely, the continued growth and availability of work in a society over time. It is only through boundless economic expansion that a highly contingent, mobile, entrepreneurial population of managers and professionals can be institutionalized and supported by the claim that employability justifies the physical, cognitive, and emotional rigors of the trades. These conditions mark the current hour. But, if history is our guide, such conditions are impermanent and cyclical. Forward-looking students of salaried professional and managerial work should begin to concern themselves with the kinds of realities employers and employees will face when a workforce whose capacity and taste for emotional labor, shaped by unregulated market processes and entrepreneurial images, encounters the dark and down side of the market that we know is waiting in the wings. The script will surely change again.

Notes

1. The change literature is enormous. It runs from the serious scholarship of Piore and Sabel's landmark study *The Second Industrial Divide* (1984) to the frankly normative and gushing promotion of new forms of work organization displayed by Tom Peter's recent *Circle of Innovation* (1997), in which loyalty to the organization is out (as are formal organizations themselves) and self-promotion is in through "the creation—and maintenance—of a BRAND CALLED YOU" (6). Solid descriptive and analytic works—both historical and contemporary—are to be found in the field of organizational change, but they are dwarfed by the prescriptive literature of the sort stocked by airport booksellers.

2. Writings on individual identification with work and organization have a long and distinguished history. Early works include Mills's influential treatment of corporate managers in *White Collar* (1956) and Whyte's powerful indictment of *The Organization Man* (1956). Recent work in much the same tradition includes Kanter 1977, Jackall 1988, and Smith 1990.

3. These more or less structural matters are covered well by Doeringer and Piore (1972), Osterman (1984, 1988), Jacoby (1985), and Kochan, Katz, and McKersie (1994).

4. It is worth noting that much of the empirical literature on emotional labor has tended to focus on the use of emotions in the context of service encounters. Service encounters—where the emotions of clients are clearly

and directly the object of work and where the emotions of service providers are its medium—obviously lend themselves to such an analytic framework, as Hochschild's groundbreaking work (1983) illustrates. Moreover, the explicit use of the language of emotion in such encounters provides an easily accessible source of data for researchers. Producing satisfied customers, however, is but a salient subset of emotional labor. Emotions—nuanced perhaps, even suppressed or denied—permeate all work that occurs in a social context, and constant efforts are required to learn, present, and shape them in acceptable ways. We believe that discovering and attending to these less noticed forms of emotional labor—in our case, the labor entailed in producing and presenting loyalty and commitment—will serve to broaden our view and enhance our understanding both of this concept and of the worlds of work within which it occurs.

5. As might be expected, the research literature on the restructuring of the workplace is growing rapidly. A few first-rate and recent empirical studies of direct relevance to our interests here include Fligstein 1994; Applebaum and Batt 1994; Gordon 1996; Useem 1996; and, especially, Osterman 1996.

6. The apparent squeeze on employee time and effort occurring in the workplace as a result—at least partly—of currently fashionable lean employment practices has generated a number of fine studies. Schor's *Overworked American* (1991) is perhaps the most recognized. But see also Nippert-Eng 1995, Hochschild 1997, and Perlow 1997 for further and more detailed studies of the time binds faced by managerial and professional employees in the contemporary workplace.

7. Our view of the current realities of the labor market is grounded, in part, in an ethnographic study of contingent work among technical professionals in Silicon Valley, currently being conducted by Gideon Kunda with Stephen Barley.

8. Andrew Pettigrew (1979) is often given credit in organization studies circles for first using the phrase "organizational culture." It is, however, a notion that has been around a long time and is, for many sociologists of work, closely linked to the Chicago School studies of work and occupations associated with Everett C. Hughes and his students (Fine 1984). A useful reading of the use of the culture concept in

organizational studies is provided by Barley, Meyer, and Gash (1988). Other good reviews include Ott 1989; Ouchi and Wilkins 1985; Frost et al. 1991; and Alvesson and Berg 1992.

9. It runs deep partly because the emotional labor of managers and professionals must carry conviction along with attitude and gesture. Such conviction must be worked at continually if successful careers are to be had. Lower-level workers usually know they are not going anywhere in a given company and therefore have little incentive to offer up heart and soul to the job. Ride operators at Disneyland, for example, put on a charming display of perky good cheer and helpfulness, but they know they will be gone from the show by summer's end. Some complain of phoniness and emotional numbness if their onstage work and overacting begin to seem bothersome. But most are able to separate feeling from display and cope easily with what Hochschild (1983) calls "emotional dissonance": a claim of having to make a display of affection (or disdain) toward something the claimant does not feel. It is precisely such dissonance that many managers and professionals in corporate worlds have trouble resolving. See Van Maanen 1991 for an analysis of the emotional labor of Disneyland employees and Kunda 1992 for a depiction of the response of lower-level employees at Tech to cultural management.

10. Such selves, of course, were not exactly what the designers of the culture had in mind. While "the engineers of culture see the ideal member as driven by strong beliefs and intense emotions, authentic experiences of loyalty, commitment, and the pleasure of work . . . they seem to produce members who have internalized ambiguity, who have made the metaphor of drama a centerpiece of their sense of self, who question authenticity of all beliefs and emotions, and who find irony in its various forms the dominant mode of everyday existence" (Kunda 1992, 216).

11. Enthusiasm for managerial control of organizational culture was widespread in the 1980s. Ouchi's popular Theory Z (1981) blended Japanese and American management techniques and promised a productive workplace based on shared values and clan solidarity. At the end of their search for excellence—the best-selling management text of all time—Peters and Waterman (1982) found culture and told readers about it in no uncertain

terms: "Without exception, the dominance and coherence of culture proved to be the essential quality of excellent companies" (16). In more prosaic terms, Deal and Kennedy (1982) told their many readers that "a strong culture enables people to feel better about what they do, so they are more likely to work harder" (21). Such enthusiasm soon waned, and, while organizational culture continues to hold considerable fascination for both researchers and practitioners alike, claims made on its behalf are now far more contingent than categorical. See, for example, Schein 1985; Martin 1992; Trice and Beyer 1993; and Watson 1995.

12. Current research suggests this is indeed happening. A number of studies document a general thinning out of managerial positions. Job security is down, fewer ranks exist, and promotions across the ranks are slower than in times past. See, for example, Cappelli 1992; Davis, Diekmann, and Tinsley 1994; Gordon 1996; and Useem 1996. On some of the individual consequences, see Newman 1993; Hirsch 1993; and Herkscher 1995. A sharp theoretical take on industrial restructuring is provided by Best (1990).

13. When learned and absorbed, the "language of enterprise," not unlike the "language of loyalty," provides a socially recognized and legitimized form of discourse through which employees can shape an identity within (and beyond) the firm. In many companies, the entrepreneurial agent is perhaps the ideologically correct identity for these times, and employees in the professional and managerial ranks give voice and support to such a figure through their language use. It is, however, only one of many kinds of language use or discourse employees can draw on and is, as Wasson 1996 so nicely illustrates, highly contingent on the settings that prompt its use. Other figures (and the languages used to articulate them) are possible as indicated in the text. Identity in the workplace is shaped, sharpened, questioned, avowed, and disavowed in the midst of other more or less organized languages (or discourses) representing different social, political, gender-based, age-based, ethnicity-based, and occupationally based perspectives. We have examined only a few of the ways employees talk about and present themselves to others in the always particular public and private settings at work. Paying close attention to the use of language in the workplace is an impor-

tant research move in organizational studies and one we have tried to promote here. Examples of recent work that gives language its due in work domains include Barker 1993; Brenneis 1994; duGay, Salaman, and Rees 1996; Wasson 1996; and Czarniawska 1997. The most influential work in the area writ large is probably Tannen 1994.

References

Alvesson, Mats and Per-Olof Berg. 1992. *Corporate Culture and Organizational Symbolism*. Berlin: De Gruyter.

Applebaum, Eileen and Rosemary Batt. 1994. *The New American Workplace*. Ithaca, NY: Cornell University Press.

Barker, James R. 1993. Tightening the Iron Cage: Concertive Control in Self-Managing Teams. *Administrative Science Quarterly* 38:408-37.

Barley, Stephen R. and Gideon Kunda. 1992. Design and Devotion: Surges of Rational and Normative Ideologies of Control in Managerial Discourse. *Administrative Science Quarterly* 37:363-99.

Barley, Stephen R., Gordon W. Meyer, and Debra C. Gash. 1988. Cultures of Culture: Academics, Practitioners and the Pragmatics of Normative Control. *Administrative Science Quarterly* 33:24-60.

Best, Michael. 1990. *The New Competition*. Cambridge, MA: Harvard University Press.

Brenneis, Donald. 1994. Discourse and Discipline at the National Research Council. *Cultural Anthropology* 9:23-36.

Cappelli, Peter. 1992. Examining Managerial Displacement. *Academy of Management Journal* 35:203-17.

Czarniawska, Barbara. 1997. *Narrating the Organization*. Chicago: University of Chicago Press.

Davis, Gerald F., Kristina A. Diekmann, and Catherine H. Tinsley. 1994. The Decline and Fall of the Conglomerate Firm in the 1980s:

De-Institutionalization of an Organizational Form. *American Sociological Review* 59:547-70.

Deal, Terrence and A. A. Kennedy. 1982. *Corporate Cultures.* Reading, MA: Addison-Wesley.

deCerteau, Michel. 1984. *The Practice of Everyday Life.* Berkeley: University of California Press.

Doeringer, Peter and Michael Piore. 1972. *Internal Labor Markets and Manpower Analysis.* Lexington, MA: D. C. Heath.

duGay, Peter, Graham Salaman, and Thomas Rees. 1996. The Conduct of Management and the Management of Conduct: Contemporary Managerial Discourse and the Constitution of the "Competent" Manager. *Journal of Management Studies* 33:263-82.

Edwards, Richard. 1979. *Contested Terrain.* New York: Basic Books.

Fine, Gary Alan. 1984. Negotiated Order and Organizational Cultures. In *Annual Review of Sociology,* vol. 10.

Fligstein, Neil. 1994. *The Transformation of Corporate Control.* Cambridge, MA: Harvard University Press.

Frost, Peter, Larry F. Moore, Meryl Reis Louis, Craig C. Lundberg, and Joanne Martin, eds. 1991. *Reframing Organizational Culture.* Newbury Park, CA: Sage.

Goffman, Erving. 1961. *Encounters.* Indianapolis, IN: Bobbs-Merrill.

Gordon, David M. 1996. *Fat and Mean.* New York: Free Press.

Herkscher, Charles. 1995. *White Collar Blues.* New York: Basic Books.

Hirsch, Paul M. 1993. Undoing the Managerial Revolution? Needed Research on the Decline of Middle Management and Internal Labor Markets. In *Explorations in Economic Sociology,* ed. Richard Swedberg. New York: Russell Sage Foundation.

Hochschild, Arlie Russell. 1983. *The Managed Heart: Commercialization of Human Feeling.* Berkeley: University of California Press.

———. 1997. *The Time Bind: When Work Becomes Home and Home Becomes Work.* New York: Metropolitan Books.

Jackall, Robert. 1988. *Moral Mazes.* New York: Oxford University Press.

Jacoby, Sanford M. 1985. *Employing Bureaucracy: Managers, Unions and the Transformation of Work in American Industry, 1900-1945.* New York: Columbia University Press.

Kanter, Rosabeth Moss. 1977. *Men and Women of the Corporation.* New York: Basic Books.

Kochan, Thomas A., Harry C. Katz, and Robert B. McKersie. 1994. *The Transformation of American Industrial Relations.* Ithaca, NY: ILR Press.

Kunda, Gideon. 1986. Ideology as a System of Meaning: The Case of the Israeli Probation Service. *International Studies of Management and Organization* 16:54-79.

———. 1992. *Engineering Culture: Control and Commitment in a High-Tech Corporation.* Philadelphia: Temple University Press.

Martin, Joanne. 1992. *Cultures in Organizations.* New York: Oxford University Press.

Miller, Peter and Nikolas Rose. 1990. Governing Economic Life. *Economy and Society* 19:1-31.

Mills, C. Wright. 1956. *White Collar.* New York: Oxford University Press.

Newman, Katherine S. 1993. *Declining Fortunes.* New York: Basic Books.

Nippert-Eng, Christena E. 1995. *Home and Work.* Chicago: University of Chicago Press.

Osterman, Paul, ed. 1984. *Internal Labor Markets.* Cambridge, MA: MIT Press.

———. 1988. *Employment Futures.* New York: Oxford University Press.

———, ed. 1996. *Broken Ladders.* New York: Oxford University Press.

Ott, J. Steven. 1989. *The Organizational Culture Perspective*. Pacific Grove, CA: Brooks/Cole.

Ouchi, William G. 1981. *Theory Z*. Reading, MA: Addison-Wesley.

Ouchi, William G. and Alan L. Wilkins. 1985. Organizational Culture. In *Annual Review of Sociology*, vol. 11.

Perlow, Leslie A. 1997. *Finding Time*. Ithaca, NY: Cornell University Press.

Peters, Tom. 1997. *The Circle of Innovation*. New York: Knopf.

Peters, Tom and Robert H. Waterman. 1982. *In Search of Excellence*. New York: Harper & Row.

Pettigrew, Andrew M. 1979. On Studying Organizational Cultures. *Administrative Science Quarterly* 24:570-81.

Piore, Michael and Charles F. Sabel. 1984. *The Second Industrial Divide*. New York: Basic Books.

Schein, Edgar H. 1985. *Organizational Culture and Leadership*. San Francisco: Jossey-Bass.

Schor, Juliet B. 1991. *The Overworked American*. New York: Basic Books.

Smith, Vicki. 1990. *Managing in the Corporate Interest*. Berkeley: University of California Press.

Tannen, Deborah. 1994. *Talking from 9 to 5: How Women's and Men's Conversational Styles Affect Who Gets Heard, Who Gets Credit, and What Gets Done at Work*. New York: William Morrow.

Trice, Harrison M. and Janice M. Beyer. 1993. *The Cultures of Work Organizations*. Englewood Cliffs, NJ: Prentice Hall.

Useem. Michael. 1996. *Investor Capitalism*. New York: Basic Books.

Van Maanen, John. 1986. Power in the Bottle: Drinking Patterns and Social Relations in a British Police Agency. In *Executive Power*, ed. S. Shrivasta. San Francisco: Jossey-Bass.

———. 1991. The Smile Factory: Work at Disneyland. In *Reframing Organizational Culture*, ed. P. Frost, L. F. Moore, M. R. Louis, C. C. Lundberg, and J. Martin. Newbury Park, CA: Sage.

———. 1992. Displacing Disney. *Qualitative Sociology* 15:5-36.

Van Maanen, John and Gideon Kunda. 1989. "Real Feelings": Emotional Expressions and Organizational Culture. In *Research in Organizational Behavior*, ed. B. M. Staw and L. L. Cummings. Vol. 11. Greenwich, CT: JAI Press.

Wasson, Christina. 1996. Covert Caution: Linguistic Traces of Organizational Control. Ph.D. diss., Yale University.

Watson, Tony J. 1995. *In Search of Management*. New York: Routledge.

Whyte, William H. 1956. *The Organization Man*. New York: Simon & Schuster.

ANNALS, *AAPSS*, **561**, January 1999

Emotional Labor
in Service Work

By ROBIN LEIDNER

ABSTRACT: Emotional labor is crucial to the performance of interactive service work, jobs that involve direct interaction with customers or clients. In such jobs, employers frequently try to manage the emotions of their workers, while workers try to control the emotional responses of service recipients. Management techniques for directing and monitoring interactive service workers extend managerial control to aspects of workers' selves usually considered outside of the scope of employer intervention. Bureaucratic controls are also extended beyond the boundaries of the organization through the management of customer behavior. While workers and consumers derive some benefits from the routinization of service interactions, its instrumental approach to human personality and social interaction raises troubling moral issues.

Robin Leidner, associate professor of sociology at the University of Pennsylvania, is the author of Fast Food, Fast Talk: Service Work and the Routinization of Everyday Life *(1993) and several articles on feminist organizations, work, and gender. She is currently researching parents' responses to advice and information on child rearing.*

NOW hiring smiling faces," says the sign outside a Kentucky Fried Chicken outlet. The phrasing calls attention to a crucial aspect of work in service occupations. While farms and factories may employ "hands," for many kinds of service work willing hands are not enough. As Arlie Hochschild brilliantly described in *The Managed Heart* (1983), producing a consistent smile for customers requires a type of effort on the part of workers who deal with people that is not asked of workers who mainly handle things or data. When that kind of effort is sold for a wage, it is what Hochschild terms emotional labor, "the management of feeling to create a publicly observable facial and bodily display" intended to produce a particular state of mind in others (7). As service jobs grow in number while those in manufacturing and agriculture continue to decline, emotional labor becomes a more and more prevalent component of work. Understanding its impact on workers, the public, and the culture at large is thus an important project for social scientists.

The service sector includes a broad spectrum of jobs, ranging from dental technicians to nannies to truck drivers to ophthalmologists. Some require emotional labor, but some do not. Moreover, the manufacturing sector includes many jobs that are service oriented and may require emotional labor, such as sales and customer service. For my purposes, it is most useful to focus on jobs rather than sector. This article addresses what I have termed interactive service work—jobs that require workers to interact directly with customers or clients, regardless of economic sector (Leidner 1993). A wide variety of jobs with varying levels of prestige fit this description, including manicurists, psychiatrists, teachers, and telemarketers.

Hochschild's introduction of the concept of emotional labor illuminated an aspect of paid work that is central to the lived experience of many workers but that had been obscured by dominant theoretical approaches to the study of work. Social scientific attention to workers' subjectivity had previously been limited to a relatively narrow range of concerns, such as employee motivation, class consciousness (as formulated by Marx), and professional identity. Conceptualizing some of the distinctive aspects of service jobs opened up fruitful avenues of investigation and analysis and facilitated the ongoing reformulation of academic understandings of work necessary to keep pace with transformations in the economy and in the nature of work.

In this article, I focus on the low- to middle-level frontline workers who are part of what Macdonald and Sirianni (1996) call "the emotional proletariat" (3). In contrast to professionals involved in interactive service work, the emotional labor of these frontline service workers is likely to be guided by employers rather than by professional norms. Employers are more likely to intervene in and supervise the emotional labor of these interactive service workers, who deal primarily with the public, than of workers who deal primarily with other members of the organization, such as clerical workers. A distinctive feature of the jobs of nonprofessional frontline service workers, then, is that they often must cope with their own emotions' being managed while they try to manage the emotional responses of others. To investigate the ramifications of such emotional management, I conducted participant observation at McDonald's and at Combined Insurance Company and also interviewed managers, trainers, and workers at those organizations (see Leidner 1993). I will draw on that research, as well as on other workplace studies, to illustrate my arguments about the work of emotional proletarians.

What makes emotional labor unusually crucial to interactive service work? In these kinds of jobs, it is impossible to draw clear distinctions between the worker, the work process, and the product or outcome, because the quality of the interaction is frequently part of the service being delivered and thus, in many cases, the product generating company profits. Producing a certain kind of response in the service recipient is integral to many such jobs, whether the desired response is pleasure, titillation, alarm, or some other state of mind (Hochschild 1983). By definition, these nonemployees—customers, clients, patients, respondents, and so on—are a part of the work process. They are not simply observers; they are generally coproducers of the interaction, whose cooperation is required for the work to go forward. Interactive service workers must expend emotional labor to produce a certain quality of interaction but also to manage the emotions of service recipients so that they do not hold up

the work. Service recipients are well positioned to act as judges of the adequacy of the workers' emotional labor and can create difficulties if they are not satisfied with it.

Holding such jobs therefore puts special burdens on even low-level workers. Macdonald and Sirianni (1996) explain:

In the past there was a clear distinction between *careers*, which required a level of personalization, emotion management, authenticity in interaction, and general integration of personal and workplace identities, and *jobs*, which required the active engagement of the body and parts of the mind while the spirit and soul of the worker might be elsewhere. Workers in service occupations are asked to inhabit jobs in ways that were formerly limited to managers and professionals alone. They are required to bring some level of personal identity and self-expression into their work, even if it is only at the level of basic interactions, and even if the job itself is only temporary. The assembly-line worker could openly hate his job, despise his supervisor, and even dislike his co-workers, and while this might be an unpleasant state of affairs, if he completed his assigned tasks efficiently, his attitude was his own problem. For the service worker, inhabiting the job means, at the very least, pretending to like it, and, at most, actually bringing his whole self into the job, liking it, and genuinely caring about the people with whom he interacts. (3)

Because interactive service workers make use of their emotions and personalities in carrying out their work, their employers generally take a direct interest in more aspects of the workers' selves than do employers of other kinds of workers. They may feel that, in exchange for wages, they are legitimately entitled to intervene in workers' looks, words, feelings, thoughts, attitudes, and demeanor, not only in the motions of their bodies and the uses of their time. While many jobs that do not involve direct contact with nonemployees require emotional labor, it is in interactive service work that employers are most likely to intervene directly in aspects of workers' selves not generally regarded as their business, because it is here that the satisfactory completion of work tasks frequently cannot be distinguished from the emotional quality of interactions.

WHEN DO EMPLOYERS INTERVENE IN SERVICE WORKERS' EMOTIONAL LABOR?

Not all employers explicitly direct and monitor the emotional labor of their interactive service workers. We can specify certain conditions that make such intervention more likely. First, do managers believe that the success of their enterprise depends on the character of interactions between workers and nonemployees? When the organization is assured of a steady demand for its services regardless of the quality of service interactions, as are government agencies and other providers with a captive customer base, employers are less likely to focus on the quality of their workers' emotional labor. Similarly, employers who believe that the quality of the service interaction does not have an appreciable impact on consumer choices (for example, taxi customers are unlikely to consider this factor) are unlikely to put a high priority on controlling emotional labor. For these reasons, most consumers have had plenty of experience with frontline service workers who, contrary to the aforementioned argument of Macdonald and Sirianni, do not put any effort into pretending to like their jobs.

Second, do managers feel that workers are willing and able to invest the emotional labor necessary to do their job well without managerial intervention? Sometimes employers may be unaware of how significant emotional labor is for the successful completion of the work; this seemed to be true, for instance, of the employers of telephone interviewers I observed engaged in collecting sociological data. Other employers may feel that they can count on workers to provide appropriate emotional labor on their own, perhaps basing their confidence on careful selection of employees. For example, a restaurant owner may judge from the appearance and manner of someone applying to be a cocktail waitress that she will convey the kind of flirtatiousness he thinks his customers appreciate, while another employer may assume that a social worker's graduate degree ensures that her treatment of clients will be guided by professional norms. Whether or not workers regulate their own emotional labor will also affect how their relationships with employers and customers are structured. Workers who have clear incentives to manage interactions with customers in ways their employers prefer, such as those whose earnings depend on commissions,[1] will require less supervision of their emotional labor than those who do not have a stake in the outcome of service interactions or those whose interests diverge from employers'. Moreover, social psychologist Barbara Gutek (1995) persuasively argues that service interactions can usefully be divided into two types: relationships and encounters. Providers who deliver services through relationships see the same customers repeatedly over an extended period of time, giving them incentives to invest emotionally in these relationships as well as knowledge that helps them provide customized emotional labor. In service encounters, by contrast, both providers and consumers are basically interchangeable. While encounters may provide speedy, efficient, and uniform service, they do not tend to foster a customer orientation among service providers, since the two participants do not count on ever seeing each other again. While many kinds of services are available through both kinds of interactions (tax preparation and hair styling, for example, may be purchased either in a first-come, first-served franchise setting or from a well-known and trusted provider), employers of those who provide services through relationships may see no need to exercise control over their emotional labor.

When employers do perceive the quality of workers' emotional labor as crucial to organizational success but they doubt either the capability or the motivation of their workers to do it well on their own, they will build in procedures intended to ensure that smiles, empathy, intimidation, or chumminess are reliably produced. The booming business literature on managing services supports the argument that controlling such work presents novel challenges (for example, Albrecht 1988; Heskett, Sasser, and Hart 1990; Zemke with Schaaf 1989). In addition to exercising control over workers' time and physical efforts, service employers frequently extend their control efforts to the details of workers' appearance (uniforms, rules about fingernail length and color, use of jewelry, hair styles, and so on), their words, and their demeanor. While some limit themselves to specifying relatively superficial aspects of workers' self-presentations, others feel that workers' moods, thoughts, feelings, attitudes, and self-conceptions must also be managed. Hochschild's distinction (1983) between surface acting, in which workers merely convey an emotion they do not necessarily feel, and deep acting, in which they try to bring their internal and external emotions into congruence, is relevant here. The workers who served McDonald's hamburgers, I found, were required to smile, make eye contact, treat every customer politely, and remain calm when they felt that they were treated badly. McDonald's management used some devices for influencing workers' feelings about the customers (for example, by referring to customers as "guests"), but, in truth, as long as workers complied outwardly with the requirements of the job, they were free to think their own thoughts, which might include inwardly cursing customers and managers. Surface acting was enough. In contrast, Combined Insurance Company believed that the psychic demands of calling on prospective customers one after another and trying to persuade them to listen to a sales pitch required reserves of determination, confidence, and enthusiasm that had to be genuine. Deep acting (or, ideally, real personal transformation) was required.

MEANS OF MANAGING INTERACTIVE SERVICE WORK

How do employers go about managing the emotional labor of interactive service workers? Like other employers, they can attempt to exert control over how the work is done in a variety of ways: by taking care in the selection of employees; through initial training and ongoing efforts at indoctrination; through the design of systems, routines, and technology that guide workers on the job; and by instituting mechanisms of monitoring or surveillance.

Selection

The traits that employers look for in job applicants vary by the kind of image the organization wants to project, as well as by the demands of the job. Hochschild records that different airlines looked for different personality types for their flight attendants—"girl-next-door," "upper class, sophisticated, and slightly reserved," "brassy, fun-loving, and sexy"—while all wanted employees who could work with a team and had sensitivity and emotional stamina. Delta Airlines gave their applicants an "animation test" to see how well they could draw others out (Hochschild 1983, 96-98). In contrast,

Combined Insurance looked for sales agents who were independent, outgoing, competitive, stubborn, cocky, "willing to fight," and determined to win. It sought out people who liked sports and competition and were dissatisfied with their current job and income (Leidner 1993, 97-98). Like other kinds of employers, organizations looking for interactive service workers can try to judge whether applicants have the desired traits based on appearance, interviews, written tests, credentials, and job experience.

Training and indoctrination

Once employees are hired, organizations use a variety of techniques to instill organizationally favored attitudes and to teach new staff how to do their jobs and comply with organizational rules. An important component of orientation programs and of ongoing employee relations efforts in many workplaces is indoctrination with company culture. Using videotapes, books and manuals, classes, meetings, and ceremonies, organizations convey approved attitudes and promote a sense of inclusion and commitment. To win the trust and emotional identification of newly hired workers, organizations may teach organizational history, often emphasizing the unique talents of the founder; commend recruits on their good fortune in joining the "team"; tell exemplary stories; highlight the distinguishing characteristics of the organization; and stress its commitment to honored values, often including customer service. Periodic rituals designed to recharge the energy and identification of continuing employees are customary in many organizations, ranging from Mary Kay Cosmetics to high-technology engineering firms (see, for example, Biggart 1989; Kunda 1992; Leidner 1993). Key personnel, such as salespeople, are frequently special targets of such efforts. Many analysts have emphasized that these attempts to win the hearts and spirits of employees should be understood as methods of control, despite their dissimilarity from more straightforward systems of regulation, incentive, and surveillance. Whether described as injections of charisma into the workplace (Biggart 1989), as systems of normative control (Etzioni 1961), or as cult-like mind control (Butterfield 1985), these practices are designed to organize the consent of workers to the objectives and policies of the organization and to encourage workers to internalize its standards and discipline. The reception of these messages is complex, so the actual organizational culture is not necessarily entirely congruent with the official version. Managerial ideology is subject to the interpretations and responses of workers, who frequently try to assert some distance between themselves and the organization. Yet, even when workers take an ironic stance toward these control efforts, the organizational culture may nevertheless powerfully shape emotions and behavior (Kunda 1992).

Scripting and feeling rules

Many employers of interactive service workers also make more pointed efforts to regulate the feelings and actions of those who work with the public through detailed pre-specification of conduct. These attempts to standardize the interactions between workers and customers parallel the processes of routinization typical of manufacturing and clerical work in that they minimize workers' autonomy and discretion (see Braverman 1974; Garson 1975, 1988). The distinctive aspects of interactive service work, however, mean that its routinization often requires different techniques and engages more aspects of the workers' selves. Scripting of speech, movement, and body language is an especially common approach to regulating emotion work. Scripting can range from simple instructions to guide brief interactions (injunctions to smile; requirements to welcome customers at the beginning of an interaction and request return business at the end) to remarkably detailed directions for longer and more complicated transactions. The training of life insurance agents that I observed was an extreme case. Trainees were required to memorize long scripts for selling specific products as well as subsidiary scripts for responding to specific customer objections and interruptions; they were taught that speaking loudly and quickly would boost their confidence; they were told how to stand when waiting for someone to answer the door and given precise movement training for entering the house; they learned exactly when to make eye contact and when to break it in the course of their speeches, how to gesture with a pen to guide prospects' eyes and attention, and how to deliver The Standard Joke. In other cases, the conduct of service interactions is technologically directed. Frequently, for example, computer software guides the work of telephone salespeople, service representatives, and interviewers, minimizing their discretion in conducting interactions. While the scripting of service interactions is openly acknowledged in some kinds of work, elsewhere workers are called on to expend emotional labor to disguise routinization or to make up for it, providing a modicum of personal service or the appearance of it.

In addition to scripting, the routines of interactive service workers frequently include a set of feeling rules (Hochschild 1983), instructions about how one should feel, which guide workers' self-presentation and their treatment of service recipients. Thus flight attendants are taught to imagine that passengers are guests in their own living rooms, family planning counselors are cautioned against conveying a judgmental attitude, and bill collectors are told to treat all debtors' claims with suspicion (Hochschild 1983; Joffe 1986). These emotion rules shaping general orientation toward consumers are only starting places, however. Service recipients often respond to routine interactions in ways that challenge the attitude of the worker, discount the front he or she is trying to project, or otherwise derail the script. Interactive service workers daily encounter behavior that angers, insults, or exasperates them. It is therefore prudent for employers to teach psychic strategies that undercut workers' resentment or at least help them control their impulses to

express it. For example, when flight attendants encounter behavior they would not tolerate in their own living rooms, they are supposed to imagine that the obnoxious passenger is probably afraid to fly and is deserving of sympathy (or, in extreme cases, to remind themselves that they do not have to go home with the jerk); sales agents are encouraged to regard yelling back at a nasty prospect not as standing up for themselves but as "letting them blow your attitude"; and many kinds of service workers are reminded that their jobs depend on not antagonizing customers (Hochschild 1983; Leidner 1993).[2] Moreover, since service scripts commonly require workers to treat consumers in ways in which they would not ordinarily behave, organizations may feel it necessary to provide feeling rules that justify interactive styles that might otherwise challenge workers' sense of dignity or ethics. Life insurance salespeople, for instance, whose job requires them to be pushy and manipulative, are taught that overriding prospects' stated wishes to disengage from an interaction is in fact a service to them, because life insurance is important even to people who prefer avoiding the thought of their own deaths (Leidner 1993; Oakes 1990). As these examples show, interactive service organizations frequently acknowledge the potentially damaging effects of emotional labor on workers' sense of self and take steps to ameliorate them.

For some kinds of interactive service work, the unpredictability or complexity of the work makes it impossible for the organization to prespecify the conduct of all interactions, so workers necessarily retain considerable discretion. One way organizations handle this situation is to hire professionals, precisely because their education and experience are supposed to have prepared them to make decisions on complex matters. My research at Combined Insurance Company uncovered another possibility: that an organization might attempt a relatively deep transformation of trainees' selves so that they would make the kinds of decisions that the organization would have chosen. At Combined, much of this transformation had to do with bolstering trainees emotionally so that they could do their work effectively. Positive Mental Attitude training— which involved chanting slogans; focusing on motivating ideas; using books, audiotapes, and team meetings to refresh enthusiasm; and striving to eliminate negative thoughts altogether—was intended to make new agents more confident, optimistic, determined, and energized so that they could weather the discouragements that salespeople face every day. In addition, the training emphasized that one's positive attitude could be compromised by unethical behavior (toward prospective customers or toward the company) and urged trainees to become the sort of polite, honest, and sensitive agents who would succeed because they had earned the community's trust and contributed to the company's good reputation. Combining this message with training in sales techniques that showed agents how to take advantage of prospective customers' po-

liteness in order to dominate interactions required some finesse.

Monitoring

Since the insurance agents worked on their own door-to-door, the company had relatively little scope for monitoring their interactive work. In many situations, however, a combination of surveillance systems controls workers' emotional labor and other behavior. These can include direct oversight by supervisors, periodic monitoring of telephone work, and electronic tracking of sales and speed of work. As Fuller and Smith (1991) have shown, service organizations also may solicit feedback on workers' performance from customers. Moreover, the presence of service recipients in itself often exerts pressure on workers to perform speedily and well. Since customers' service preferences do not necessarily coincide with managerial wishes, however, interactive service workers are often subject to cross-pressures.

Employers' choices about strategies for controlling interactive service work are contingent and interrelated. If careful selection procedures can supply the organization with workers able and willing to perform as desired, the need for indoctrination and training is lessened. If close monitoring is possible and most decisions can be made in advance, there is little need to try to effect transformations in workers' characters. The possibilities for predetermining desired worker behavior, in turn, depend on the interests and abilities of the service recipients.

CONTROL AND RESISTANCE

Routinization requires that the demands of work be relatively predictable. Since nonemployees are part of the work process in interactive service work, the smooth functioning of routines depends on customers' willingness and capacity to comply with organizational expectations. In addition to controlling workers' efforts, then, service organizations must somehow regulate the behavior of nonemployees as well. In many cases, little effort is required to guide customers or clients. Most adults are familiar with a variety of service systems and are willing to play their parts by making appointments, waiting their turn, not ordering items that are not on the menu, and otherwise cooperating. However, if the nonemployees have not chosen to involve themselves in the service interaction (sales prospects, fundraising targets), are not able to understand or comply with the rules (children, people in great pain), or are not happy with routine treatment (picky customers, clients with problems that do not fit a standard organizational solution), their cooperation is problematic. The balance of power between workers and service recipients varies among workplaces (and among individuals within workplaces) based on such factors as the availability of alternative service-providers, the importance to the organization of the business or goodwill of the particular customer, the transparency of the processes by which the work is accomplished, the workers' skill, and the nature of the organizational routines. Frequently, emotional labor is the means by which workers try to control the behavior of potentially troublesome service recipients.

Sociologists and labor historians have emphasized the importance of autonomy to workers' satisfaction and the importance of skill to their power in the workplace. Hence they have depicted routinization, which systematically diminishes both autonomy and skill, as invariably undermining both workers' bargaining power and their pride in their work (see, for example, Edwards 1979; Montgomery 1979). According to Hochschild's analysis (1983), the demands of emotional labor intensify workers' alienation, estranging them from their own feelings as the organization encroaches on previously sacrosanct parts of the self. In most discussions of either routinization or emotional labor, resistance to organizational demands seems the only self-respecting response open to workers.

Nevertheless, Wharton (1993) did not find that demands for emotional labor inevitably lowered workers' satisfaction with their jobs; in fact, emotional labor was positively related to job satisfaction in her sample. She did find, however, that workers in jobs requiring emotional labor who did not have much job autonomy suffered more emotional exhaustion than did emotion workers with some autonomy. This finding supports the presumption that the combination of routinization and emotion work would indeed affect workers negatively, and is in accord with Hochschild's arguments.

When I studied workers in highly routinized jobs that demanded emotional labor, I expected to find a great deal of resistance, both practical and psychological. I certainly did find some: McDonald's workers who refused to smile and who regularly omitted the part of the required routine most likely to irritate customers and provoke nasty comments; insurance agents who eliminated parts of scripts that they disliked; and trainees and experienced workers who were ironic about company ideology. Moreover, there was extremely high labor turnover among both the fast-food workers and the insurance salespeople, whose jobs, of course, had a variety of unappealing features beyond the ones under discussion here. However, the responses of the workers I met were considerably less negative and more varied than I had expected. Why did more workers not refuse to go along with organizational scripts and emotion rules? Why were they not more indignant about organizational practices that seemed to challenge their intelligence, their individuality, and their personal dignity?

Anthropologist Greta Foff Paules (1991) describes a group of waitresses who brassily rejected both deference to customers and submission to managerial demands. While Paules applauds their triumphant resistance, she does not analyze what gave them such an unusual degree of autonomy. First, the waitresses were in an extremely strong position in the labor market because a local boom in service businesses had created a shortage of workers. Second, since the restaurant had a transient customer base, the waitresses were not dependent on regular customers. Since McDonald's workers were closely supervised and relatively easy to replace, and since Combined Insurance agents' incomes depended on how prospective customers reacted to them, as a practical matter neither group could have resisted the emotional demands of their jobs as overtly as the waitresses without much greater risk, even had they so desired.

Still, why did so many of the workers apparently accept their service routines quite willingly? The answer lies in the distinctive nature of interactive service work. In this setting, the power dynamic of the workplace shifts from a tug-of-war between workers and management to a three-way contest for control between workers, management, and service recipients. While routinization does diminish the power of workers relative to management, its effect on the balance of power between workers and service recipients varies. The degree to which workers experience emotional labor as threatening to their sense of self varies as well, in part based on its usefulness in exercising power over customers or in protecting them from customers' power.

At Combined Insurance, agents had good reason to appreciate their scripts and their lessons in emotional labor. Because the nonemployees they met with were people on their own turf who had not chosen to participate in the service interactions, it was entirely up to the agents to try to manage prospective customers so that they would allow the interactions to continue and, ideally, buy some insurance. Virtually every element of the agents' routine was designed to help them maintain control over these interactions, to outmaneuver the nonemployees who might wish to cut them off at any moment. Combined's trainees were led to believe that if they followed both the precepts of Positive Mental Attitude training and the verbal, physical, and emotional elements of their routines, they would succeed in selling policies and earn "as much as they were worth." Some were initially uncomfortable with the regimentation expected of them, a few had scruples about the pressure they had to put on prospective customers, but they were aware that they would be free to modify the scripts when they were out on their own and they were reassured by the interpretation of their emotional transformation as a shift to a smoother, more successful self. The organizational emphasis on the gladiatorial clash of wills beneath the polite surface of the interactions also allowed the agents to construe as inherently masculine a job that involved a good deal of flattery, ingratiation, and acceptance of poor treatment. The agents all appreciated the power their training gave them over their work and the edge they gained over the people they met.

In contrast, McDonald's routines were not designed to give workers power over customers. The workers had to focus more on controlling themselves than on controlling others. Not surprisingly, they were less likely to embrace their routines and emotion work enthusiastically than were the insurance agents, but there was less need for them to do so. While the agents really did have to generate optimism and assertiveness to succeed at their jobs, the McDonald's workers could easily carry out their routines without investing themselves deeply in the parts. Some workers appreciated the confidence the routines gave them that they could do their job well; others did try to engage their personalities on the job, embellishing the script and injecting a bit of individuality into the interactions. Many, however, used various techniques to establish role distance (Goffman 1961), finding ways to convey, or at least to remind themselves, that their words and actions did not reflect their true selves. Unlike Hochschild's flight attendants, they did not express discomfort about acting like phonies; their difficulties were more likely to concern having to repress their resentment of having to be servile or being insulted. Given that McDonald's workers lacked what Hochschild (1983, 163) calls a status shield to protect them from customers' expression of feelings of impatience, contempt, and annoyance, the ability to maintain some role distance had clear benefits. In fact, the extreme routinization of the job and standardization of the interactions made it easier for workers to avoid taking mistreatment personally or seeing themselves as deserving the low regard in which many obviously held them.

I argue, then, that if interactive service workers do not always resist routinization and managerial interference with their personalities, it is not necessarily because they suffer from false consciousness. Under some conditions, scripted emotional labor can help workers enforce their will over others, protect them from mistreatment, bolster their confidence in their abilities, or at least offer them some psychological distance from disagreeable interactions. My point is not to deny that there are significant costs to workers whose feelings and thoughts are manipulated by their employers and who are asked to manipulate others. The loss of autonomy, the requirement to behave like someone the worker does not want to be, the sense of indignity, the depersonalization, and the inauthenticity that many interactive service workers suffer can be painful and stressful (perhaps all the more so because the managerial interventions and scripted interactions often seem absurd and comic). The standardization of the self required in these jobs is at odds with values that are especially strongly emphasized in American society, such as individuality, sincerity, and self-direction. Acknowledging the practical and psychological benefits that workers accrue from routinized emotional labor in some circumstances helps us understand why resistance may be muted, but it does not resolve the moral questions raised by a blatantly instrumental approach to human personality and to social interaction. Under what conditions is it acceptable for organizations to disregard the usual boundaries protecting employees' selves, and how far can they go in reshaping those selves? When is it justifiable for organizations and their employees to manipulate taken-for-granted social rules in managing the behavior of service recipients? Norms of individual autonomy and interpersonal respect may be put at risk by some forms of routinized emotional labor.

FURTHER QUESTIONS

Future research in this area should extend preliminary efforts to map out the variables that determine the forms that emotional labor takes in different kinds of service jobs, the choices employers make about techniques for controlling interactions between workers and service recipients, the balance of power between the three parties to service interactions, and the kinds of responses available to workers and to customers as well. Moreover, given the direct involvement of nonemployees in the work processes of service organizations, much further investigation is called for of the cultural effects of the management of service work. Are cynicism and defensiveness fostered by frequent encounters with workers whose jobs involve emotional manipulation? Will an increasingly instrumental attitude toward the self gain greater acceptance? Alternatively, will sincerity be more highly valued because it is under threat? Since many service organizations call on workers to turn relatives and friends into customers, will the boundary between business and personal relationships be further eroded? Does organizational management of interaction tend to undermine or reinforce inequality based on gender, class, and race?

The defining qualities of interactive service work—the inseparability of the worker from the product or service and the involvement of nonemployees in the work process—require that scholars recast some of the questions they have traditionally brought to the study of work, such as those concerning power in the workplace and processes of routinization. In addition, investigating this sort of work links those matters to broader questions concerning the construction of identities, the moral underpinnings of social interaction, and the scope of organizational power to shape social life.

Notes

1. In fact, the interests of workers and employers are sometimes partly aligned and partly divergent. For example, life insurance sales agents and their employers both benefited when the agents sold a lot of policies, but the two parties' interests diverged when the agent tried to maximize his income by selling a policy to someone whose eligibility for the coverage was marginal (see Leidner 1993).

2. A particularly telling example is what Macdonald and Sirianni (1996) call "a legendary training session at Harvard" in which clerical workers who were upset with students' treatment of them were counseled to "think of yourself as a trash can. Take everyone's little bits of anger all day, put it inside you, and at the end of the day, just pour it in the dumpster on your way out the door" (17). Evidently this bit of instruction did not have the desired effect on the clerical workers.

References

Albrecht, Karl. 1988. *At America's Service: How Corporations Can Revolutionize the Way They Treat Their Customers*. Homewood, IL: Dow Jones–Irwin.

Biggart, Nicole Woolsey. 1989. *Charismatic Capitalism: Direct Selling Organizations in America*. Chicago: University of Chicago Press.

Braverman, Harry. 1974. *Labor and Monopoly Capital: The Degradation of Work in the Twentieth Century*. New York: Monthly Review Press.

Butterfield, Steve. 1985. *Amway: The Cult of Free Enterprise*. Boston: South End Press.

Edwards, Richard. 1979. *Contested Terrain: The Transformation of the Workplace in the Twentieth Century*. New York: Basic Books.

Etzioni, Amitai. 1961. *A Comparative Analysis of Complex Organizations*. New York: Free Press.

Fuller, Linda and Vicki Smith. 1991. Consumers' Reports: Management by Customers in a Changing Economy. *Work, Employment, and Society* 15:1-16.

Garson, Barbara. 1975. *All the Livelong Day: The Meaning and Demeaning of Routine Work*. New York: Doubleday.

———. 1988. *The Electronic Sweatshop: How Computers Are Transforming the Office of the Future into the Factory of the Past*. New York: Simon & Schuster.

Goffman, Erving. 1961. Role Distance. In *Encounters: Two Studies in the Sociology of Interaction*. Indianapolis, IN: Bobbs-Merrill.

Gutek, Barbara. 1995. *The Dynamics of Service: Reflections on the Changing Nature of Customer / Provider Interactions*. San Francisco: Jossey-Bass.

Heskett, James L., W. Earl Sasser, Jr., and Christopher W. L. Hart. 1990. *Service Breakthroughs: Changing the Rules of the Game*. New York: Free Press.

Hochschild, Arlie Russell. 1983. *The Managed Heart: Commercialization of Human Feeling*. Berkeley: University of California Press.

Joffe, Carole. 1986. *The Regulation of Sexuality: Experiences of Family Planning Workers*. Philadelphia: Temple University Press.

Kunda, Gideon. 1992. *Engineering Culture: Control and Commitment in a*

High-Tech Corporation. Philadelphia: Temple University Press.

Leidner, Robin. 1993. *Fast Food, Fast Talk: Service Work and the Routinization of Everyday Life*. Berkeley: University of California Press.

Macdonald, Cameron Lynne and Carmen Sirianni. 1996. The Service Society and the Changing Experience of Work. In *Working in the Service Society*, ed. Cameron Lynne Macdonald and Carmen Sirianni. Philadelphia: Temple University Press.

Montgomery, David. 1979. *Workers' Control in America: Studies in the History of Work, Technology, and Labor Struggles*. New York: Cambridge University Press.

Oakes, Guy. 1990. *The Soul of the Salesman: The Moral Ethos of Personal Sales*. Atlantic Highlands, NJ: Humanities Press International.

Paules, Greta Foff. 1991. *Dishing It Out: Power and Resistance Among Waitresses in a New Jersey Restaurant*. Philadelphia: Temple University Press.

Wharton, Amy S. 1993. The Affective Consequences of Service Work: Managing Emotions on the Job. *Work and Occupations* 20(2):205-32.

Zemke, Ron with Dick Schaaf. 1989. *The Service Edge: 101 Companies That Profit from Customer Care*. New York: NAL Books.

ANNALS, *AAPSS*, **561**, January 1999

Emotional Labor in Academia: The Case of Professors

By MARCIA L. BELLAS

ABSTRACT: Most professors divide their time between teaching, research, service, and, for some, administration. As in the nonacademic labor market, there is a gendered reward structure in academia. Teaching and service are most closely aligned with characteristics and behaviors culturally defined as feminine, and, in the aggregate, women spend more time in these activities than men. Teaching and service clearly involve substantial amounts of emotional labor, but this labor is generally not seen as involving valued skills and is consequently poorly rewarded. In contrast, research and administration are associated with traits culturally defined as masculine, and, on average, men spend more time in these activities. Although research and administration also involve emotional labor, their emotional aspects are largely ignored, while intellectual, technical, or leadership skills are emphasized and highly compensated. Aside from differences in the propensity of women and men to engage in different activities and the gendered reward structure associated with these activities, even when the tasks are the same, the type and intensity of emotional labor required of the sexes may differ.

Marcia L. Bellas is an assistant professor of sociology at the University of Cincinnati. Her research interests include gender stratification in labor markets and households, with a focus on academia and the work of professors.

I N her groundbreaking book, *The Managed Heart* (1983), Arlie Hochschild estimated that approximately one-third of all jobs require substantial amounts of emotional labor and that women are more likely to hold such jobs than are men. Hochschild stipulated that jobs requiring emotional labor involve face-to-face or voice-to-voice contact with the public; require that workers produce an emotional state in another person; and allow employers to control (at least to some extent) the emotional activities of workers.[1] She considered the occupation of professor to require substantial amounts of emotional labor. Clearly, professors have face-to-face or voice-to-voice contact with students, colleagues, administrators, staff, and, at times, the public. Professors often try to elicit emotions in people with whom they interact, which involves managing their own emotional expression. Although professors have considerable autonomy, administrators exert some control over their emotional activities, for example, by assessing performance with evaluations by students and colleagues. According to Hochschild (1983), emotional labor involves following certain prescriptions or "feeling rules." Professors learn these feeling rules through professional socialization and explicit organizational or occupational codes of conduct. Those who do not may be subject to poor evaluations, informal or formal sanctions, and, in extreme cases, termination from employment.

In this article, I examine the activities in which professors engage and the emotional labor required by each. Specifically, I assess the emotional labor required by teaching (both inside and outside the classroom), service, research, and administration and how expectations for and experiences of emotional labor may differ for the sexes. I suggest that professors' work activities are gendered, and so, too, is the academic reward structure. Teaching and service are most closely aligned with social prescriptions of appropriate feminine activities, and, on average, women spend more time in these activities than men (Bellas and Toutkoushian Forthcoming). Teaching and service clearly involve substantial amounts of emotional labor—labor that is generally not viewed as involving valuable skills and is consequently poorly rewarded. As a result, teaching "is either a negative factor in compensation or . . . unrelated to compensation" (Fairweather 1993, 64; see also Bellas 1994). As professors recognize, there are also few rewards for service (Fairweather 1993).

In contrast, research and administration are culturally defined as masculine activities, and, in the aggregate, men spend more time in these activities (Bellas and Toutkoushian Forthcoming). Although research and administration also require substantial amounts of emotional labor, it is typically minimized or overlooked while other more highly rewarded skills are emphasized. Studies of faculty salaries invariably show that higher numbers of publications and holding an administrative position contribute to higher salaries (Bellas 1994; Fairweather 1993). Thus, as Feldberg

(1984) recognizes, "far from being an objective fact, skill is often an ideological category imposed on certain types of work by virtue of the sex and power of the workers who perform it" (322).

EMOTIONAL LABOR AND TEACHING

Both teaching and mothering entail social expectations of nurturance, altruism, and self-abnegation (Acker 1995; Grumet 1988). Although the conflation between teaching and mothering lessens as the age of the students and the likelihood that teachers will be male increase, it is apparent to some extent throughout the education system. As at other levels, postsecondary teaching involves far more than simply imparting knowledge. Professors help students mature intellectually and emotionally; they motivate and stimulate student interest. In short, professors nurture young minds.

Despite the skills involved in effective teaching, like so much of so-called women's work teaching appears to draw on natural abilities. Most colleges and universities do not offer on-the-job training for professors, or, if they do, the amount of resources used pales in comparison to those devoted to research (Rau and Baker 1989). Professors who improve their teaching tend to do so through trial and error and feedback from students. While discussions about teaching techniques may be common at some types of institutions, they are infrequent at the more prestigious (that is, more research-oriented) institutions (Statham, Richardson, and Cook 1991).

Emotional labor in the classroom

An award-winning teacher and former editor of *Teaching Sociology*, sociologist Kathleen McKinney (1988) suggests that one of the five components of quality teaching is entertainment. She advises professors to "show your enjoyment and entertain your students through impression management techniques. Show a sense of humor, wear diverse and visually interesting clothes, alter your vocabulary, and make use of paralanguage and nonverbal behaviors (gestures, facial expressions, body movement, eye contact)" (300). In other words, put on a show. Being knowledgeable about one's subject matter is not enough; professors must convey that knowledge. Maintaining student interest and motivation is crucial to accomplishing this task. Professors are, in effect, on stage and required to perform whether they feel like it at the time or not.

One's orientation to teaching and repertoire of communication and human relations skills undoubtedly mediate the classroom experience and demands for emotional labor. Professors who thrive on teaching may not feel that they are acting or performing at all. It may be invigorating and genuinely elicit positive emotions. For those less oriented toward teaching, however, the task may entail "surface acting" (pretending to hold certain feelings) or "deep acting" (conjuring feelings up so that the actor in fact experiences them)

(Hochschild 1983). The extent to which either kind of acting is emotionally draining or results in feelings of alienation from self probably depends on the extent of one's identification with teaching, as well as other personality factors. Emotional labor need not be a negative experience, as Hochschild suggested, but may be moderated by individual and work characteristics (Wharton 1993; Stenross and Kleinman 1989; Rafaeli and Sutton 1987).

The association between teaching and mothering and the lower status and authority of women may cause male and female professors to experience emotional labor in the classroom quite differently. The extent to which gender differences in professors' behavior and orientation reflect different socialization experiences versus conformity to organizational and work role standards and expectations is unclear. Both can create pressures for female professors, in particular, not only to perform enthusiastically but to exhibit friendly, caring behaviors, and they appear to be more likely to do so (Statham, Richardson, and Cook 1991). Women are more likely than men to interact with students in the classroom—to pose questions, encourage students to ask questions, mediate discussions, and encourage passive students while curbing overbearing ones.[2]

Women also tend to be more concerned than men with student learning, rather than with teaching per se (Statham, Richardson, and Cook 1991). Consequently, women allow students to speak significantly more than men (twice as long, according to

Brooks [1982]). Women tend to view classroom interaction as a means of helping students become independent thinkers and to see this as an important goal. In contrast, men tend "to regard students' participation as a requirement or sometimes as a time waste" (Statham, Richardson, and Cook 1991, 126). Students appear to expect and reward such gendered behavior. Students reward female professors, but sanction male professors, for exhibiting interactive behavior (Basow 1995; Statham, Richardson, and Cook 1991; Kierstead, D'Agostino, and Dill 1988; Bennett 1982).

Male professors are less likely than females to relate personal experiences in the classroom, and, when they do, their self-revelations tend to be less personal (for example, offering information about their careers rather than their families). Female professors are also more likely than males to exhibit warm, reinforcing behavior in the classroom. Not surprisingly, students expect female professors to be nicer than male professors and judge them more harshly when they are not. Kierstead, D'Agostino, and Dill (1988) found that friendly behavior elevated students' ratings of women but had no effect for men.

Women are far more likely than men to report that students evaluate them on their personalities (Statham, Richardson, and Cook 1991; see also Martin 1984). Reminiscent of Hochschild's interviews with flight attendants (1983), female professors report that students criticize them for "not smiling enough," for being "dull" or "unexciting"

(Statham, Richardson, and Cook 1991, 110-11). Thus women are more engaged with students in the classroom and engaged at a more personal level, one that may require greater investments in emotional labor. Interestingly, Statham, Richardson, and Cook (1991) found that men and women do not appear to experience teaching in the same way. Female professors "frequently mention the emotional consequences of dedicated teaching in terms of their feelings of well-being or depression. Dedicated males, on the other hand, focus on teaching as a technical problem" (48).

Not only must professors display positive emotions, but they must also work to control negative emotions—both their own and their students'. At times, professors are expected to exhibit neutrality, for example, in treating students equitably. Like other professionals, such as paralegals (Pierce 1995), detectives (Stenross and Kleinman 1989), salespersons (Leidner 1993), and bill collectors (Hochschild 1983; Rafaeli and Sutton 1991), professors must at times suppress their negative (or positive) feelings toward students and avoid displays of impatience, annoyance, and even anger. When students do not take their studies seriously, are rude, or confront professors' belief systems, professors must control their frustration and hostility. While occasional displays of annoyance may be effective in getting students to toe the line, professors—particularly women— cannot display real anger without negative repercussions, if only on student evaluations.

Diffusing volatile situations clearly requires interpersonal skills such as humor and tact. Sometimes professors can anticipate hostile reactions, as when handing back a set of poor exams, but at other times tempers may flair unexpectedly, compounding the stress of teaching. The risk of unexpected "eruptions" is probably greater in such courses as women's studies and ethnic studies, which women are more likely to teach than men (Astin, Korn, and Dey 1991). Even when women and men teach the same course, students may be more resistant to the message of women professors (Moore 1997). In addition, men are twice as likely as women to have graduate teaching assistants (Astin, Korn, and Dey 1991), who can serve as "emotional shields," deflecting student hostility. In addition, dealing with an irate (male) student may be far more unsettling for female than for male professors because of the level of violence against women in our society.

Women's lower social status may result in a weaker "status shield" for female professors (Hochschild 1983). Women are less protected from affronts to their authority, even when in the same occupational position as men. Students tend to rate female professors as less knowledgeable than their male counterparts (Feldman 1993) and appear to demand a higher standard of preparation from them (Bennett 1982). Brooks (1982) found significant differences in the aggressiveness of male graduate students toward female professors relative to male professors. She suggests that some male graduate students have difficulty dealing with professional women who exhibit characteristics that are culturally defined as male, such as self-confidence, assertiveness, and ambition. Thus women have the difficult task of establishing their authority and reducing opportunities for students to challenge it, while at the same time establishing a warm, interactive classroom environment.

Emotional labor
outside the classroom

Since cultural expectations dictate that women be polite and listen to other people's problems, students may expect such behavior of their female professors outside the classroom. Some female professors complain that students expect hand-holding or mothering, which they may or may not have the time, inclination, or emotional energy to provide. Although most professors recognize that personal problems can influence classroom performance and many believe that students deserve to be heard, there is also a perception that students value male professors' time more than female professors' (Tierney and Bensimon 1996).

Men and women may send different messages to students about their willingness to listen to personal problems. Statham, Richardson, and Cook (1991) found that men tend to avoid counseling students and discourage students from conveying personal problems. One male professor explained his strategy: "If they begin to talk about personal problems, I tell them that I am not trained to deal with those kinds of problems, I'm not comfortable dealing with that" (96). Another male professor reported that he responds to students' attempts to discuss personal matters by saying, "I have to do some other things. I have other things to do and you'll have to excuse me" (96). In contrast, women are less likely to cut students' time in their office short. One female professor in the same study lamented that "all the students that have ever had nervous breakdowns in this place have had them in [her] office" (95).

Despite evidence to the contrary, students rate their female professors as being less available than men. Furthermore, Bennett (1982) found a relationship between amount of personal contact and student satisfaction for female professors but not for males, indicating that women are penalized if they do not meet students' expectations for personal contact. This is consistent with DeVault's observation (1991) that "caring work is exceptional or optional for men while it is obligatory for women" (151). The extent to which professors should listen to their students' personal problems is less at issue than the consequences of gender differences in professors' behavior and the toll women's behavior may take on their emotions and time when they expend so much of both on activities that are little recognized or financially rewarded.

EMOTIONAL LABOR AND SERVICE

Service, a catchall category that typically encompasses everything that is not clearly teaching or research, includes activities both internal and external to the institution (Blackburn and Lawrence 1995). Student advising and committee work are the most common forms of internal service performed by faculty, and I discuss some of the emotional labor required in these activities later. Professors may also engage in public relations work for their college or university. Favorable personal interactions between faculty and students, parents, alumni, potential donors, legislators, and other constituents help "sell the institution"; can increase student enrollment, retention, and financial contributions; and can improve community relations.[3] External service typically involves public service; professional activities, such as reviewing manuscripts for journals; and serving as an officer or com- mittee member for professional organizations.

Studies of faculty time expenditures show that, in the aggregate, women spend more time in service work than men (Bellas and Toutkoushian Forthcoming). Like teaching, service appears to require no special training (Seldin 1980). Although service is often routine, little noticed, and unrewarded, it can be an important means of networking, facilitating research, and otherwise enhancing one's career (Lawson 1990). Service activities can also be a route to higher status for faculty (for example, by attaining visibility within institutions) and higher salaries (for example, by leading to an administrative position).

Student advising

Student advising is quite similar to interacting with one's own students outside the classroom. Seldin's discussion of what constitutes a good adviser (1980) points to the emotional labor involved in this endeavor. In addition to verbal and nonverbal communication skills and knowledge about the curriculum, he stipulates that advisers should have a "genuine interest in working with students . . ., the ability to deal with students as individuals and human beings . . ., empathy, warmth, intuition and flexibility, the patience to listen . . ., and the ability to give as much time as necessary to counsel students [who may be frustrated and angry] on courses, careers, and personal problems" (121).

In view of the requirements Seldin describes, it is not surprising that women spend more hours per week advising students than do men (Astin, Korn, and Dey 1991). Statham, Richardson, and Cook (1991) found that male university professors are more likely than female professors to view interactions with students outside the classroom negatively. Consequently, women may appear more welcoming to students and more willing to listen to their concerns. To create a positive experience for students, professors may need to engage in deep acting or surface acting, unless feelings and emotions are genuine (Hochschild 1983).

Committee work

Serving on committees requires both communication skills (for example, the ability to convey ideas succinctly and clearly) and human relations skills (for example, diplomacy and sociability). The degree of emotional labor required will vary depending on the charge of the committee, the issues involved, committee composition, and the level of consensus among members. Norms dictate that professors should act professionally in committee meetings and while conducting related work. Acting professionally may require one to control negative emotions and express positive ones (or, at a minimum, exhibit cordiality) and to show respect for differences of opinion, whether or not this reflects one's true feelings. Seldin (1980) suggests that evaluations of faculty service should include the dimensions of "faculty relations" as well as a "cooperative attitude": "Is the faculty member always civil toward his [sic] colleagues? Toward others? Does he show respect for differing opinions? Is he cooperative? Does he offer department peers help with their problems? Does he appear interested and pleased to carry out assignments? Is he positive and forward-looking? Responsive to others' needs?" (126; see also Blackburn and Lawrence 1995, 226).

This emphasis on collegiality raises the questions of whether different behaviors are expected of the sexes, and whether men's and women's interpersonal styles and their contributions to committees are judged differently. Tierney and Bensimon (1996) refer to women's efforts to fit into patriarchal work settings as doing "smile work"—the "symbolic management of behavior to present oneself as being pleasing

and agreeable." They argue that "male dominated cultures encourage feminine stereotypical behaviors that make women appear 'unobjectionable,' congenial and cheerful rather than strident and unpredictable" (83).[4] As in teaching, women may be expected to exhibit facial displays of emotion to a greater extent than men to convey a pleasant and agreeable demeanor (Hochschild 1983). While untenured faculty, among whom women are disproportionately represented, are at greatest risk if they do not conform to gendered expectations, tenured faculty are also vulnerable since promotions and merit increases require review by colleagues and department heads (Johnsrud 1993).

In general, women are disadvantaged in mixed-sex groups. Structurally, men are more likely to hold higher ranks and administrative posts and therefore be in positions to evaluate, reward, and punish women. This may place greater demands for emotional labor on women as women attempt to convey, justify, and legitimize their contributions and, indeed, their presence. Men's communication styles are associated with power and professionalism, while women's styles are associated with weakness (Tannen 1994). Men's deeper voices and larger size contribute to these perceptions, as well as their tendency to speak more, interrupt more, and control the topic of conversation. Women's comments and suggestions tend not to be accorded the same weight as men's (Sandler 1992; Henley and Freeman 1989). Some women faculty and administrators report that they may go unrecognized in meetings, be interrupted, or have their comments ignored or dismissed. To have their ideas heard or motions passed, women may have to find a man to present them (Olsen, Maple, and Stage 1995; Sandler 1992). Ironically, although women's communication styles are devalued, if women adopt a more masculine style they risk being viewed as overly aggressive, insensitive, or even uncollegial. All this may place additional demands for emotional labor on faculty women, especially women in the lower ranks and women of color, who may suffer devaluation in interactive as well as financial contexts.

EMOTIONAL LABOR AND RESEARCH

At first glance, research appears to involve little emotional labor relative to teaching and service. This perception stems from the strong association between science and objectivity, as well as the view that emotions are an impediment or contaminant to the scientific process (Jayaratne and Stewart 1991; Oakley 1981; Smith 1974). The polarity between "objective science" and "subjective emotions" parallels gender stereotypes.

Women are characterised as sensitive, intuitive, incapable of objectivity and emotional detachment and as immersed in the business of making and sustaining personal relationships. Men are thought superior through their capacity for rationality and scientific objectivity and are thus seen to be possessed of an instrumental orientation in their relationships with others. (Oakley 1981, 38)

Scientists, including social scientists, are trained to suppress emotions and, when necessary, to manipulate emotions in subjects so as to obtain their cooperation. Consider examples in the popular textbook *The Practice of Social Research*, by Earl Babbie (1995). When research requires direct interchange between researcher and subject, the interviewer should be a *"neutral* medium through which questions and answers are transmitted"* (264, italics in original). Interviewers should not display emotions even when respondents do. Interviewers strive for neutrality by following a script, since changes in wording may influence what they are trying to find out from those they are studying. The interviewer should "become the kind of person the respondent is comfortable with" since respondents "deserve the most enjoyable experience the researcher and interviewer can provide" (266). Babbie also emphasizes good listening skills; the interviewer should "be more interested than interesting" (290). Clearly, a substantial element of impression management is evident in these interviewing techniques.

Despite the emphasis on emotional detachment and neutrality, researchers can become deeply involved in their subjects' lives, particularly when there is sustained contact between researchers and subjects. As Marie Corbin (1971) described:

In theory it should be possible to establish confidence simply by courtesy towards and interest in the interviewees. In practice it can be difficult to spend eight hours in a person's home, share their meals and listen to their problems and at the same time remain polite, detached and largely uncommunicative. (Reported in Oakley 1981, 53)

Neutrality may be especially difficult when the research topic is emotionally charged or related to one's personal experiences. For example, sociologist Becky Thompson (1990) conveys the following regarding her response while interviewing women with eating disorders: "I sometimes found myself trying to escape from the pain of their stories as they spoke. Many of the women have been multiply victimized including enduring poverty, sexual abuse, exposure to high levels of violence, and emotional and physical torture." She said this often left her completely drained after the interviews. Sociologist Barbara Katz Rothman (1986) describes her study of women who underwent amniocentesis to diagnose fetal abnormalities: "It was like lifting the proverbial rock and having it all crawl out—ugliness, pain, grief, horror, anger, anguish, fear, sadness. . . . It was a nightmare." These are but two of the examples cited in *Feminist Methods in Social Research* by Shulamit Reinharz (1992, 34-36). These examples demonstrate that the interview experience can elicit powerful emotions both in the interviewee and the researcher. Yet social scientists largely ignore the emotional aspects of the research process or learn to minimize and even deny them by becoming mere "tools" or "instruments" (Oakley 1981, 32).

Qualitative methods such as interviews, fieldwork, and participant-observation are most prevalent in the social sciences and the humanities, and it is precisely these methods that researchers employ in the study of emotional labor (for example, Pierce 1995; Leidner 1993; DeVault 1991; Hochschild 1983). Yet quantitative methods such as analysis of secondary data and controlled experiments (also prevalent in the social sciences but most characteristic of the physical sciences) are not totally devoid of emotion.[5] Professors are typically invested in their research and must manage their emotions regarding the interpretation and potential impact of their findings. Thus emotional detachment, so often associated with quantitative methods, may in reality be deep acting—and a convenient way of distancing oneself from emotional issues.

Other aspects of research, whether qualitative or quantitative, involve emotional labor. Professors may have research assistants, with whom they must communicate. Professors must provide instructions and training and be concerned with issues of morale and motivation. Collaboration and coauthorship involve communication and interpersonal skills, too. However, collaboration, thought to be more common among women than men, conflicts with the normative view of science as an autonomous pursuit (Ward and Grant 1991). Collaborative efforts may require more emotional labor than does individual work but are likely to be accorded less value, with negative consequences for women.

Professional conferences also require emotional labor. Like teachers, presenters of papers are on stage, but the stakes are generally higher. A poor professional presentation may have negative consequences for one's reputation. Authors must communicate clearly, suppress any fear or anxiety, and elicit positive emotions from their audience. Professional conferences also provide an opportunity for networking and self-promotion. Due to differences in gender socialization, self-promotional behavior is thought to be easier for most men than for most women and may be better received by others if it comes from men (McIlwee and Robinson 1992). Thus, contrary to the image of research and publishing as requiring little if any emotional labor, scholarly activities involve both emotional labor and intellectual labor, though the latter is recognized and rewarded far more than the former.[6]

ADMINISTRATION

The role of faculty in administration has received little research attention, although studies show that men are far more likely to serve in administrative positions than women, particularly in the upper echelons (Kaplan and Tinsley 1989; Chamberlain 1988). This is not surprising given the strong association in people's minds between leadership characteristics and masculine attributes. Because the mental image of a leader is male, people may find it incongruous for a woman to be an administrator (Sandler 1986). As discussed in the section on committee work, the behavior of female administrators may be judged differently from males' even when it is the same,

creating different and perhaps greater demands for emotional labor on women.

Although administration involves some solitary activities such as preparing budgets and reports, it also typically involves supervising subordinates and reporting to people in higher positions. Thus communication skills and human relations skills are paramount, though these are generally valued less than strong leadership abilities. Although women administrators may be more adept than men at interpersonal relations, they are nevertheless most likely disadvantaged in their interpersonal interactions since gender role expectations can influence interactions with students, colleagues, and the public.

The style of women administrators, like that of women professors, appears to be more inclusive and egalitarian than men's, but such tendencies are frequently interpreted as a sign of weakness (Tannen 1994). Similarly, women's less forceful presentation styles, along with their higher voices and smaller physical size, tend to be judged less appropriate than more masculine characteristics (Sandler 1992; Henley and Freeman 1989). This may have negative consequences for women's effectiveness in the job. Yet, as noted previously, if women assume more masculine styles, they are likely to be sanctioned for deviating from gender-appropriate behavior. As Sandler (1986) observes, "We are not surprised when men are powerful, assertive, ambitious, and achieving, but we may be uncomfortable when women exhibit these traits . . . we 'expect' women to be nurturing, passive, accommodating" (4). Thus women administrators, like women faculty and other professional women generally, appear to face a double bind. Women are expected to be nice and accommodating, but if they are too nice, they are not respected. These problems may interfere with the ability of women administrators to carry out their work effectively, and they may even contribute to a self-fulfilling prophecy.

CONCLUSION

Research demonstrates that gendered reward structures can arise when specific job tasks are valued more or less because of the gendered nature of the work. Skills and responsibilities defined as feminine, such as nurturance and face-to-face service to clients or customers (emotional labor), are typically unappreciated and unrewarded by employers and stigmatized even when male workers perform them. In contrast, employers tend to appreciate and reward skills and responsibilities defined as masculine, such as technical expertise and management responsibilities (England et al. 1994; Steinberg 1990; Feldberg 1984).

Most professors divide their time between teaching, research, service, and, for some, administration. As in the nonacademic labor market, there is a gendered reward structure in academia. Teaching and service are most closely aligned with characteristics and behaviors culturally defined as feminine, and, in the aggregate, women spend more time in these activities than men. Teaching and service clearly involve substan-

tial amounts of emotional labor but are generally not seen as involving valued skills and are consequently poorly rewarded. In contrast, research and administration are associated with traits culturally defined as masculine, and, on average, men spend more time in these activities (Bellas and Toutkoushian Forthcoming). Although I have suggested that research and administration also involve emotional labor, their emotional aspects tend to be largely ignored, while intellectual, technical, and leadership skills are emphasized and highly compensated. Aside from differences in the propensity of women and men to engage in different activities and the gendered reward structure associated with these activities, even when the tasks are the same, the type and intensity of emotional labor required of the sexes may differ.

Notes

1. Although Hochschild defined emotional labor as involving situations where employees have face-to-face or voice-to-voice contact with the public, others have expanded this conceptualization to include interaction with coworkers (for example, Rafaeli 1989).

2. An interesting study by Canada and Pringle (1995) found that interactive behaviors on the part of both female and male professors are sensitive to the sex composition of classes. Female and male professors initiated comparable numbers of interactions in all-female classrooms, but female professors initiated more and male professors fewer interactions in mixed-sex classrooms. In addition, the more male students, the fewer the number of professor (and student) interactions.

3. Institutional promises of quality faculty-student interactions in their recruitment materials may influence student expectations for personal contact with professors.

4. Gendered expectations may extend beyond smile work, of course, to include serving as secretary for committees or performing wifely duties such as making coffee or cleaning up after meetings (Sandler 1992). These activities all constitute "doing gender" (West and Zimmerman 1987).

5. Note that women faculty and women students are concentrated in fields where expectations for emotional labor and expression are greatest (such as the humanities, social work, and education), while men are concentrated in presumably unemotional fields (such as engineering and physics).

6. Written communications may also involve emotional labor; examples of such communications are responses to journal reviewers' comments and exchanges between authors who disagree.

References

Acker, Sandra. 1995. Carry on Caring: The Work of Women Teachers. *British Journal of Sociology of Education* 16(1):21-36.

Astin, Alexander, William S. Korn, and Eric L. Dey. 1991. *The American College Teacher: National Norms for the 1989-90 HERI Faculty Survey.* Los Angeles: University of California at Los Angeles, Graduate School of Education, Higher Education Research Institute.

Babbie, Earl. 1995. *The Practice of Social Research.* Belmont, CA: Wadsworth.

Basow, Susan A. 1995. Student Evaluations of College Professors: When Gender Matters. *Journal of Educational Psychology* 87(4):656-65.

Bellas, Marcia L. 1994. Comparable Worth in Academe: The Effects on Faculty Salaries of the Sex Composition and Labor-Market Conditions of Academic Disciplines. *American Sociological Review* 59(6):807-21.

Bellas, Marcia L. and Robert K. Toutkoushian. Faculty Time Allocations and Research Productivity: Gender, Race and Family Effects. Forthcoming Review of Higher Education.

Bennett, Sheila Kishler. 1982. Student Perceptions of and Expectations for Male and Female Instructors: Evidence Relating to the Question of Gender Bias in Teaching Evaluation. *Journal of Educational Psychology* 74(2):170-79.

Blackburn, Robert T. and Janet H. Lawrence. 1995. *Faculty at Work.* Baltimore, MD: Johns Hopkins University Press.

Brooks, Virginia. 1982. Sex Differences in Student Dominance Behavior in Female and Male Professors' Classrooms. *Sex Roles* 8(7):683-90.

Canada, Katherine and Richard Pringle. 1995. The Role of Gender in College Classroom Interactions: A Social Context Approach. *Sociology of Education* 68(3):161-86.

Chamberlain, Marian K. 1988. *Women in Academe: Progress and Prospects.* New York: Russell Sage Foundation.

Corbin, Marie. 1971. Appendix 3. In *Managers and Their Wives,* by Jan M. Pahl and Raymond E. Pahl. London: Allen Lane.

DeVault, Marjorie L. 1991. *Feeding the Family: The Social Organization of Caring as Gendered Work.* Chicago: University of Chicago Press.

England, Paula, Melissa S. Herbert, Barbara Stanek Kilbourne, Lori L. Reid, and Lori McCreary Megdal. 1994. The Gendered Valuation of Occupations and Skills: Earnings in 1980 Census Occupations. *Social Forces* 73(1):65-99.

Fairweather, James S. 1993. Academic Values and Faculty Rewards. *Review of Higher Education* 17(1):43-68.

Feldberg, Roslyn L. 1984. Comparable Worth: Toward Theory and Practice in the United States. *Signs: Journal of Women in Culture and Society* 10(2):311-28.

Feldman, Kenneth A. 1993. College Students' Views of Male and Female College Teachers: Part II—Evidence from

Students' Evaluations of Their Classroom Teachers. *Research in Higher Education* 34(2):151-211.

Grumet, Madeline R. 1988. *Bitter Milk: Women and Teaching.* Amherst: University of Massachusetts Press.

Henley, Nancy and Jo Freeman. 1989. The Sexual Politics of Interpersonal Behavior. In *Women: A Feminist Perspective*, ed. Jo Freeman. Mountain View, CA: Mayfield.

Hochschild, Arlie Russell. 1983. *The Managed Heart: Commercialization of Human Feeling.* Berkeley: University of California Press.

Jayaratne, Toby Epstein and Abigail J. Stewart. 1991. Quantitative and Qualitative Methods in the Social Sciences: Current Feminist Issues and Practical Strategies. In *Beyond Methodology: Feminist Scholarship as Lived Research*, ed. Mary Margaret Fonow and Judith A. Cook. Bloomington: Indiana University Press.

Johnsrud, Linda K. 1993. Women and Minority Faculty Experiences: Defining and Responding to Diverse Realities. In *Building a Diverse Faculty*, ed. Joanne Gainen and Robert Boice. Vol. 53. New Directions for Teaching and Learning. San Francisco, CA: Jossey-Bass.

Kaplan, Sheila and Adrian Tinsley. 1989. The Unfinished Agenda: Women in Higher Education Administration. *Academe*, Jan.-Feb.:18-22.

Kierstead, Diane, Patti D'Agostino, and Heidi Dill. 1988. Sex Role Stereotyping of College Professors: Bias in Students' Ratings of Instructors. *Journal of Educational Psychology* 80(3):342-44.

Lawson, Hal A. 1990. Constraints on the Professional Service of Education Faculty. *Journal of Teacher Education* 41(4):57-70.

Leidner, Robin. 1993. *Fast Food, Fast Talk: Service Work and the Routinization of Everyday Life.* Berkeley: University of California Press.

Martin, Elaine. 1984. Power and Authority in the Classroom: Sexist Stereotypes in Teaching Evaluations. *Signs: Journal of Women in Culture and Society* 9(3):482-92.

McIlwee, Judith S. and J. Gregg Robinson. 1992. *Women in Engineering: Gender, Power, and Workplace Culture.* Albany: State University of New York Press.

McKinney, Kathleen. 1988. Faces: Five Components of Quality Teaching. *Teaching Sociology* 16(3):298-301.

Moore, Melanie. 1997. Student Resistance to Course Content: Reactions to the Gender of the Messenger. *Teaching Sociology* 25(2):128-33.

Oakley, Ann. 1981. Interviewing Women: A Contradiction in Terms. In *Doing Feminist Research*, ed. Helen Roberts. London: Routledge.

Olsen, Deborah, Sue A. Maple, and Frances K. Stage. 1995. Women and Minority Faculty Job Satisfaction: Professional Role Interests, Professional Satisfactions, and Institutional Fit. *Journal of Higher Education* 66(3):267-93.

Pierce, Jennifer L. 1995. *Gender Trials: Emotional Lives in Contemporary Law Firms.* Berkeley: University of California Press.

Rafaeli, Anat. 1989. When Cashiers Meet Customers: An Analysis of the Role of Supermarket Cashiers. *Academy of Management Review* 32(2):245-73.

Rafaeli, Anat and Robert I. Sutton. 1987. Expression of Emotion as Part of the Work Role. *Academy of Management Review* 12(1):23-37.

———. 1991. Emotional Contrast Strategies as Means of Social Interest: Lessons from Criminal Interrogators and Bill Collectors. *Academy of Management Journal* 34(4):749-75.

Rau, William and Paul J. Baker. 1989. The Organized Contradictions of Academe: Barriers Facing the Next Academic Revolution. *Teaching Sociology* 17(Apr.):161-75.

Reinharz, Shulamit. 1992. *Feminist Methods in Social Research*. New York: Oxford University Press.

Rothman, Barbara Katz. 1986. Reflections on Hard Work. *Qualitative Sociology* 9(1):48-53.

Sandler, Bernice Resnick. 1986. *The Campus Climate Revisited: Chilly for Women Faculty, Administrators, and Graduate Students*. Washington, DC: Association of American Colleges, Project on the Status and Education of Women.

———. 1992. *Success and Survival Strategies for Women Faculty Members*. Washington, DC: Association of American Colleges.

Seldin, Peter. 1980. *Successful Faculty Evaluation Programs: A Practical Guide to Improve Faculty Performance and Promotion/Tenure Decisions*. Crugers, NY: Coventry Press.

Smith, Dorothy E. 1974. Women's Perspective as a Radical Critique of Sociology. *Sociological Inquiry* 44(1):7-13.

Statham, Anne, Laurel Richardson, and Judith A. Cook. 1991. *Gender and University Teaching: A Negotiated Difference*. Albany: State University of New York Press.

Steinberg, Ronnie J. 1990. Social Construction of Skill: Gender, Power, and Comparable Worth. *Work and Occupations* 17(4):449-82.

Stenross, Barbara and Sherryl Kleinman. 1989. The Highs and Lows of Emotional Labor: Detectives' Encounters with Criminals and Victims. *Journal of Contemporary Ethnography* 17(4):435-52.

Tannen, Deborah. 1994. *Talking from 9 to 5: How Women's and Men's Conversational Styles Affect Who Gets Heard, Who Gets Credit, and What Gets Done at Work*. New York: William Morrow.

Thompson, Becky. 1990. Raisins and Smiles for Me and My Sister: A Feminist Theory of Eating Problems, Trauma, and Recovery in Women's Lives. Ph.D. diss., Brandeis University.

Tierney, William G. and Estela Mara Bensimon. 1996. *Promotion and Tenure: Community and Socialization in Academe*. Albany: State University of New York Press.

Ward, Kathryn B. and Linda Grant. 1991. Co-authorship, Gender, and Publication Among Sociologists. In *Beyond Methodology: Feminist Scholarship as Lived Research*, ed. Mary Margaret Fonow and Judith A. Cook. Bloomington: Indiana University Press.

West, Candace and Don H. Zimmerman. 1987. Doing Gender. *Gender & Society* 1(2):125-51.

Wharton, Amy S. 1993. The Affective Consequences of Service Work: Managing Emotions on the Job. *Work and Occupations* 20(2):205-32.

ANNALS, *AAPSS*, **561**, January 1999

Police Force or Police Service?
Gender and Emotional Labor

By SUSAN EHRLICH MARTIN

ABSTRACT: Police work involves substantial emotional labor by officers, who must control their own emotional displays and those of citizens, who often are encountered at their worst—injured, upset, or angry. Although policing often is viewed as masculine work that focuses on fighting crime, it also requires that officers maintain order and provide diverse services, which officers tend to disdain as feminine activities. This article explores the varieties of emotional labor, the rules regulating emotional displays in policing, and the role of gender in shaping these occupational and organizational norms. It identifies variations in the norms regulating emotional labor across policing assignments, interactional situations, and the gender of both the officers and the citizens in an encounter. It also reviews coping mechanisms for regulating emotions—including socialization, organizational rituals, humor, and off-duty social activities—and the dilemmas that norms related to emotional labor pose for women officers.

Susan Ehrlich Martin received her Ph.D. in sociology from American University. She wrote "Breaking and Entering": Policewomen on Patrol *(1980) and* Doing Justice, Doing Gender *(1996), coauthored with Nancy Jurik. She has been a study director at the National Research Council and at the Police Foundation. She currently directs a research program on alcohol and violence at the National Institute on Alcohol Abuse and Alcoholism and continues writing on women, work, and violence.*

P OLICE work involves extensive emotional labor since it requires the officer "to induce or suppress feelings in order to sustain the outward countenance that produces the proper state of mind in others" (Hochschild 1983, 7). To be effective, officers must control both their own feelings and the emotional displays of citizens. The importance, skills, and scope demanded of police in performing emotional labor often are overlooked or downplayed by both the police and the public for two closely linked reasons. First, policing has been defined in terms of fighting crime or catching criminals, although it involves a far wider variety of tasks. Second, the occupation has long been dominated by men and closely associated with the stereotypical inexpressive masculinity of Sergeant Friday, although women have served as sworn officers since 1910 and been on street patrol since 1972. Despite the professional (that is, unemotional) image that the police have cultivated, the activities and incidents that police encounter often arouse deep emotions in themselves and the citizens with whom they come into contact. A cop's failure to manage these emotions may have high costs, as illustrated by the disturbance ensuing from officers' lack of self-restraint in their interaction with Rodney King in Los Angeles, California.

This article explores the feeling and display rules that regulate emotional expression in police work, the ways these are made masculine, and how this affects occupational and organizational norms. Norms regarding emotional labor vary across police interactions with both coworkers and the public and are affected by the gender of the officer and of the person the officer encounters. Although policing is a traditionally male job, it requires frequent performance of emotional labor affecting both the hard and soft emotions (Price 1996). Since these, in turn, are associated, respectively, with masculinity and femininity, this article explores how gender contributes to the apparent division of emotional labor in policing.

EMOTIONAL LABOR: DEFINITIONS AND THEORETICAL ISSUES

Emotions are feelings that people experience, interpret, reflect on, express, and manage (Thoits 1989; Mills and Kleinman 1988). They arise through social interaction; are influenced by social, cultural, interpersonal, and situational conditions; and are managed by workers along with physical and mental labor on the job.

Workers do emotional labor (that is, manage feelings to create a publicly observable display) on the job. Hochschild (1983) emphasized how employees are required to manage their own feelings in order to create displays that affect others in desired ways. England and Farkas (1986) underscored the effect of emotion work on others. Increasingly, research on emotional labor addresses the emotions of both the employee and those with whom he or she interacts since these are linked through the performance of emotional labor.

The earliest studies of emotional labor focused on women service workers interacting with their clients or patients. More recent studies have recognized that a far wider group of occupations than those identified by Hochschild (1983) involve emotional labor and that jobs demand emotional labor to a greater or lesser degree, rather than as an all-or-nothing phenomenon (Steinberg and Figart 1997). For example, Fineman (1993) observed:

Many professional workers . . . are . . . paid for their skill in emotion management. They are to look serious, understanding, controlled, cool, empathetic and so forth with clients or patients. . . . Benign detachment disguises, and defends against, any private feelings of pain, despair, fear, attraction, revulsion or love; feelings which would otherwise interfere with the professional relationship. (19)

As this statement suggests, there are organizational norms governing both the appropriate expression and the suppression or management of emotions. The work of supervisors and professionals includes serving as emotional managers and enforcing the feeling rules associated with subordinates' roles. Feeling rules are norms regarding what emotions should be experienced by workers. In contrast, display rules are norms guiding which emotions ought to be publicly expressed and how; thus these norms are observable.

Both feeling rules and display rules are essential parts of the broader occupational and organizational work cultures in which they are embedded (Van Maanen and Kunda 1989). Cultures are created by groups to give meaning and to order behavior. Many occupations have cultures or sets of taken-for-granted emotionally charged beliefs or ideologies based on shared experiences and specific technical knowledge as well as prescribed mechanisms or cultural forms for expressing what they believe (Trice 1993). Occupations and organizations create myths, stage-manage events like award ceremonies and retirement parties, and use occasions such as police funerals to ritually handle emotion, support a collective identity, and reinforce organizational values and bonds.

Organizations also exercise cultural control through recruitment, selection, socialization, and supervisory practices. Potential employees are screened not only on skills but for temperamental fit with the emotional demands of the job. Through socialization, individuals learn the rules regarding the content, intensity, and variety of emotions demanded in performing their work role; once these are internalized, the work and desire for success provide incentive for conforming with display rules. When display rules are not congruent with workers' inner feelings, organizations manage those emotionally dissonant feelings through monitoring, rewards (for example, raises and promotions), inculcating psychological defense mechanisms, and occasional punishments (such as transfers and terminations) (Sutton 1991). Psychological defense mechanisms include techniques for displacing an emotion through actions such as cursing after an unpleasant encounter, joking to release tension, or physical exercise, and escape through drinking, eating, or sexuality.

Ritualized expression of emotion also may be part of the informal culture of occupations or work groups. Opportunities for venting may occur in backstage areas of the work site such as the locker room or nursing station, or in offstage areas such as a local bar or parking lot where workers socialize together after work.

Setting and situation also affect emotional displays. As an interactional sequence unfolds, the actor receives feedback from the target person. In addition, the actor is affected by transaction-defining cues from both the target person and the setting; these, in turn, are affected by feedback from the target person (Rafaeli and Sutton 1989).

In sum, jobs that involve emotional labor require contact with other workers or customers; the use of skills and the performance of tasks and activities that are associated with the expression of an emotion by the employee or its suppression through self-management; and production of an emotional state in another person. Emotional displays are shaped by employers through their control of selection, training, supervision, and rituals; by occupational cultures and informal work groups through their norms regulating emotional expression; and by the immediate situation, setting, and feedback as an interaction unfolds.

Jobs also vary in the amount of emotional labor and the type of emotion they require or permit employees to express. These variations are related to the gender of the worker and the gendered stereotype of the job. In brief, service workers, who are primarily women, are expected to display soft emotions such as nurturance; professionals and others in jobs dominated by men are expected to display no emotion or to manage emotional displays that revolve around anger and implied threats in order to induce fear and compliance in others (Hochschild 1983; Pierce 1995; Sutton 1991; Wharton 1996). At the same time, because gender assumptions transfer from the workers to their jobs, workers simultaneously construct, or do, gender through their work, and the culturally shaped gender designations of work activities are reinterpreted in ways that support the jobholders' gender identities (Leidner 1991).

The association between many jobs and gender-stereotyped characteristics has obscured the actual content of the work itself, including the emotional demands. As Steinberg and Figart (1997) observed:

Both male and female jobs can incorporate similar ranges and degrees of emotional labor. This supports the argument that the gender of the job can influence our perceptions of job content to some extent independently of actual job content. The very way that we characterize jobs in terms of their prototypical content is thus socially constructed on the basis of our common sense understandings of characteristics of the gender of the typical job incumbent. (2)

EMOTIONAL LABOR, GENDER, AND POLICE WORK

This section examines the myth and reality of police work, the ways policing is stereotyped as masculine and provides male officers a tool for doing gender, and what this means for the emotional labor involved in the job.

There is a wide gap between the work that the police actually do and the public image of policing, which is associated with crime fighting and stereotyped as masculine. Police not only enforce the law and arrest offenders; they also are responsible for preventing crime, protecting life and property, maintaining peace and public order, and providing a wide range of services to citizens 24 hours a day. Across these tasks, an essential part of policing is taking charge of situations. Depending on the circumstances, cops may seek to gain control by "hitting, shooting, referring, rescuing, tending, separating, handcuffing, humoring, threatening, placating, and discussing" (Bayley and Bittner 1984, quoted in Dunham and Alpert 1993, 111). The objective is to minimize the disruption of normal life.

While most calls to the police do not clearly refer to a crime or result in invocation of officers' legal powers, most incidents do deal with an element of latent conflict and the potential ingredients of a criminal offense (Reiner 1992). This enables an officer to interpret an event either as a conflict requiring an aggressive response or as an interpersonal dispute requiring informal conflict resolution. Since the character of the incident often is in the eye of the beholder, policing becomes a site for competing ways of doing gender.

Aggressive crime fighting is viewed by both police and the public as real police work and is visible, val-

ued, and rewarded. The association of catching criminals with danger and bravery is what marks police work as "men's work."

In reality, however, much of police work is dirty, insignificant, boring, or unpleasant. Most calls involve a request for service or order-maintenance tasks (Brown 1981) and involve officers interacting with people at their worst—when they have been victimized, are injured or helpless, or are guilty and seeking escape. This means officers must restore order in volatile situations and use interpersonal skills to gain citizen compliance.

The unique combination of occupational activities and unpredictable threats to their safety also has led to a set of attitudes and behaviors characteristic of police termed the "working personality" (Skolnick 1966). Cops tend to be suspicious of and isolated from the public, which fears them and which they view as hostile. This situation has resulted in a close and cohesive occupational culture that offers officers physical protection, support, solidarity, and social identity. The informal norms of this work culture include the expectations that an officer will remain silent about others' illicit behavior, will provide physical backup to other officers, and will punish displays of disrespect for the police (Westley 1970). In addition, they include a norm of emotional self-management. An officer who displays too much anger, sympathy, or other emotion in dealing with danger or tragedy on the job will not be accepted as a "regular cop" or viewed as someone able to withstand the pressures of police work (Pogrebin and Poole 1995).

The solidarity of the homogeneous group of white working-class men who previously composed police forces has eroded over the past 25 years due to both the recruitment of many female and ethnic-minority male officers and an organizational shift in focus from detached crime fighting to community policing. These changes have, among other things, feminized policing and have met resistance from many male rank-and-file officers who still believe women are unfit to handle the work either physically or emotionally (Martin 1980) and whose informal culture continues to demand that women officers adopt " 'male characteristics' to achieve even a limited social acceptability" (Young 1991, 193).

"The logic of sexism" among police rests on the men's dualistic worldview that associates gender-stereotyped oppositions (masculinity versus femininity) with various organizational symbols (such as street versus station house), occupational themes, and work activities (for example, crime fighting versus service and order maintenance) (Hunt 1990). From this dualistic view, men create an idealized image of real police work, which involves crime fighting that takes place on the street, celebrates physical prowess, and demands emotional control in the face of danger and injury. In contrast, station house and supervisory assignments are associated with feminine labor involving inside work and interpersonal skills. Although crime fighting and service work each demand management of emotions, the emotions associated with the former

are the hard (read "masculine") emotions requiring control of fear, anger, and hostility; those associated with service tasks often evoke the soft (read "feminine") emotions of compassion and sadness (Price 1996).

The norms of the department and of the informal culture demand that police officers severely limit expression of emotions. Even talking about pain, guilt, or fear is rare since officers who reveal their feelings to other officers may be viewed as weak or inadequate. Nevertheless, there are variations in the amount of emotional labor and emotion management performed by officers that are related to the immediate situation, its interactional demands, and the role of the citizen as victim, suspect, or third party in that interaction. Situations vary, for example, in terms of the extent to which they involve citizens who are upset, angry, injured, or disoriented; are perceived as threatening to the officer; and whether they require the officer to take immediate action (as with a robbery in progress or family fight) or involve the officer primarily in the collection of information and the provision of emotional support to the victim.

In addition to onstage interactions with citizens, police do emotion work with fellow officers in backstage interactions in the locker room and offstage informal social activities. Tales told either in the locker room or with drinking buddies after work recount sexual exploits and war stories as ways that both displace emotions and contribute to a man's status among the men. In interactions with both citizens and fellow police, the gender of the officer and the gender of the other participants affect interactional norms, including those related to emotion work, and which emotion is evoked.

DOING GENDER AND EMOTIONAL LABOR IN POLICE WORK

Officers do emotional labor in their encounters with citizens that are affected by the gender of the participants. They also do emotional labor in their backstage interactions with other officers. This section looks at the ways gender affects officers' performance of emotional labor.

Gender and police-citizen encounters

When women enter jobs traditionally defined as men's work, they usually implicitly are expected to accept work role definitions and behavioral scripts patterning interactions that are designed for and by men. They may act as police officers, but the job tasks and service styles remain gendered. Since a key element of policing—gaining and maintaining control of situations—remains associated with manhood, male officers do gender along with doing dominance. For women officers, however, this means finding ways to take control while dealing with uncertainties arising from citizens' assumptions (for example, that women are nicer or more emotional), the unfolding situation itself, occasional challenges to their authority, and their own emotional reactions to citizens' behavior (Martin and Jurik 1996).

Citizens generally defer to police, but in some instances they may seek to disrupt normal interaction by disavowing the officer's police identity and relate person to person by refocusing the interaction on irrelevant statuses, such as age, race, ethnicity, or gender, to gain an advantage (Goffman 1961). Such interruptions are more prevalent and problematic for women because of the close association of authority and control with masculinity. Thus women must find ways to turn these interactions to their advantage, by minimizing attention to their sex category or by taking advantage of it.

What qualifies as good police work varies across situations but involves gaining and maintaining control with minimal use of force. It requires skills both in crime-fighting encounters with mostly male offenders and in service-related encounters that demand emotional support for victims and their families. Because the service aspect of the work is regarded as feminine, it is devalued (Hunt 1990; Stenross and Kleinman 1989). In addition to gendered scripts in police work related to the definition of the encounter and the citizen, within each of these types of police-citizen interactions, the gender of the officer and the citizen affects their expectations and behaviors and poses specific management problems (Martin and Jurik 1996). Each of these four combinations of gender and social category will be examined.

Male officer, male citizen. As officers, male police have status superiority over male citizens, who are obligated to defer and comply. As men, however, both may draw on masculinity as an interactional resource, thereby implying a reduction in social distance, which generally is to the citizen's advantage. If a man displays inappropriate emotions, tactics for getting him to express appropriate emotions include rationalizing the other's emotions, offering alternative solutions, ignoring him, or not acknowledging his emotional expression (Price 1996). For example, to get a man to stop cursing the officer may assert, "Pull yourself together," saying, in effect, "Act like a man (that is, exercise self-control) and I won't have to exert my authority as an officer to overpower you." This benefits both the citizen and the officer by reducing the use of force and risk of injury, and it enables the officer to act as a "good guy," giving a little to gain compliance. Similarly, with male victims, the invocation of shared masculine norms of emotional self-control permits the officer to limit the emotional labor (that is, expressions of compassion, sympathy, or support) demanded of him in the interaction. Thus, drawing on shared manhood is an effective control technique used in some situations by male officers.

Sometimes when a suspect or offender attempts to define the situation in terms of shared manhood, however, the officer may perceive it as a denial of the deference owed to his office. Rejection of a male citizen's effort to be treated as a man may result in a "duel of manhood" (Martin 1980), which has a high probability of a verbal or physical confrontation since the man who backs down first fails the test of masculinity (Price 1996). When young male "street dudes" bait or challenge a male officer, the officer may manage his own reaction by drawing on his age superiority and treating the challenger as too young to merit a response. Alternatively, he may dispense so-called street justice, reflecting a failure to maintain emotional self-control but displaying police authority.

For detectives (who are usually men), the most rewarding part of their work is handling criminals (who are mostly men). This not only enables them to gain insights into the world of crime; it also provides an "emotional high" as they redefine their interaction with seasoned criminals as "higher mental work" (Stenross and Kleinman 1989). Criminals do not make detectives' jobs easy; they curse, refuse to talk, and sometimes cry. Detectives deal with criminals' emotional outbursts by discounting their expressive displays as feigned "strategic interaction" (Goffman 1969). They may finagle information out of a criminal by getting him or her to boast about a crime, hinting at leniency, or employing "strategic friendliness" (Pierce 1995). By interpreting the emotional labor they do with criminals as "higher status mental work," detectives are able to enjoy it as a challenging intellectual game (Stenross and Kleinman 1989).

Male officer, female citizen. Male officers' double-status superiority over female citizens enables the men to gain control by choosing to use the authority of their office or the authority of their gender. They can do gender by, for example, seeking compliance from "shrill" (that is, verbally abusive) female citizens by asserting, "Act like a lady (that is, behave in a calm, dignified manner) and I will treat you like one"—such treatment being to display respect owed to "the fair sex" rather than use physical force. If this gender-based strategy works, the officer maintains control while enhancing his sense of manly generosity. If it fails, he still may ignore minor displays of unilateral disrespect, treat the woman as a wayward girl on whom he will not waste his time, or use force.

Sometimes male officers use a flirting script or sexual flattery to gain control. This strategy is most notable in male officers' relations with prostitutes with whom they may exchange information about others' criminal activities for leniency in enforcing loitering laws.

Interactions with female victims that require displays of support, compassion, or empathy, however, create emotional demands that many men seek to avoid. Men's discomfort arises both because of the emotional hardness they have developed in response to their continual work exposure to the worst in humanity and because of the norms of emotional reserve included in their definition of masculinity. Victims of rape and domestic violence, for example, often have criticized police for their demeanor when they seek "just the facts, ma'am," or show outright insensitivity to victims' complaints. Even if male officers were more willing to convey more sympathy, service work may be emotionally stressful. Some women victims of partner violence may want the presence of an officer to level the playing field but

turn against the cop if he attempts to arrest the abuser. Abused and neglected children may physically resist being removed from their homes and abusive parents.

Many police recognize that the victims' pain is genuine, but they feel powerless in dealing with emotional outbursts (Stenross and Kleinman 1989) and regard providing emotional support as low-status women's work (Hunt 1984); others fail to feel sympathy because what is traumatic for the victim is routine for the officer. Their emotionality aside, victims can be troublesome to police in other ways. Even when an officer spends a great deal of time with a victim, the latter may complain of police inefficiency despite the absence of leads to solve the case, try to tell the officer or detective what to do, hound him or her with ideas and leads to follow up, fail to show up in court, and even be ungrateful when his or her property is returned. Thus, despite sympathy for the victims' plight, victims are an emotional burden to police.

Female officer, male citizen. Interactions between female officers and male citizens are problematic because men defer to the office but may resist being controlled by or deferential to a woman. Women police usually are given deference either out of gender-blind respect for the uniform or a sense of chivalry that enhances a male citizen's sense of self. Fighting a woman (particularly when there are male witnesses) is viewed as unmanly and so may cause a male citizen's loss of status, whether he wins or loses the fight. Still, given women's physical disadvantage, female officers must find alternative ways to control situations when they encounter male citizens' resistance.

Women officers generally ignore sexist or sexual comments that intrude on but do not alter the outcome of an interaction. In dealing with offenders, some women draw on citizens' stereotypes, including the fear that women are "trigger happy" or are emotional in the face of danger (Martin 1980). Others, particularly older black women, draw on social stereotypes such as that of "matriarch" or "aggressive bitch" (Collins 1991) in asserting authority.

Women's situational control strategies include a variety of verbal and nonverbal cues involving use of their voice, appearance, facial expression, and body postures to convey that they are to be taken seriously regardless of their physical stature. This often requires changing habits such as learning not to smile and how to literally "stand up to people" (Martin 1980).

Female officer, female citizen. Female officers get both greater cooperation and more resistance from women citizens than do male officers. They may draw on their common female status to reduce social distance and gain cooperation, particularly from women victims who refuse to talk to male officers. But female officers also revoke the special consideration given to female citizens by chivalrous male officers and, for that reason, may need to control a female citizen angered at not being able to flirt or manipulate her way out of a situation.

Effective officers of both genders are flexible, able to use both the crime-fighter script (associated with masculinity) and the service script (associated with femininity) to gain and maintain emotional control of situations and thereby physical control. By accurately reading the citizen's emotional state and responding to it, they use all the interpersonal resources available to them, actively seeking control by appealing both to gender-appropriate behavior and to the citizen's respect for the officer's authority. They use the citizen's expectations and values to their advantage, do gender so as to simultaneously diminish social distance and maintain control, often by invoking gendered familial roles (such as the role of mother or big brother), and limit reliance on the authority of the badge and the tools of policing. Ineffective officers either too rigidly rely on their formal authority, enact only the crime-fighting aspects of policing, and fail to provide emotional support to citizens when it is needed or, conversely, provide service and support to citizens but are unable to deal with defiance and back off from challenges.

The link between emotional labor and policing assignments

There is a close association between the emotional demands of various policing assignments and the status of those assignments. Most desirable are assignments that involve organizational functions most closely aligned with what is thought of as real policing (that is, fighting crime) and that emphasize control of the hard emotions. Detectives, for example, are able to avoid or deflect citizens' emotional demands onto the patrol officers taking the report at the crime scene. In contrast, caring assignments that demand control of the soft emotions (for example, missing-persons cases and victim services) or make limited emotional demands (such as work at a training academy and administrative assignments) tend to be devalued as feminized, judged as appropriate for women officers, and regarded as assignments in which women tend to be overrepresented (Martin 1990). Similarly, within patrol work, women officers are especially valued in domestic disputes since they are believed to be better able than men to calm an angry man, understand him, and prevent violence (Kennedy and Homant 1983).

Neither the rise of community policing nor the growing presence of women in policing has led to explicit discussion of the emotional component of the work. Male antipathy for the social service aspects of police work continues, and women either share the men's views or adapt to the fact that crime control rather than social service persists as the central occupational image.

Police organizations, gender, and strategies for discharging emotions

Police organizations manage officers' emotions through a number of mechanisms, including selection, socialization, supervision, reward systems, and ritual or ceremony. These indicate occupational norms and provide emotion management techniques.

Selection, socialization, and gender. All police departments carefully screen applicants. One important selection criterion is emotional stability. Candidates usually undergo extensive background investigations, psychological testing (for example, via the Minnesota Multiphasic Personality Inventory [MMPI]), and an interview with a psychologist (Scrivner 1994).

Socialization occurs in several phases, each of which teaches alternative ways to manage feelings. In the police academy, rookies learn that professional behavior and demeanor include the repression of emotional displays. This is conveyed largely through instructors' war stories that emphasize the importance of solidarity, teamwork, toughness, and stoicism in the face of pain. They also stress the importance of viewing the public in a detached manner and the belief that both hard and soft emotions are an occupational weakness in performing their duties (Pogrebin and Poole 1995).

On the street, rookies first work under supervision of a training officer. Through observation, instruction, experience, and correction, they become increasingly aware of their isolation from the community, and they develop verbal and nonverbal skills in managing situations. The primary concern in the early weeks is how the rookie handles the "hot" call (an in-progress crime or officer in trouble). Such calls constitute a behavioral test. To pass, the recruit must show willingness to share the risks of police work.

Policing norms reinforce the wider norms that men must hide fear in frightening situations and take action or face humiliation for failure to "act like a man." Women, in contrast, are permitted a greater range of self-expression and are expected to show fear. They are allowed to cry and seek exemption from duties felt to be too difficult or frightening, and they even are encouraged to be helpless. If they accept this paternalistic bargain, however, they fail to meet the occupational expectations of officers. Thus new women officers must adopt new patterns of behavior and simultaneously ignore the "double messages" and double standards for male and female competence and emotional displays on the job (Martin and Jurik 1996).

Women also must learn new behavior regarding verbal, facial, and bodily displays that convey their authority to citizens. This includes learning not to smile (smiling may cool a situation but signals deference, so usually is inappropriate) and to avoid postures that indicate hesitation or unreadiness to act.

Officers also need to learn techniques for dampening their own anger or annoyance at citizens' comments or taunts. Both male and female officers maintain calm by "thinking of the source" (that is, reminding themselves that the citizen in question is immature, ignorant, or unworthy of a rejoinder) and thus remain "above it all" (Martin 1980, 172).

Police also learn the norm of emotional restraint in relating to peers in backstage and offstage interactions. All newcomers want to fit in when they enter an occupation. In work where one's personal safety may depend on others' responses, the pressure to conform to informal behavioral norms is even greater. This means expressing emotions through off-color humor (Young 1991) and replacing fear, sorrow, and revulsion with a show of bravado and practical competence (Brown and Grover 1998). Even discussing fear, sadness, or anger in the locker room can be a dangerous breach of the norm of assuming a "stoic posture" by repressing emotions (Pogrebin and Poole 1995, 159).

Mechanisms for coping. Emotions remain, and undesirable feelings need to be discharged. Organizational mechanisms that help officers deal with work-related emotional stresses include psychological counseling services (including mandatory counseling for officers involved in a shooting) (Scrivner 1994) and elaborate rituals and ceremonies related to the death of an officer on duty that facilitate collective coping with stressful or tragic events.

The death of an officer in the line of duty and the funeral of that officer become invested with symbolic meaning for both the public and the police. The ritual of a police funeral reinforces the "sacred canopy . . . drawn over police work suffusing it with a moral integrity" (Manning 1997, 21), reaffirms for the officers their vulnerability and their isolation from the public, and offers individual officers reassurance about the way society would honor them should they die in the line of duty. Moreover, the funeral provides a period during which the rules of emotional reserve are suspended and a collective emotional catharsis occurs. Officers who are otherwise expected to mask feelings and manage both their own and others' emotions are permitted, even expected, to shed emotional reserve and cry or vent anger.

The informal culture permits coping with emotions that must be repressed on the job through humor, and displacement of emotional energy through physical and social activity. However, gendered norms for expressing feelings may lead to differences in the activities that are acceptable for men and women officers.

To conform with the demands of masculinity, the men mask their feelings of affection for and dependency on each other. "They guard themselves from the emotionally wrenching situations they face with slogans like 'don't let it get to you' and seek acceptable manly outlets such as heavy drinking, cursing, sexual exploits, fast driving and other dangerous sports, and displacing anger onto others" (Martin 1980, 97).

The presence of women threatens to expose the activities that men use to deal with emotions and so magnifies men's fear of losing self-control. At the same time, because men often find it easier to express emotions to a woman than to another man, they frequently cast women into the stereotypical role of "nurturant mother." Such women face the di-

lemma that they are "thrust into the role of emotional specialist, and then criticized for being emotional" (Martin 1980, 152).

Humor often is used to vent feelings, avoid the impression of vulnerability, and lessen the harshness of the tragic experience. Joking about tragic events offers a way to express emotions without damaging the professional image and enables police collectively to empathize with each other's feelings through gallows humor, a communicative conduit for "translating an individual experience into a group experience" (Pogrebin and Poole 1995, 161). It also helps normalize a tragic event by couching it as just another conventional part of the job and fosters the sense that tragedies can be routinely handled. Emotional tensions are neutralized through a collective coping strategy that reinforces group solidarity; laughter serves as a tension reliever in the face of the awful.

Rather than verbalize feelings, police may discharge tension through athletic activity or escape from feelings through drinking and sexual escapades. Officers often unwind after a tour of duty by working out or socializing with other police. While men compete (do masculinity) and act out feelings through athletic competition in the numerous police sports leagues, women have far fewer opportunities for participation in these aspects of the informal culture.

Similarly, both male and female officers believe that socializing and drinking together promote feelings of group unity, trust, and camaraderie. In addition, alcohol is widely used to relieve stress. Thus drinking serves two distinct but important functions in the police culture: as a social lubricant involved in bonding rituals and as a stress reliever. However, while heavy drinking and the ability to hold one's liquor are ways of enhancing masculinity, women who drink heavily fail to meet the social ideals of feminine behavior. Because of this defeminization, women officers risk criticism if they seek acceptance by conforming to the drinking norms for releasing work-related tensions and are the subjects of contempt rather than admiration for sexual behavior similar to that of male officers.

CONCLUSION

Policing makes great emotional demands on officers, who are required to deal with a wide variety of situations involving people in crisis while maintaining order, providing service, and controlling crime. Even more than bravery and physical strength (qualities associated with masculinity), the work demands communication and human relations skills that often are both unrecognized and undervalued by police managers and officers themselves. This occurs, in large part, because these skills are associated with femininity. Nevertheless, both masculine- and feminine-typed skills are essential for officers to be effective. They must have a command presence that enables them to act decisively to maintain control in volatile situations, and they must have the ability to actively listen and talk to people.

Currently, officers are judged by their peers largely on the basis of their responses to and management of danger-related situations. It is this unique aspect of the work that sets police apart, is associated with masculinity, and is rewarded by society. Because of this association, men interpret their work tasks so as to enhance their gender identity, downplay the service tasks and emotional demands labeled feminine, and mask or displace expression of emotion.

Women entering policing still encounter gender-related dilemmas in coping with norms related to emotional labor. On the street, they must not be too emotional in responding to volatile situations; yet the woman who conforms to emotional display rules of policing (that is, is inexpressive) is regarded as unfeminine. In informal interaction with other officers, women are cast into the mother or confidante role, expected to be supportive of a man's emotional venting, but criticized for expressing similar feelings. In addition, their opportunities to participate in social activities through which other officers discharge emotional stresses are limited, and, when they join in, they are criticized for acting like men. Despite changes in the number of women and minority men officers and in departmental policies and practices over the past two decades, the informal police culture has remained resistant to changing the definition of the core aspects of the work. Thus the police continue to emphasize that they constitute a police force and downplay the fact that they also comprise a police service.

References

Bayley, David H. and Egon Bittner. 1984. Learning the Skills of Policing. *Law and Contemporary Problems* 47:35-59. Reprinted in *Critical Issues in Policing*, ed. Roger G. Dunham and Geoffrey P. Alpert. Prospect Heights, IL: Waveland Press.

Brown, Jennifer and Jennifer Grover. 1998. Stress and the Woman Sergeant. *Police Journal* 71:47-54.

Brown, Michael K. 1981. *Working the Street: Police Discretion and the Dilemmas of Reform*. New York: Russell Sage Foundation.

Collins, Patricia H. 1991. *Black Feminist Thought: Knowledge, Consciousness and the Politics of Empowerment*. New York: Routledge.

England, Paula and George Farkas. 1986. *Households, Employment, and Gender: A Social, Economic, and Demographic View*. New York: Aldine.

Fineman, Stephen. 1993. Organizations as Emotional Arenas. In *Emotion in Organizations*, ed. S. Fineman. Newbury Park, CA: Sage.

Goffman, Erving. 1961. *Encounters*. Indianapolis: Bobbs-Merrill.

———. 1969. *Strategic Interaction*. Philadelphia: University of Pennsylvania Press.

Hochschild, Arlie Russell. 1983. *The Managed Heart: Commercialization of Human Feeling*. Berkeley: University of California Press.

Hunt, Jennifer. 1984. The Development of Rapport Through Negotiation of Gender in Field Work Among Police. *Human Organization* 43:283-96.

———. 1990. The Logic of Sexism Among Police. *Women and Criminal Justice* 1:3-30.

Kennedy, David and R. Homant. 1983. Attitudes of Abused Women Toward Male and Female Police. *Criminal Justice and Behavior* 10:391-405.

Leidner, Robin. 1991. Serving Hamburgers and Selling Insurance: Gender, Work, and Identity in Interactive Service Jobs. *Gender & Society* 5(2):154-77.

Manning, Peter. 1997. *Police Work: The Social Organization of Policing*. 2d ed. Prospect Heights, IL: Waveland Press.

Martin, Susan E. 1980. *"Breaking and Entering": Policewomen on Patrol*. Berkeley: University of California Press.

———. 1990. *On the Move: The Status of Women in Policing*. Washington, DC: Police Foundation.

Martin, Susan E. and Nancy C. Jurik. 1996. *Doing Justice, Doing Gender: Women in Law and Criminal Justice Occupations*. Thousand Oaks, CA: Sage.

Mills, Trudy and Sherryl Kleinman. 1988. Emotions, Reflexivity, and Action: An Interactionist Analysis. *Social Forces* 66:1009-27.

Pierce, Jennifer L. 1995. *Gender Trials: Emotional Lives in Contemporary Law Firms*. Berkeley: University of California Press.

Pogrebin, Mark R. and Eric D. Poole. 1995. Emotion Management: A Study of Police Response to Tragic Events. *Social Perspectives on Emotion*. Vol. 3. Greenwich, CT: JAI.

Price, Jammie. 1996. Doing Gender: Men and Emotion. Paper presented at the annual meeting of the American Sociological Association.

Rafaeli, Anat and Robert I. Sutton. 1989. The Expression of Emotion in Organizational Life. In *Research in Organizational Behavior*, ed. Barry M. Staw and L. L. Cummings. Vol. 11. Greenwich, CT: JAI Press.

Reiner, Robert. 1992. Police Research in the United Kingdom. In *Modern Policing*, ed. M. Tonry and N. Morris. Chicago: University of Chicago Press.

Scrivner, Ellen. 1994. *The Role of Police Psychology in Controlling Excessive*

Force. Washington, DC: Department of Justice.

Skolnick, Jerome. 1966. *Justice Without Trial.* New York: John Wiley.

Steinberg, Ronnie J. and Deborah M. Figart. 1997. The Range of Emotional Labor at the Workplace: A Job Content Analysis. Paper presented at the annual meeting of the Eastern Sociological Society, Baltimore, MD.

Stenross, Barbara and Sherryl Kleinman. 1989. The Highs and Lows of Emotional Labor: Detectives' Encounters with Criminals and Victims. *Journal of Contemporary Ethnography* 17(4):435-52.

Sutton, Robert I. 1991. Maintaining Norms about Expressed Emotions: The Case of Bill Collectors. *Administrative Science Quarterly* 36(June): 245-68.

Thoits, Peggy A. 1989. The Sociology of Emotions. *Annual Review of Sociology* 15:317-42.

Trice, Harrison. 1993. *Occupational Subcultures in the Workplace.* Ithaca, NY: ILR Press.

Van Maanen, John and Gideon Kunda. 1989. "Real Feelings": Emotional Expression and Organizational Culture. In *Research in Organizational Behavior,* ed. Barry M. Staw and L. L. Cummings. Vol. 11. Greenwich, CT: JAI Press.

Westley, William. 1970. *Violence and the Police.* Cambridge, MA: MIT Press.

Wharton, Carol S. 1996. Making People Feel Good: Workers' Constructions of Meaning in Interactive Service Jobs. *Qualitative Sociology* 19:217-33.

Young, Malcolm. 1991. *An Inside Job: Policing and Police Culture in Britain.* Oxford: Clarendon.

ANNALS, *AAPSS*, **561**, January 1999

Emotional Labor Among Paralegals

By JENNIFER L. PIERCE

ABSTRACT: Despite the invisibility of emotional labor among paralegals, this dimension of work has significant consequences for the reproduction of the labor process in the large bureaucratic firm and for the psychological well-being of paralegals. These legal workers function to support and maintain the emotional stability of the lawyers for whom they work through deferential treatment and caretaking. By affirming the status of lawyers, paralegals also reproduce gender relations in the law firm. Most attorneys who receive caretaking and support are men, and the majority of the legal assistants who provide these emotional services are women. In this way, the emotional labor required of paralegals serves to reproduce the sex-segregated structure of law firms.

Jennifer L. Pierce is associate professor of sociology and American studies at the University of Minnesota. She is also affiliated with the Center for Advanced Feminist Studies. Her most recent book is Gender Trials: Emotional Lives in Contemporary Law Firms. *She has published articles on women and work, feminist theory and method and has completed the work for an anthology,* Social Justice, Feminism and the Politics of Location.

I N the late 1960s, the increasingly competitive market for legal services helped create a niche for a new job category: paralegals, or legal assistants. Typically college-educated women, these new legal workers performed many of the same tasks that lawyers did, such as doing legal research, summarizing court transcripts and depositions, and reviewing and analyzing documents produced in large litigation cases—but they carried out these tasks at a fraction of the cost in annual salary to law firms (Johnstone and Wenglinsky 1985; Larbalestrier 1986; Shirp 1989). As I discovered in my 15 months of fieldwork at two large law offices in the San Francisco Bay Area, what often distinguished the work of paralegals from that of attorneys was not a set of mental tasks related to semiprofessional and professional status but, rather, the socioemotional requirements of each job.[1] Unlike lawyers, who were expected to be alternately intimidating and strategically friendly, paralegals were expected to nurture or mother their bosses.

As I will argue in this article, this emotional dimension of labor is important to studies of women in the workplace. Arlie Hochschild (1983), who coined the influential concept emotional labor, found not only that women are more likely than men to be in jobs requiring this type of labor but also that such work carries with it a psychological cost. For Hochschild, emotional labor "requires one to induce or suppress feeling" in paid jobs in order to influence others, specifically clients or customers (7). Flight attendants in her study, for instance, suppressed their own feelings of irritation with difficult passengers by inducing feelings of care and concern. As Hochschild argues, though emotional labor is often an invisible feature of many job descriptions in the service sector, it can pose serious psychological consequences for workers, many of them women, including estrangement from self, burnout, and feelings of emotional numbness.

Like Hochschild, I find that despite the invisibility of emotional labor among paralegals, such labor has consequences for their psychological well-being. In their workplace setting, however, paralegals do not perform emotional labor for customers but for their bosses. Further, their emotional labor plays a crucial role in the reproduction of the labor process in the large bureaucratic firm.[2] Legal assistants are expected to support and maintain the emotional stability of the lawyers for whom they work through deferential treatment and caretaking. By affirming the status of lawyers, paralegals also reproduce gender relations in the law firm. Most attorneys who receive caretaking and support are men, and the majority of legal assistants who provide these emotional services are women. In this way, the emotional labor required of paralegals serves to reproduce the sex-segregated structure of law firms.

PARALEGALS AND
EMOTIONAL LABOR

In contrast to Max Weber's classic conception ([1922] 1946) of a rationalized, depersonalized bureaucracy, the relationship between paralegal and attorney in the large law firm is a highly personal one. This fact is supported by the numerous statements lawyers made during my fieldwork, emphasizing the importance of personality traits over work performance skills in hiring decisions. For example, Richard, an attorney, highlighted his paralegal Sarah's "intuitive qualities" as most important to him. Personnel directors discussed the importance of being "pleasant" and being able to work with "difficult" attorneys. Similarly, when I asked attorneys what qualities they considered important for a good legal assistant, they invariably listed personal characteristics such as "pleasant" or "unflappable" before they mentioned task-related skills such as "good organizer" or "detail oriented."

From my fieldwork and interviews, I identified two specific components of emotional labor: deference and caretaking behavior. The first component reflects the structure of the relationship between the attorney and the paralegal; the attorney is the authority and the paralegal, the subordinate. As such, legal assistants are expected to be deferential. In his article The Nature of Deference and Demeanor (1956), Erving Goffman defines deference as a type of ceremonial activity which "functions as symbolic means by which appreciation is regularly conveyed to the recipient" (477). For Goffman, the distinctive element of deferential behavior between subordinate and superordinate is that it reproduces the hierarchical nature of the relationship by confirming each person's position within it. This is also true of legal assistants and attorneys; however, for paralegals, deference involves not only a facial display of subservience but an emotional one as well. A paralegal may show deference by averting the eyes, but he or she must also suppress feelings such as anger or irritation to make attorneys feel competent, knowledgeable, and powerful.

Although deferential behavior is required of workers in other service occupations, in paralegal work, deference reflects the adversarial nature of the legal profession itself: it requires that paralegals be treated "as if" they were adversaries by attorneys.[3] Just as opposing counsel, clients, and witnesses are interrogated, intimidated, grilled, and regarded with great suspicion and distrust, so, too, are legal assistants. Marguerite, a 26-year-old paralegal, describes her discussion with Eric, a partner, in this way:

I feel like I am on the witness stand when I am talking to him about the trial. After I give him detail after detail [in answer] to his questions, he says: "Anything else? Anything else?" in this aggressive way.... He can't turn off this adversarial style.... He just persists in cross-examining me.

Although paralegals are subjected to adversarial practices, they are not allowed to respond in a like manner. As subordinates, they must recognize the attorney as the authority and not challenge him or her as would an equal. Thus they affirm the attorney's status by enduring the degradation of being treated as, one legal assistant told me, "the lawyer's emotional punching bag."

To do so, paralegals must manage anger—their own and that of the attorneys. Whenever a lawyer is angry about something, the paralegal is liable to be the recipient of that anger—even when the fault lies elsewhere. The majority of legal assistants I interviewed reported daily incidences of managing anger. Law firms recognize this aspect of the job; they specifically seek to hire legal assistants who can deal gracefully with irate attorneys. When I was interviewing for paralegal positions, the question that came up in each of the five interviews was, "How do you feel about working with a difficult attorney?" In fact, in one office, I was asked this question by the personnel director, her administrative assistant, and one of the interviewing attorneys. An experienced paralegal told me the question implied the attorney I was to work with "must be a jerk." Employers, on the other hand, were trying to discern how a prospective employee would handle such a personality. Bonhomie Corporation's personnel director told me, "We like to hire people who know how to get along with the lawyers. The litigation department is a pressure cooker, we don't have time for girls who take everything personally." Thus part of deferential work is the skill and effort involved in managing one's own and others' anger.

Whereas deference is the first major component of emotional labor, playing a caretaking role vis-à-vis the attorneys and, to a certain extent, witnesses and clients is the second. This form of emotional labor also reflects the asymmetry of the attorney-paralegal relationship: the

attorney is the recipient of care; the paralegal, the caregiver. It also reflects a particular cultural construction of motherhood, what Nancy Chodorow and Susan Contratto (1982) as well as Jessica Benjamin (1989) refer to as the "mother as object." This cultural representation is the "fantasy of the perfect mother" (Chodorow and Contratto 1982, 71) who meets all her children's needs and wishes while suppressing her own. She is the ultimate caregiver, but no one takes care of her. Thus caretaking, like deference, serves to reproduce the gendered nature of the relationship between attorneys and paralegals.

One element of the caretaking dimension of emotional labor is being pleasant. As one paralegal described her job, "I was trying to be pleasant, pay attention and take notes [while the witness was talking]. Not an easy feat, [because] I felt like I was next to a human time bomb [the attorney]." Being pleasant or cheerful is an attitude paralegals are expected to convey while trying to accomplish other aspects of their jobs. As the personnel director for the private firm told me in a job interview, "It's important to maintain a pleasant manner while attending to the not-so-pleasant side of the job, don't you think?" Being pleasant not only involves inducing a feeling—cheerfulness—but also calls for a specific facial display, a smile. Like the women flight attendants in Hochschild's study (1983), women paralegals grimly reported the consequences of not smiling: "Why aren't you smiling today?" "What's the matter with you, give me a smile!" "You look like someone just died." Such remarks were typically made by male attorneys, clients, and witnesses to female legal assistants. However, the personnel director who was a woman could also be counted on to make comments about a paralegal's demeanor. A female paralegal wryly observed, "Sometimes I think she thinks smiling is supposed to be part of my job."

Another element of caretaking is reassurance. This is accomplished by alleviating the anxiety of the attorneys for whom one works. For example, Jenna spent most of an afternoon doing what she called "handholding." By this she meant repeatedly reassuring John, an attorney, that he would make his five o'clock filing deadline. Similarly, Debbie spent a lot of her time acting as Michael's therapist. She listened patiently to all his work-related anxieties and concerns, gently asked questions, and offered reassurance. Of course, this form of emotional labor went only one way. Lawyers rarely, if ever, reassured paralegals about work-related matters.

GENDERING CONSTRAINT AND CONSENT

Historically, most paralegals have been women, and employers often expect that paralegals will be women. However, some men also perform the job of paralegal and are treated as tokens. For Rosabeth Moss Kanter (1977), tokenism emerges in groups that are highly skewed, with a preponderance of one group of workers, the dominants, over another, the tokens.[4] Kanter's thesis further suggests that tokens face greater per-

formance pressures in jobs because they encounter more scrutiny than their counterparts in the numerical majority. For example, in response to their greater conspicuousness, women managers in her study attempted to limit their visibility by being more secretive, less independent, and less oppositional. Both in the private firm and in the legal department at Bonhomie Corporation, male legal assistants as token members of the occupation are treated in dissimilar ways from women, face divergent expectations, and do different kinds of emotional labor.

However, upon closer examination, these differences do not concur with Kanter's explanations about organizational behavior. Unlike the female managers in Kanter's study, male paralegals do not attempt to limit their visibility within the occupation or conform to the behavior of the numerically dominant group. Nor do they encounter the exclusionary practices Kanter's women executives faced.

These findings corroborate recent feminist scholarship in sociology that suggests that the experiences of male and female tokens are not equivalent (Zimmer 1988; Williams 1989, 1993). My research also considers how male tokens reproduce their gender even while being in a feminized occupation. However, rather than looking at gender only as a difference between workers in a given occupation, I conceptualize gender as an aspect of occupational structure, behavior, and identity. Gender as an aspect of organizational structure shapes the experiences of paralegals in law firms by posing different normative expectations for male and female workers. At the level of behavior, paralegals perform different kinds of emotional labor as a way of "doing gender," that is, as West and Zimmerman (1987) suggest, a way of interacting that is consistent with their notions of gender-appropriate behavior. By doing gender, males and females not only affirm their own gender identities as men and as women but reproduce gender relations in law firms.

The first gender difference at work is reflected in the occupational structure. Specifically, there is stratification within the occupation: male paralegals were more likely to be found in positions of authority or influence than female paralegals. This suggests that among paralegals, much like other occupations and professions such as nursing and social work, an "internal stratification" exists wherein men occupy the "good" jobs and women, the "bad" ones even within the same broad occupational category (Bielby and Baron 1986; Reskin and Roos 1990; Williams 1989). For example, both at the private firm and in the legal department at Bonhomie Corporation, male paralegals held the most influential, highly valued, and highly paid positions. Among paralegals, this finding is especially striking given that this occupation is female dominated and only a few such positions existed in any one firm.

Men not only found themselves in different positions within the occupational hierarchy, but they were also treated differently by virtue of their status as male. Male paralegals were often mistaken for attorneys because they were men. By contrast, be-cause most secretaries are women, female paralegals were often mistaken for secretaries. Many female paralegals reported that they were asked to type things for attorneys. Not surprisingly, women resented this assumption. The male legal assistants frequently viewed this behavior as humorous. These examples illustrate how the gender of a paralegal affected the perception of the paralegal's occupational roles. Being male inflated the perception of one's occupational status, whereas being female deflated it.

These status differences were also played out informally in that male legal assistants were often included with male attorneys to go out for drinks after work, to play on the firm softball team, or to go to sporting events together. These informal get-togethers served an important function. They became a means of getting to know better the attorney who might write a letter of recommendation for professional school or provide more interesting work assignments. One male paralegal, for example, managed to finagle his way out of a boring case into a more interesting assignment. Women were rarely included in these events.

Female paralegals socialized together and sometimes with secretaries; male legal assistants often chose not to do so. Their choice not to socialize within their own occupational group challenges one of Kanter's findings (1977). She describes how members of a dominant group heighten boundaries between themselves and the token to exaggerate differences. This is not the case with female and male paralegals. Women actively sought to include the men in lunches, breaks, and other social activities. Although the men sometimes participated, they often opted out because they were bored with the women's discussions. Other men said they preferred to reserve time outside the office for friends, as opposed to coworkers. Although male para-legals were included by the women, they chose to emphasize their difference as men and downplay any presumption of similarity.

These differences in status also resulted in a gendered division of labor, especially around socioemotional behavior. Women were expected to be more nurturing than men were. Attorneys were more likely to confide their personal problems in women paralegals. Several women, in fact, were referred to as this or that attorney's "therapist." Men were not relied upon as therapists, but as political advisers and "yes men." They were expected to provide political information and gossip to protect their boss's interests. Theirs was a less personal, seemingly rational mode of conduct. Thus men and women were expected to do different kinds of emotional labor.

The basis for gender-appropriate emotional labor among legal assistants lies in the degree of affective engagement. Being affectively neutral or polite is acceptable for men but not for women. As a consequence, men must put a lid on expressing deep emotion. For example, attorneys repeatedly criticized one male paralegal for his "giddy" and "flamboyant" behavior. While other paralegals and secretaries found his imitations of the "church lady" from the

television show *Saturday Night Live* amusing, the attorneys did not. As he said to me in his interview, "They're always telling me to tone it down. Attorneys are so serious. . . . You'd think this place was a funeral parlor or something." This "feeling rule" for male inexpressivity reflects largely cultural conceptions of what Robert Connell (1987) has called hegemonic masculinity.[5]

By contrast, women are expected to be affectively engaged. This can be demonstrated through behavior such as being nice or facial displays such as smiling. Not only were women repeatedly admonished to express their engagement by smiling, but they were also prodded to humor attorneys, flirt with them, or pay special attention to them. One 27-year-old woman said, "David [the attorney] always says things like, 'Did you notice my new tie or my new office furniture or my new car. . . .' He's always trying to get me to pay attention to him!" An older woman commented, "After Mark [a 26-year-old associate] gives me an assignment, he just stands around in my office like this little boy waiting for something. . . . When I ask 'What's up,' he'll say, 'Oh, nothing.' But he keeps standing there looking hopeful."

These descriptions are reminiscent of the early mother-child relationship. Mothers coo and smile at their babies, and babies coo and smile back. As the infant gets older and begins to take its first steps away from mother, he or she continues looking back to mother for recognition and support (Mahler, Pine, and Bergman 1975). Similarly, male attorneys look to female paralegals for recognition—to be noticed, to be smiled at—as if the paralegals were actually their mothers. As Hochschild (1983) writes, "The world turns to women for mothering, and this fact silently attaches itself to many a job description" (170).

While smiling and being nice are required of women, anger is prohibited. The job requires that paralegals manage anger—their own and that of attorneys. For example, when attorneys yell at paralegals, legal assistants, as subordinates, are not expected to respond in the same way but to suppress their own anger. However, as Hochschild (1983) observes, there is a double standard in the perception of anger. "When a man expresses anger, it is deemed rational. . . . When women express an equivalent degree of anger, it is more likely to be interpreted as a sign of emotional instability" (173). In my findings, this double standard appeared in the form of an invisible threshold. Both men and women paralegals were expected to manage their anger. However, men were given more leeway than women to express anger. For male paralegals, it was not until they blew up in response to the attorney's needling them that they were sanctioned for their behavior. For women, this threshold occurred sooner. Women were much more likely than men to be sanctioned for simply responding coolly to an attorney's unreasonable request.

Status differences also translated into differential expectations about intellectual ability. Male paralegals were taken more seriously than women paralegals were. Although

both women and men had to contend with being treated as if they could not understand the finer points of the law, women tended to be denigrated more frequently than men. Male attorneys referred to various women paralegals as "bimbos," "ditzy," and "Barbie dolls," implying they were sexually attractive but dumb. Male paralegals were sometimes criticized for being "weird" or lacking social skills, but no one called them names implying they lacked intelligence.

Some men felt embarrassed or defensive about being a legal assistant. Being a member of a female-dominated profession does not approximate the masculine ideal of success. When I asked a 26-year-old what he told people he did for a living, he laughed nervously and said, "I just tell them I work for Lyman, Lyman and Portia and they're impressed. You know it's a big San Francisco financial district law firm. If I told them I was just a paralegal, they wouldn't be." Another male legal assistant told me that he believed male paralegals were treated quite favorably compared to female paralegals. "The attorneys always asked me *when* I planned to go to law school." He interpreted this as a sign of their confidence in his abilities. On the other hand, a 30-year-old who described himself as an artist and not a paralegal said, "Lawyers always think you should be a lawyer. I used to be offended. Now, I think they lack imagination—they can't imagine anybody would want to be anything else!" By contrast, the lawyers never indicated that they thought any of the female paralegals should be lawyers.

The differences paralegals faced in expectations correspond roughly to actual gender differences in emotional labor. Women performed what I term a more relational style of emotional labor, which emphasized their concern for others. Men, on the other hand, had a less relational style of emotional labor, which underscored their difference from others as well as their own achievements.

Paralegals are expected to take care of their bosses, but men and women do this differently. Women were more likely to be what I call "nice" or affectively engaged, whereas men were more likely to be polite or affectively neutral. Lisa, for example, was the prototypical nice female paralegal. She was warm, friendly, and outgoing. Whenever I saw her in the office hallways, she was always cheerful. She tried to please people by remembering their birthdays and cheering them up when they were down. After our interview, she came back several times the following day to tell me more personal stories that she thought might be "helpful." Bill, on the other hand, was the ideal of the polite male paralegal. He was always tactful, courteous, and considerate of other people's feelings but never overly solicitous. Although he did not smile much, he gave the appearance of being interested and concerned. However, I never saw him standing in the hallways to socialize with coworkers.

Being polite is more aloof than being nice. The male paralegal is pleasant but distant. He does what Hochschild (1983) calls "surface acting" which involves acting as if one has a feeling through facial display, body movement, or tone of voice (37). Daniel, another male paralegal, describes his behavior toward an attorney in this way:

I was waiting outside his door to talk to him while he was on the phone. As he talked, I began to imagine the face I wanted to present—calm, serious, competent. I watched my reflection in the plate glass window and tried out various looks. As Mark [the attorney] said good-bye and hung up the telephone, I entered with what I imagined to be the proper politesse [and asked], "Can I have a word with you Mark? It's about the American Bank case."

Greg, another male legal assistant, who was far more outgoing than either Bill or Daniel, greeted paralegals and secretaries with a booming hello. Whereas he was openly flirtatious with women paralegals and secretaries, with attorneys he was subdued. "I turn down the volume with them and put on my serious face."

Whereas men do "surface acting" by presenting a particular face or turning down the volume, women do what Hochschild (1983) calls "deep acting," that is, actually evoking the feeling itself (38). Lisa does not just smile but "psyches" herself up to be cheerful and friendly to those around her. In describing herself, she says, "Everyone thinks I'm nice and cheerful all the time, but I'm not. On my bad days I try and think about how they're feeling and what I can do to make them feel better." Over two-thirds of the women I interviewed described their attempts to make themselves actually feel "nice," "pleasant," or "cheerful."

In addition to surface acting, male paralegals also distance themselves from the niceness required of paralegals through criticism and contempt. Most men regarded "being nice" as "taking shit." For example, Tony, a male paralegal, was openly contemptuous of the behavior of a paralegal named Jane. He denigrated her for being "sugar sweet" and refusing to stand up for herself when the attorneys treated her badly. When Jane received a higher raise than Tony did, he was furious: "She doesn't even deserve the raise. She just pretends to be nicey-nice and sweet." He then went to the managing partner and complained politely about his raise, arguing that he was as qualified as Jane, if not more so. He also threatened to quit if he did not get the raise. He received the raise.

Men could get away with being polite instead of nice and bowing out of some of the caretaking, but women could not. Karen was a bright, competent paralegal whose behavior in many ways more closely resembled that of the men. She was somewhat aloof and businesslike in her presentation of self. She did not smile much and expressed no interest in the personal problems of the attorneys she worked for. She was regarded by the partner for whom she worked as "uncooperative" and was given a raise that reflected as much. When she inquired about the low raise, she was told that she had an "attitude problem." Concerned that she may have severed working relations, Karen pressed to find out what precisely this meant. "If they think I'm not doing my job, I'd like to know about it and if I've hurt someone's feelings, I'd

like to know about that too." However, neither her boss nor anyone else would tell her anything more specific. She eventually left the firm.

Women paralegals were well aware of this gendered division of labor and how it affected them psychologically. The vast majority complained about the implicit expectation that they mother attorneys. Mary Ann, for example, said, "To him [the attorney], a paralegal is a mother. He could never understand why I didn't want to 'play mom.' He didn't like that about me. A lot of attorneys are like that." Despite this common complaint, most women found themselves engaged to some degree in doing this type of emotional labor. At one end of the continuum were women like Karen who refused to have any part in it. (Ten percent of the women fell into this category.) Next, were the women who grudgingly went through the motions but complained. (They represented over half of the women.) Finally, at the other end of the continuum, there were the women like Lisa who were the prototype of niceness.

Why do some women feel compelled to perform this aspect of emotional labor and others do not? To answer this question, the experiences of women paralegals must be theorized as a dynamic relationship between the macrolevel of occupational structure and microlevel of behavior and identity. Structurally, a female-dominated job such as paralegal work demands specific types of emotional labor from women. Not only are women expected to be deferential and carry out caretaking, but they are further expected to be cheerful, reassuring, and attentive to the moods and feelings of others. On the most basic level, women must perform such emotional labor if they intend to keep their jobs. A woman who is not friendly, pleasant, and nurturing develops "bad working relations" with attorneys, is regarded as uncooperative, may not receive raises, or may be forced out of the law firm altogether. Thus women comply with feeling rules because they cannot afford to do otherwise if they entered this occupation to stay.

The structural part of my argument outlines the gendered constraints women paralegals encounter in the occupation. Further, it suggests powerful economic incentives for women to comply with feeling rules. However, reliance only on structural explanations denies the agency to social actors that is also observed. It assumes that legal assistants are in some sense forced to perform emotional labor. To improve upon this theoretical weakness, I introduce a behavioral component to my structural explanation.

Women perform different kinds of emotional labor as a way of doing gender, that is, as West and Zimmerman (1987) suggest, a way of interacting that is consistent with their notions of gender-appropriate behavior. In this explanation, the feminized structure of paralegal work sets gendered limits on women's behavior. Unlike male legal workers, female legal workers are expected to be affectively engaged. Yet, the women vary among themselves. Women like Lisa remain safely and unambivalently within these boundaries by doing gender in accordance with the tradi-tional female caregiving role. Others do gender by adopting a more distanced relation to these limits, performing the requisite feminized labor nonetheless. Finally, a small group of women, like Karen, cross over these boundaries, refusing to heed the limits. Women in this group do gender by being professional—in other words, acting more like their male counterparts—and by downplaying any association with the traditional female role.

Despite this variation in behavior, these women have a common concern with relationships. For those who conform to the feminized socioemotional requirements, ambivalently or not, a relational or feminine style of emotional labor serves to emphasize connection with others through reassurance, by attentiveness to the moods and feelings of others and by being nice. On the other hand, women like Karen who do not behave relationally remain psychologically preoccupied with these issues. Although her behavior approximates that of male paralegals, when relationships break down, she still expresses concern. Chodorow's theory of gender identity (1978) helps us to understand this common concern. In her psychoanalytic understanding, women develop a sense of self as empathic and nurturant through the early mother-daughter relationship. As a consequence, feminine identity comes to be defined through attachment and relation to others. For some women paralegals, this sense of self is expressed through the performance of emotional labor, and, for others, in their continuing preoccupation with relational issues.

Chodorow's theory alone cannot explain why women are relational in some contexts and not in others. Her theory cannot address such behavior because it does not explain the relationship between occupational structure and personality. However, by integrating her concept of gender identity with this specific occupational context, the continuity and variation in women's behavior can be explained by theorizing a dynamic relationship between occupational structure, behavior, and gender identity. In a dynamic understanding, the paralegal occupation places gendered limits on behavior. Women respond actively and creatively to these limits to construct an emotional style that is congruent with their notion of gender-appropriate behavior.

Furthermore, their choice of doing gender is in some way informed by their sense of self as relational or feminine. In this dynamic account, gender shapes the structure of the occupation by setting limits on women's behavior. At the same time, women negotiate within and around these limits, reproducing gender in their interactions with others by being nice, reassuring, and attentive to the feelings of others or simply through their preoccupation with relational issues.

This argument also applies to the behavior of male paralegals. In structural terms, men must also comply with emotional norms. However, as male workers in this female-dominated occupation, men have different experiences from those of women. As I have shown, there is a double standard in terms of how women and men are treated by lawyers. Male paralegals, for example, are assumed to be more qualified for positions of authority within the occupation, more career oriented, and more intelligent. Consequently, men are often able to get away with being polite rather than nice, playing the role of political adviser rather than the nurturing therapist, and so on. Furthermore, they also accrue a number of advantages simply by virtue of being male. Informal socializing with male attorneys sometimes leads to more interesting work assignments, letters of recommendation for professional school, and personal recognition and affirmation for their work.

Doing gender in a female-dominated job means male paralegals, unlike women, must contend with the contradictions of being men in a woman's job. Their contradictory location explains, in part, why they choose to exclude themselves from women's social activities as well as their contempt for their "nicey-nice" female counterparts. They do gender in these ways to emphasize their differences as men and downplay any similarity to their women coworkers.

The concept of doing gender is further informed by the assumption that men have a gender-specific identity. In other words, men do gender because they have a sense of self as masculine. Chodorow's theory of gender identity (1978) suggests that masculine gender identity emerges through a definition of self as separate from the mother—as not female. A masculine style of emotional labor emphasizes difference and self-assertion through mechanisms such as politeness, contempt for niceness, and surface acting, which distance men from the feminine aspects of the job. Moreover, men further emphasize difference by choosing to exclude themselves from all-female, informal social activities. While men accrue benefits structurally by engaging in such exclusionary practices, doing gender in this way also serves to affirm and enhance their gender identity as masculine.

Such an explanation analyzes the experiences of paralegals at the level of occupational structure, behavior, and identity. Gender is an integral part of this analysis. The occupational structure itself is gendered, posing divergent experiences for women and men. By doing gender through emotional labor, paralegals, in turn, reproduce gender relations in law firms. At the level of face-to-face interactions, deference and mothering serve to enhance the status and psychological well-being of lawyers. However, because more attorneys who receive caretaking and support are men, and the majority of legal assistants who provide these services are women, emotional labor also serves to reproduce the sex-segregated structure of law firms.

CONCLUSION

Paradoxically, though emotional labor is a crucial feature of paralegal work, it is not formally acknowledged in job descriptions or position announcements. Employers advertise for workers who have competence in litigation practice, but they do not call for the emotional skills of a full-time mother.[6] On the job, however, women paralegals who do not "play mom" face sanctions in terms of lower raises, the types of work assignments they receive, or, in the extreme, termination for their "attitude problems." What this means is that emotional labor is often treated as if it were invisible.

One consequence of invisibility is a lack of financial compensation to women workers. Women are paid less than male paralegals with comparable years of experience. Yet men do not have to fulfill the same emotional requirements as women do. They do not have to "play mom." In fact, they are able to bow out of the feminized aspects of emotional labor without any cost. This suggests that women face a double bind that men do not. Institutional norms require them to "play mom" but do not reward them for it. In this way, mothering as emotional labor is simultaneously required and devalued.

This contradiction lies at the heart of American cultural beliefs about women and mothering. On one hand, motherhood is typically expected of women and celebrated as an important aspect of feminine identity (Hays 1996, 7). On the other, motherhood and the practice of mothering are devalued in a culture that celebrates the autonomy of the individual, achievement, and "rational" thought (Bellah et al. 1985, 11). That such a contradiction arises in the American workplace should therefore come as no great surprise. As other feminist scholars have noted, nurturing on the job is often undervalued, if not unrecognized, in many jobs and occupations (Steinberg

1990; James 1989). Nevertheless, this finding raises several important questions for social policy. First, what kinds of social policy steps can be taken to address this problem for women workers? Should women be financially compensated for such labor? Or does the explicit call for mothering skills reinscribe the very stereotypes that women already face in the paid labor force?

Finally, the simultaneous requirement and devaluation of nurturing on the job point to a subtle, yet insidious, form of discrimination against women. Women paralegals are penalized when they do not display a traditionally feminine presentation of self. They are encouraged and, in some situations, even harassed to take on this emotional aspect of the job. Many paralegals reported, for example, that the question, "Why don't you smile for me, honey?" was repeated constantly by the lawyers and supervisors for whom they worked. While the constant demand to smile may not appear to be harassment, consider the fact that the women who were not "nice enough" did not receive good raises. Unfortunately, laws such as Title VII do not protect women from harassment that is not overtly sexual. Nevertheless, it is precisely these stereotypical beliefs about women as mothers that make the workplace inhospitable to them. In seems, then, that a necessary first step in transforming the lives of women legal workers lies in moving beyond the fixed and static conceptions embodied in male "fantasy of the perfect mother" (Chodorow and Contratto 1982, 7) and recognizing the diversity and complexity in women's experiences and identities. As feminist scholars and policymakers, we need to consider expanding the scope of harassment to include the systematic forms of gender stereotyping, thereby providing women workers with a broader range of legal remedies to institutionalized sexism.

Notes

1. Between 1988 and 1989, I worked for six months at a private firm, which I will call "Lyman, Lyman and Portia," and nine months in the legal department of a large corporation, "Bonhomie Corporation." Names of organizations and individuals have been changed throughout this article to protect confidentiality.

2. Burawoy conceptualizes the labor process as both "relational," that is, referring to structural relations between subordinates and superordinates, and "practical," referring to what workers actually do (1979, 15).

3. Under the American adversarial model, the main objective of the lawyer, or the "zealous advocate," is to persuade an impartial third party (the judge) that his or her client's interests should prevail (Luban 1988; Menkel-Meadow 1985).

4. For Kanter, tokenism occurs in situations where dominants outnumber tokens in a ratio of up to 85:15 (1977, 209).

5. Connell defines "hegemonic masculinity" as "always constructed in relation to various subordinated masculinities as well as in relation to women" (1987, 183). Comparing male professionals to the working class, Connell writes that these men are "emotionally flat, centered on a specialized skill, insistent on professional esteem and technically based dominance over other workers, and requiring . . . complete freedom from childcare and domestic work" (181).

6. After reviewing more than 100 ads in legal trade dailies in the San Francisco Bay Area, I found that most job descriptions for paralegal positions asked for experience in general litigation and good organizational and writing skills. The one atypical ad I found appeared in the *Recorder* (1988); it called for a

paralegal who "had the patience of Job and a sense of humor."

References

Bellah, Robert, Richard Madsen, William Sullivan, Ann Swidler, and Steven Tipton. 1985. *Habits of the Heart: Individualism and Commitment in American Life*. Berkeley: University of California Press.

Benjamin, Jessica. 1989. *The Bonds of Love: Psychoanalysis, Feminism and the Problem of Domination*. New York: Pantheon.

Bielby, William and James Baron. 1986. A Woman's Place Is with Other Women: Sex Segregation with Organizations. In *Women's Work, Men's Work: Sex Segregation on the Job*, ed. Barbara Reskin and Heidi Hartmann. Washington, DC: National Academy Press.

Burawoy, Michael. 1979. *Manufacturing Consent*. Chicago: University of Chicago Press.

Chodorow, Nancy. 1978. *The Reproduction of Mothering: Psychoanalysis and the Sociology of Gender*. Berkeley: University of California Press.

Chodorow, Nancy and Susan Contratto. 1982. The Fantasy of the Perfect Mother. In *Rethinking the Family: Some Feminist Questions*, ed. Barrie Thorne with Marilyn Yalom. New York: Longman.

Connell, Robert. 1987. *Gender and Power: Society, the Person and Sexual Politics*. Stanford, CA: Stanford University Press.

Goffman, Erving. 1956. The Nature of Deference and Demeanor. *American Anthropologist* 58(3):473-502.

Hays, Sharon. 1996. *The Cultural Contradictions of Motherhood*. New Haven, CT: Yale University Press.

Hochschild, Arlie Russell. 1983. *The Managed Heart: Commercialization of Human Feeling*. Berkeley: University of California Press.

James, Nicky. 1989. Emotional Labour: Skill and Work in the Social Regulation of Feelings. *Sociological Review* 37(1):15-42.

Johnstone, Quintin and Martin Wenglinsky. 1985. *Paralegals: Progress and Prospects of a Satellite Occupation*. Westport, CT: Greenwood Press.

Kanter, Rosabeth Moss. 1977. *Men and Women of the Corporation*. New York: Basic Books.

Larbalestrier, Deborah. 1986. *Paralegal Practice and Procedure: A Practical Guide for the Legal Assistant*. 2d ed. Englewood Cliffs, NJ: Prentice Hall.

Luban, David. 1988. *Lawyers and Justice: An Ethical Study*. Princeton, NJ: Princeton University Press.

Mahler, Margaret, Fred Pine, and Anni Bergman. 1975. *The Psychological Birth of the Human Infant*. New York: Basic Books.

Menkel-Meadow, Carrie. 1985. Portia in a Different Voice: Speculations on a Women's Lawyering Process. *Berkeley Women's Law Review* (Fall):39-63.

Recorder (1988). 13 June.

Reskin, Barbara and Patricia Roos. 1990. *Job Queues, Gender Queues: Explaining Women's Inroads into Male Occupations*. Philadelphia: Temple University Press.

Shirp, A. R. 1989. Paralegals Show Strength in Numbers. *San Francisco Banner*, 30 Aug.

Steinberg, Ronnie J. 1990. Social Construction of Skill: Gender, Power, and Comparable Worth. *Work and Occupations* 17(4):449-82.

Weber, Max. [1922] 1946. Bureaucracy. In *From Max Weber: Essays in Sociology*, ed. Hans Gerth and C. Wright Mills. New York: Oxford University Press.

West, Candace and Don Zimmerman. 1987. Doing Gender. *Gender & Society* 1(2):125-51.

Williams, Christine. 1989. *Gender Differences at Work: Women and Men in Nontraditional Occupations.* Berkeley: University of California Press.

———, ed. 1993. *Doing "Women's Work": Men in Nontraditional Occupations.* Newbury Park, CA: Sage.

Zimmer, Lyn. 1988. Tokenism and Women in the Workplace: The Limits of a Gender-Neutral Theory. *Social Problems* 35(1):64-77.

ANNALS, *AAPSS*, **561**, January 1999

Emotional Labor in Job Evaluation: Redesigning Compensation Practices

By RONNIE J. STEINBERG

ABSTRACT: Few client-oriented organizations compensate those who perform emotional labor. Traditional job evaluation systems, used by employers to construct a wage hierarchy, fail to recognize the value of emotional labor. Through the pay equity movement, this bias was identified. This article offers a technical attempt to design a new job content questionnaire and evaluation framework that measure the actual tasks, activities, and situations in which incumbents of differentially female jobs perform emotional labor. Four general dimensions of emotional labor are discussed: human relations skills, communication skills, emotional effort, and responsibility for client well-being. These instruments offer the most detailed measurement of the components of emotional labor available and represent a starting point for refinement of this increasingly important type of work.

Ronnie Steinberg, professor of sociology and director of the Women's Studies Program at Vanderbilt University, has provided technical assistance on job evaluation in 40 pay equity initiatives and consulted with religious denominations, feminist organizations, and trade unions. She received the Promotion of Human Welfare Award from Emory University and the Southern Sociological Society in 1995 for the design of the Gender Neutral Compensation System.

E MOTIONAL labor is a very important job characteristic differentially found in historically female service sector and retail sales work. A billboard in front of one of the largest U.S. fast-food chains announces, "Hiring Smiles." Within three blocks, two smaller retail stores post signs with generic smiling faces, also noting that they are "hiring smiling faces." Indeed, the objectives of most client-oriented organizations, whether profit making or nonprofit, are integrally tied to the effective performance of emotional labor. Yet few employees in jobs requiring this form of work are compensated for the skills and effort involved in its performance. Why is this the case?

A majority of employers use some form of job evaluation as the basis for constructing a wage structure. Job evaluation is a systematic set of procedures for ordering jobs from least complex to most complex according to a predetermined set of job content factors identified as important to firm productivity. Jobs are first described in terms of the characteristics of the work required. They are then assessed along a defined metric of levels of complexity for each work dimension. These work dimensions, often called factors, are organized in terms of a set of skills, the effort demanded, responsibilities, and undesirable working conditions. Wage rates are based on these assessments of recognized job content. The more complex the work, the higher the wage or salary.

Few off-the-shelf job evaluation systems in use today recognize the skills, effort, and responsibilities associated with emotional labor. If this type of work is recognized, it is defined, without justification, as involving low levels of these broad factors, and those who do the work get little for it. Not paying employees for the performance of work that is critical to the accomplishment of organizational objectives and even the survival of the organization is wage discrimination. The invisibility of emotional labor as a compensable job requirement contributes to the gap in wages by gender.

U.S. working women working full-time year-round in 1996 earned 73.8 percent of the pay of the average man employed full-time year-round, according to the Institute for Women's Policy Research. To understand what this statistic means, consider that it took the average working woman over 15 months (until the second week in April of the subsequent year) to match the wages the average man earned over a 12-month period. That day in April is now Equal Pay Day, to recognize the pay inequities by gender. In dollar terms, in 1996, working women lost almost $100 million in earnings due to these inequities. Over a lifetime, the average working woman loses about $525,000 because she is not paid fairly for the work she performs. A portion of this loss of income is due to the failure to compensate disproportionately female employees for the performance of emotional labor.

HISTORICAL BACKGROUND

These pay disparities and their institutionalization in job evaluation have a long history. Evidence suggests that employers developed separate pay scales by the gender of the job, embedding in their compensation practices cultural assumptions about the male breadwinner and female homemaker roles along with other market and power considerations (Kessler-Harris 1990; Milkman 1987; Schwab 1985). Many early job evaluation textbooks overtly recommended procedures that would maintain customary low wages for historically female work (Taylor 1989). One expert commented on the proceedings of a 1937 conference:

The conferees noted with approval that most occupations in their companies were filled respectively by men or by women. . . . The conference favored the segregation of men's and women's jobs for valuation purposes. The representatives held that men's jobs should be valued with reference to market rates for similar types of men's work, and women's jobs should be valued with reference to market rates for similar types of women's work. (Riegel 1937, 21)

These informal practices and the cultural assumptions about women's work on which they were built were routinely embedded in job evaluation systems because the systems were constructed to reward, as valuable work, those types of job content found in high-paying jobs. In other words, early job evaluation systems chose factors and factor weights to best reproduce and rationalize an existing wage hierarchy (Beatty and Beatty 1984; Remick 1981; Schwab 1985; Treiman 1979). Thus, skills, demands, and responsibilities associ-

ated with historically male managerial jobs and with engineering, law, and medicine were regarded as complex. In turn, because women's work was especially low paying at the time of the development of these systems, this method for constructing job evaluation systems ensured that the content characteristics differentially associated with historically female jobs would not be treated as valuable.

Current off-the-shelf systems of job evaluation were developed prior to the emergence of the service sector. Most of them have been modified with cosmetic changes that have little effect on wages and fail to give full value to the distinctive skills, effort demands, and responsibilities associated with client-oriented service work. The job evaluation systems used today to set compensation standards rest on highly selective and unjustified assumptions about what constitutes job complexity and valuable work. Emotional labor remains invisible. It is not viewed as complex. It is not treated as valuable.

PAY EQUITY

Pay equity, also called comparable worth, emerged in the late 1970s as a reform to correct for that portion of the wage gap that results from lack of recognition and inadequate compensation for the work performed in historically female jobs. While early research established the presence of wage discrimination in the labor market and linked it to traditional systems of job evaluation (Remick 1979; Treiman 1979; Treiman and Hartmann 1981), a second phase of studies identified the specific sources of gender bias in job evaluation that resulted in wage discrimination (Remick 1984a, 1984b; Steinberg 1984; Steinberg and Haignere 1985, 1987), including the invisibility and lack of compensation for emotional labor. Indeed, research on gender bias in compensation practices was one route through which emotional labor was discovered by social scientists.

A third phase of research, which is still under way, attempts to correct for the sources of gender bias in traditional job evaluation. Oftentimes, it is necessary to design a new job evaluation system to capture successfully and value positively the range of job content found in historically female jobs. In general, gender-neutral job evaluation requires consistency in the description and evaluation of all jobs as well as in pay setting, and it requires inclusiveness, which refers to a set of design objectives to ensure that the work requirements of both historically female and historically male jobs are fully described and fairly assessed. (See Steinberg and Walter 1992 for a fuller discussion of these issues.)

What follows is a case study of a pay equity initiative that involved the design of a new gender-neutral job evaluation system (GNJES), including the design of a new set of factors that attempt to measure the actual tasks, activities, and situations associated with performing emotional labor. The discussion of the development of this system will focus on those portions of the GNJES that measure emotional labor.

THE LAW, THE UNION, THE CONTEXT

The opportunity to develop the GNJES emerged out of a complaint taken by the Ontario Nurses' Association (ONA) against the municipality of Haldimand-Norfolk (HN) over the issue of gender neutrality in job evaluation, especially in relation to the work performed by the 54,000 registered nurses who constituted the union's membership. The 1987 Ontario Pay Equity Act requires that job evaluation systems used to meet the objectives of the act be gender neutral, although it is silent on what constitutes gender neutrality. One criterion for gender neutrality is consensus between labor and management, something ONA and HN could not achieve. Their conflict ended up in the Pay Equity Tribunal established by the act.

The complaint taken by ONA was the first heard by the tribunal on the issue of gender-neutral job evaluation. In their negotiations with HN, ONA rejected the off-the-shelf job evaluation system HN wanted to use. ONA leadership in general also wanted to be involved in all aspects of the design and implementation of the job evaluation system that would be used to assess the complexity and demands of the work of the nurses they represented. Municipal management wanted ONA to sign off on the system and allow the consulting firm to conduct the research exercise to determine if registered nurses and other historically female job classes in the municipality were systematically undervalued. The system proposed by HN relied very heavily on managerial job content as the standard of complex work. Using the HN system would have resulted in compressing nonmanagerial jobs into the lower-complexity levels of its factor hierarchies.

After more than a year of testimony, on 29 May 1991, the Pay Equity Tribunal upheld ONA's position. It found the municipality's proposed system inadequate for the purposes of assessing the job content of registered nurses. The HN system did not identify or positively value characteristics of work, like emotional labor, that had historically been invisible. Thus it did not meet the requirements of gender neutrality. As the tribunal defined gender neutrality, "if the skill, effort, responsibility, and working conditions are required for the normal performance of work, they must be of value to the organization whether or not those requirements have been consciously recognized or previously valued by the Employer" (Ontario Pay Equity Hearings Tribunal 1991, 113).

Specific references to the lack of recognition of the emotional labor required in the different jobs performed by registered nurses were sprinkled throughout the tribunal's decision. Consider three examples. Although the HN-proposed system includes a factor on "oral communication skills," the tribunal found that

the . . . nurses . . . could not locate their communication skill requirements on the questionnaire. . . . [which] does not collect . . . skills required to deal with seriously ill or infirm patients, those in drug induced states, or low functioning clients. . . . [or] skills required in counseling; for example, encouraging or persuading a client or patient to follow a particular programme. "Non-verbal" communication skills . . . could not be found . . ., specifically the need for patience, caring and listening skills. (Ontario Pay Equity Hearings Tribunal 1991, 15-16)

The tribunal also was critical of the way a subfactor on "internal contacts" overlooked the types and the quality of contacts required of registered nurses, which "include emotional responsibility for patients and clients, . . . often the core of nursing work. . . . [It] fails to collect the requirements . . . to include contacts with respect to socially and politically delicate issues such as AIDS programmes, sex education and family planning" (19). Finally, the tribunal cited the lack of recognition of "the physical, emotional and psychological aspects of death as well as the emotional aspects in providing support to families" (21).

The tribunal ordered ONA and HN each to develop a new or revised job evaluation system sensitive to the concerns identified in its decision. The parties were to negotiate a new system from their separate starting points. ONA contracted with me to develop the system they would present to management. Under my supervision and with the assistance of Lawrence Walter, an ONA research specialist on job evaluation, a questionnaire and evaluation framework were developed as a first effort at a gender-neutral evaluation system. HN failed to deliver a modified system. The tribunal then issued a second decision, in which the power to resolve the controversy was transferred to the Pay Equity Commission, and ONA's GNJES would form the basis for an evaluation system to measure wage discrimination in the work of registered nurses. I was retained by the commission to refine the evaluation system initially submitted by ONA.

INFORMATION GATHERING

The development of a GNJES and the inclusion of measures of emotional labor were built on factors developed in the 1990s found in other gender-neutral systems. We supplemented these broad categories of job content with detailed information about the work performed by registered nurses in six job classes and about the work performed in 17 historically male job classes in HN. Focus groups, averaging three and a half hours in duration, were organized with school nurses, home health care nurses, nurses from homes for the aged, public health nurses, and public health nurses specializing in sex education. In addition, we conducted several focus groups with registered nurses who worked in different units in three provincial hospitals (in conjunction with a second court case initiated by ONA).

Based on this information and on information from published sources describing the skills required of registered nurses (Benner 1984), a pilot questionnaire was developed and distributed to 31 incumbents in 22 classes: 4 of the registered nurse classes and 18 male classes. (These are listed in the appendix of Steinberg and Figart, this volume, Emotional Demands at Work.) Follow-up interviews ranging from two to four hours in length were conducted, individually or in groups, with each incumbent who filled out the questionnaire. Based on this pilot survey, the questionnaire was redesigned. In addition, detailed information about job content was used as the basis for constructing scales of job complexity within categories of job factors.

Creating scales of complexity across dissimilar types of job content inevitably requires judgment about what types of job content are more complex than other types of work. One criterion against which job content can be assessed for levels of complexity is existing wages. The higher the wage, the more complex the work. That criterion is problematic, however, not only because the wage embeds culturally based gender biases about the value of work but also because the wage is a function of many influences, only one of which is job complexity. Another way that hierarchies of complexity have been constructed involves some use of a forced-choice exercise conducted with experts—job evaluators, managers of firms, and personnel specialists. Yet others who design job complexity hierarchies borrow hierarchies from other, readily available systems of evaluation. These second and third approaches rely on groups whose definitions of complexity have been shaped by traditional job evaluation.

In constructing complex hierarchies within each factor, I used what might be called "expert" judgment, backed by political muscle. Since the government agency responsible for implementing the tribunal decision retained me, it was my task to establish equivalencies of complexity across dissimilar job content as well as hierarchies of complexity within each job factor. To make it possible for ONA, the municipality, and the Pay Equity Commission to review the equivalencies I established, I made each factor-level definition as concrete and explicit as possible. Ultimately, however, in constructing these hierarchies, I relied heavily on face validity, believing that, in negotiation, the parties or the government would modify equivalencies they regarded as being out of alignment.

The GNJES described in this article is organized into 17 broad categories of work or factors.[1] In keeping with the requirements of the Pay Equity Act, these factors are divided into four areas: skills, effort, responsibility, and working conditions. Skill factors include education and skill updating; technical skills; organization-specific knowledge; human relations skills; communication skills; and physical skills. Four factors fall under the category of effort: problem complexity, physical demands, mental demands, and emotional demands. Under the category of responsibility are coordination and supervision; planning, organization, and development; responsibility for information and material resources; and responsibility for client, resident, patient, or citizen well-being. Under the category of working conditions are three factors: work environment; hazards; and work pressure and stress.

EMOTIONAL LABOR IN MUNICIPAL WORK

Emotional labor is relational work. It involves managing the emotions of others to achieve a desired state of mind or a desired course of action in them. It also involves managing one's own emotions to project the appropriate emotions for the situation at hand. Emotional labor involves interaction, whether face-to-face or voice-to-voice. Therefore, among the skill factors developed in the GNJES, emotional labor is encompassed within human relations skills and communication skills. A third factor, emotional effort, also measures emotional labor in that it captures the degree to which human relations and communication skills are applied. Finally, consistent with the orientation of England and Farkas (1986), who focus on the effects of emotional labor on others, emotional labor encompasses a responsibility for the well-being of those whose emotions and actions are being managed. Thus, in the GNJES, four factors, in whole or in part, capture the detailed content of emotional labor.

These factors also differentiate between many levels of complexity to determine how complex the work requirements are in relation to the job factor being examined.

Human relations and communication skills

Human relations skills encompass both those skills necessary to supervise subordinates and the skills required to deal effectively with or care for others or to shape, affect, or influence others' feelings, actions, or decisions. While the human relations skills necessary to supervise other employees involve emotional labor, these skills are not limited to such work. Thus the questions posed under this factor extend beyond skills that could reasonably be considered to be emotional labor.

The questionnaire, for this and other factors, combines closed-ended, forced-choice questions; closed-ended questions accompanied by a space to provide specific examples; and open-ended questions. The use of examples and open-ended questions allows those reviewing the questionnaire to ground their evaluations of complexity level in more accurate and complete information. It constrains job evaluators from imposing stereotypes about jobs and causes them to rely, instead, on information about actual job content.

A first set of questions deals with the types of skills used in interacting with others on the job, broadly defined. It asks not only if such skills are used but how often job incumbents must use them (as measured by a five-point scale). Skills include considerable tact, nurturance, coaching, counseling, interviewing, and persuading. Incumbents are asked to provide examples. A second and third set of questions, which also use a five-point frequency scale and request examples, asks about situations in which the incumbent must interact with coworkers or with clients, residents, or patients. The assumption here is that dealing effectively with others in these situations requires some level of human relations skills. Incumbents are asked

how often and under what circumstances they must settle minor disagreements or differences of opinions or negotiate solutions to complex human relations problems, for instance. Another set of questions asks about the frequency of dealing in person with people who are, for example, uncooperative, very upset, very angry, threatening or verbally abusive, or physically violent. These questions are followed by a similar set asking if an incumbent's job requires her or him to deal with such people on the telephone. The questionnaire also asks how often the job incumbent must tell others things they do not want to hear and to whom the incumbent must tell these things.

Based on these and other questions, a human relations skills factor was constructed. It includes five levels of complexity. Because most jobs require the use of human relations skills at different levels of complexity, we asked evaluators to select "the appropriate level for each job . . . by assessing which level captures the essential . . . skills required." The following hierarchy, drawn from the GNJES, illustrates how levels of complexity of human relations skills that involve emotional labor vary.

Level A: [The job includes] discussion of factual information [and] ordinary personal courtesy. . . . Contacts with clients or the public are incidental, not integral.

Level B: [The job requires the incumbent to] exhibit polished courtesy, [to] promote and maintain good relations, build trust and maintain credibility, [to conduct] relations with the public to maintain organizational image. . . . Conflict management is incidental.

Level C: [The job requires the incumbent to] motivate, mentor, coach or train employees and the public. [It] may require hand-holding, reassurance, compassion, empathy and rapport in non-sensitive . . . situations. [It] may require resolution of minor conflicts.

Level D: [The job requires the incumbent to exercise] considerable tact, patience, understanding, ability to reassure, compassion, empathy and rapport in providing direct services or comfort in sensitive situations or in situations where people are uncooperative or in guiding clients in building new habits that affect quality of life. . . . OR [it requires] the use of persuasion techniques, networking, . . . a developed understanding of group . . . dynamics. [It] may involve dealing with . . . emotionally charged issues in public forums . . . conducting extensive consultations with external groups over sensitive political or other emotionally charged issues on a periodic basis, as a regular and critical dimension of the job. OR [it may involve] subduing or restraining others in moderately difficult circumstances.

Level E: [The job requires the incumbent to exercise] interpersonal skills *in combination*, creating a climate for and establishing a commitment to the welfare of clients or the public . . . coaching and guiding clients through difficult emotional, attitudinal and developmental change around issues that are sensitive, controversial, and about which there is . . . individual resistance. [It requires] providing comfort . . . where

people are in considerable pain, dying or gravely ill, angry, distraught, . . ., in drug-induced states, or otherwise unpredictable, physically violent or emotional. . . . crowd control when crowd gets out of hand.

Note that skill complexity is defined in relation to not only the skills required in performing the job but also the situations in which the skills must be used and the character of the emotional state of those with whom the incumbent is interacting. A similar hierarchy is used for communication skills.

The communication skills factor recognizes different forms of communication, including writing and speaking skills as well as nonverbal skills, reading, listening, and the requirement to use another language. The factor also differentiates levels of complexity in the types of information and in the method in which it is conveyed. For example, presentation of information to clients with serious communication impairment or to groups where the level of understanding of the material presented is varied requires a higher level of skill in communicating with others than presenting information to unproblematic clients or to a group of technical peers with equal facility with the materials presented. Thus communicating or listening to the same types of information would involve different levels of complexity of communication skills depending on the circumstances under which the communication is imparted or received and the characteristics of the nonincumbents receiving the communication. The skills involved in verbal and nonverbal communication and in listening are central to the measurement of emotional labor, as is gaining the cooperation of others without formal authority.

In constructing the factor-level definitions for the communication skills factor, we first provided a general overview of the level of complexity. We followed this overview with a range of specific skills assigned to each level. We added illustrations of specific job content, cautioning those using the system to use these as a guide, not a straitjacket. Once again, we asked evaluators to choose the level of complexity that best captures the essential characteristics of the job. The communication skills factor comprises six levels of complexity. At the higher levels, emotional labor is differentiated in terms of the variety of communication skills necessary (that is, the use of these skills separately or in combination), the degree of the sensitivity of the situation in which listening or communicating is involved, the frequency with which these skills are used, and the degree to which the job requires switching levels of communication complexity due to varied levels of client understanding.

Some off-the-shelf job evaluation systems include factors on human relations and communication skills. However, human relations skills are defined in terms of the "personal contacts," with factor-level definitions built on the assumption that the higher the level of the person with whom one is communicating in the organizational hierarchy, the more complex the human relations skills. Similarly, communication skills are defined in terms of the level of the sophistication of the material, with more complex technical information treated as involving more complex communication skills. Neither of these definitions takes the emotional labor associated with such skills into account. Rather, it values location in the organizational hierarchy and technical competence. Thus, in designing the GNJES, we redefined factor definitions to encompass the actual skills involved in human relations and communication skills that were previously invisible. First and foremost, these redefinitions meant recognizing, defining, and assessing the relative complexity of emotional labor.

Emotional effort

The construction of a job content factor measuring emotional effort is new to job evaluation. It emerged as a result of studies of gender bias in job evaluation. When pay equity technical proponents examined what people actually did on their jobs, they found that emotional effort was an important component of many jobs. Gender-neutral evaluation systems, like the one described here, attempted to measure its contours and to differentiate its levels of complexity. The GNJES built on the work of Janice Burns and Martha Coleman, then of the State Services Commission and the Department of Labor in New Zealand, and their system of gender-neutral evaluation, *Equity at Work: An Approach to Gender Neutral Job Evaluation*. It also relied heavily on several earlier evaluation systems developed by Lawrence Walter at ONA with sociologist Lynda

Ames. The most important sources of information, however, were our focus groups, the pilot testing of the questionnaire, and debriefing interviews with respondents.

Effort factors in general measure the application of skills and the demands that these applications make on the job incumbent. Such factors therefore are closely tied to skill categories. The emotional demands factor captures the degree of intensity, frequency, duration, and the cumulative effect of the emotional effort required to deal directly with the needs of clients for assistance, instruction, care, or comfort. Intensity of effort is defined as a function of the type of client needs and the circumstances under which the needs arise and assistance is given. Effort can result from dealing directly with people and groups who are difficult (confused, angry, distrustful, upset, unreasonable, demanding); psychologically or emotionally impaired; under the influence of drugs or alcohol; or dangerous. This factor attempts to measure the actual work that specifically requires emotional responses and not the consequences of the demanding or conflicting work situations on job incumbents. For example, dealing with clients who are unpredictably hostile or confused or working with and discussing death with the terminally ill and their families is defined as requiring more emotional effort than dealing directly with and meeting the needs of clients with sensory barriers.

The questions begin by asking the frequency of working in situations involving clients who would be more or less emotionally demanding.

These include people with disabilities; those who are distressed; those with severe psychological problems; those who are scared, in trouble, or in danger; or those who are in constant pain or unpredictably hostile. They then ask how much of the total work time is spent meeting the needs of people external to the organization. Throughout, the questionnaire asks incumbents to describe examples of the emotional demands of their work that occur often and very often.

Emotional demands are divided into five levels of effort:

Level A: [Incumbents] occasionally deal with unfriendly people.

Level B: [Incumbents] may deal occasionally with people or groups who are in difficult or sensitive or controversial circumstances. [Incumbents] never deal with emotionally impaired or dangerous individuals or groups or individuals under the influence of drugs or alcohol.

Level C: [Incumbents] deal regularly with people who are difficult or with people who are emotionally impaired (such that considerable patience is required). [They] may work directly with people under the influence of drugs or alcohol.

Level D: [Incumbents] may deal with physically dangerous or unpredictably hostile or violent people or groups (including those on drugs or intoxicated) or work directly with people who are in constant pain or facing near-death emergencies or work in highly sensitive or highly controversial circumstances.

Level E: [Incumbents] deal regularly with highly physically dangerous and unpredictably hostile or violent people or groups. [They] may also work directly to meet the needs of people (including family members) who are facing death, through caring for or discussing this or other, comparable, extremely sensitive topics with them.

Responsibility for client well-being

Most discussions of emotional labor recognize the skills and effort involved in managing one's own and others' emotions. Less often recognized are the responsibilities inherent in emotional labor. Furthermore, in traditional job evaluation, responsibility factors are given heavy weight in determining compensation, especially responsibility for moneys or equipment or for the supervision of a large number of subordinates. But consider the consequences for an alcohol and drug treatment center or a hospital or even a department store or a restaurant of staff who fail to exhibit the necessary human relations skills or to expend the energy required to perform their client-oriented tasks effectively. Clients may take their business elsewhere. The well-being of clients may also be undermined by negative interactions with staff. The competent performance of emotional labor has significant consequences, not only for the bottom line but also for the clients who are affected by displays of inappropriate emotional labor.

No traditional job evaluation system of which I am aware includes a factor for the responsibility for the well-being of clients. At best, several systems include a definition within a broad responsibility factor recognizing (at lower factor level) responsibility for those who are sick or dying. To fully recognize the responsibility accompanying the skills and effort associated with emotional labor, we created a factor that takes client well-being into account and that values it in the same way that responsibility for information and material resources is valued. This factor acknowledges and constructs a complexity hierarchy around the responsibility (direct and indirect) for the well-being of clients who receive services from the organization. It measures the actual (as opposed to formal) responsibility involved in informing, training, advising, counseling, teaching, nurturing, and regulating the behavior of clients to ensure their well-being. Levels within the factor are differentiated in terms of the extent of responsibility (such as "minimal," "moderate," "integral," "major," "full," each of which is defined with reference to certain client needs and situations) and the seriousness of the client condition (for example, "short term health needs," "immediate effects," "immediate service," or "treatment of life threatening situations").

Were nurses rewarded for their emotional labor?

Did this exercise in gender-neutral job evaluation bear fruit for the registered nurses working for the municipality of HN? The answer is yes and no.

The GNJES questionnaire was delivered to the Pay Equity Commission, the administrative agency responsible for resolving the conflict between ONA and HN, in October 1993, almost five years after ONA made its original complaint against HN. The commission used the questionnaire with only minor modifications to collect the job content information from historically male job classes and from the registered nurse job classes it needed to arrive at a decision about the amount of wage adjustment. The GNJES factors and factor-level definitions were submitted to the commission in March 1994. Those responsible for resolving this initiative again made what appeared to be small changes in the system and applied it to determine the extent to which registered nurse job classes suffered wage discrimination. The results of their job evaluation exercise were never made public, however, nor was there any recognition or endorsement of the system developed for their use.

Instead, according to ONA, in mid-1995, ONA and HN signed a memorandum of agreement to accept a uniform and collectively bargained wage adjustment for all registered nurse job classes. The adjustment included some back pay. Neither the adjustment nor the back pay came close to the levels of wage discrimination uncovered by the GNJES, again according to ONA. Thus the Ontario government agency responsible for implementing pay equity was able to sidestep any endorsement of a technical pay equity proponent's evaluation system as gender neutral. The system has yet to be tested in an explicitly political context.

The resistance in this and other efforts to assess this system is, not surprisingly, felt by employers. Those who support pay equity and the full valuation of the work differentially found in historically female jobs have enough power to get a law on the books but insufficient power to get the law implemented. We have made emotional labor visible, but we have not yet made it compensable.

CONCLUSION

The recognition of emotional labor as skilled, demanding, and responsible work is ultimately about the achievement of long-term shifts in power relations in the labor market. Achieving this transformation in relative power requires, as a first step, making visible characteristics of women's work and demonstrating concretely the positive value of that work to organizational objectives. Full documentation of the details of emotional labor is absolutely critical to the longer-term goal of ensuring equitable compensation. Detailed studies such as the one conducted in HN cumulatively make it more difficult for employers to ignore and discount the significance and value of this work.

The four factors of the GNJES possibly offer the fullest measurement of the specific job content of emotional labor available. The GNJES differentiates levels of complexity involved in performing emotional labor. It recognizes that there is an important category of work performed by employees for which they receive no compensation. It describes what is involved in carrying out that work. It can serve as the basis for correcting this costly (to those who perform emotional labor) oversight. Others need to build on this and other starting points to further investigate and refine the measurement of emotional labor. Future research needs to measure emotional labor independently of any specific job so that variations in emotional labor between jobs can be observed. But whether or not these efforts to modify job evaluation practices to recognize and compensate emotional labor will bear fruit will depend less on technical concerns and more on political will.

Of course, without the support of women workers for pay equity, and without their understanding of the significant contribution that their emotional labor makes to organizational effectiveness, employers and policymakers will continue to ignore the evidence. There will be no political will. Thus the question of whether emotional labor will be valued is an open one—much less clear than our technical understanding of what this work entails.

Note

1. The GNJES described in this article is a revised version of the questionnaire used in Steinberg and Figart, this volume, Emotional Demands at Work.

References

Beatty, R. and J. Beatty. 1984. Some Problems in Contemporary Job Evaluation. In *Comparable Worth and Wage Discrimination*, ed. Helen Remick. Philadelphia: Temple University Press.

Benner, Patricia. 1984. *From Novice to Expert: Excellence and Power in Clinical Nursing Practice*. Menlo Park, CA: Addison-Wesley.

England, Paula and George Farkas. 1986. *Households, Employment, and Gender: A Social Economic and Demographic View*. New York: Aldine.

Kessler-Harris, Alice. 1990. *A Woman's Wage: Historical Meanings and Social Consequences*. Lexington: University of Kentucky Press.

Milkman, Ruth. 1987. *Gender at Work: The Dynamics of Job Segregation by Sex During World War II*. Urbana: University of Illinois Press.

Ontario Pay Equity Hearings Tribunal. 1991. *Haldimand-Norfolk*. No. 6, 2 P.E.R. 105 at 117.

Remick, Helen. 1979. Strategies for Creating Sound, Bias Free Job Evaluation Plans. In *Job Evaluation and EEO: The Emerging Issues*, ed. Industrial Relations Counselors. New York: Industrial Relations Counselors.

———. 1981. The Comparable Worth Controversy. *Public Personnel Management* 10:371-83.

———. 1984a. Dilemmas of Implementation: The Case of Nursing. In *Comparable Worth and Wage Discrimination*, ed. Helen Remick. Philadelphia: Temple University Press.

———. 1984b. Major Issues in *a Priori* Applications. In *Comparable Worth and Wage Discrimination*, ed. Helen Remick. Philadelphia: Temple University Press.

Riegel, John W. 1937. *Wage Determination*. Ann Arbor, MI: Bureau of Industrial Relations.

Schwab, D. 1985. Job Evaluation Research and Research Needs. In *Comparable Worth: New Directions for Research*, ed. H. Hartman. Washington, DC: National Academy Press.

Steinberg, Ronnie J. 1984. Identifying Wage Discrimination and Implementing Pay Equity Adjustments. In *Com-*

parable Worth: Issues for the '80s, ed. U.S. Commission on Civil Rights. Washington, DC: Government Printing Office.

Steinberg, Ronnie J. and Lois Haignere. 1985. Testimony on Comparable Worth. Testimony before the Subcommittee on Compensation and Employee Benefits, Committee on Post Office and Civil Service, U.S. House of Representatives. 99th Cong., 1st sess., 28 Mar.

———. 1987. Equitable Compensation: Methodological Criteria for Comparable Worth. In *Ingredients for Women's Employment Policy*, ed. Christine Bose and Glenna Spitze. Albany: State University of New York Press.

Steinberg, Ronnie J. and W. Lawrence Walter. 1992. Making Women's Work Visible: The Case of Nursing—First Steps in the Design of a Gender-Neutral Job Comparison System. In *Exploring the Quincentenniel: The Policy Challenges of Gender, Diversity, and International Exchange*. Washington, DC: Institute for Women's Policy Research.

Taylor, Susan. 1989. The Case for Comparable Worth. *Journal of Social Issues* 45(4):23-37.

Treiman, Donald. 1979. *Job Evaluation: An Analytic Review*. Washington, DC: National Academy of Sciences, National Research Council.

Treiman, Donald and Heidi Hartmann. 1981. *Women, Work and Wages: Equal Pay for Jobs of Equal Value*. Washington, DC: National Academy Press.

ANNALS, *AAPSS*, **561**, January 1999

The Psychosocial Consequences
of Emotional Labor

By AMY S. WHARTON

ABSTRACT: Understanding the psychological consequences of emotional labor for workers has been an ongoing project among students of emotional labor. Drawing on Hochschild's pathbreaking work in this area, five major streams of qualitative and quantitative research have emerged, including (1) the experiences of workers who perform emotional labor; (2) comparisons between performers and nonperformers of emotional labor; (3) the conditions under which emotional labor may be positive or negative; (4) variations between workers that condition their responses to emotional labor; and (5) consequences of emotional labor at work for workers' private lives. This article reviews each area and concludes with suggestions for future research on the psychological consequences of emotional labor.

Amy S. Wharton is associate professor of sociology at Washington State University. Her research on the psychological consequences of emotional labor has appeared in Work and Occupations; Sociological Quarterly; Social Problems; *and the* Academy of Management Review. *In addition to emotional labor, Wharton's research interests include organizational demography, social relations, and the construction of difference in work groups; the use and consequences of corporate work-family policies; and gender and racial inequality in the workplace.*

I N her now classic 1983 book, *The Managed Heart*, Arlie Hochschild warned readers of the potentially negative social and psychological consequences of emotional labor for workers. Hochschild's arguments inspired many ensuing studies of emotional labor, most of which paid at least some attention to the significance of this labor for those who perform it. As Steinberg and Figart (this volume, Emotional Labor Since *The Managed Heart*) note, it is appropriate that we reexamine Hochschild's concerns in light of the 15 or so years of research since *The Managed Heart*.

Understanding the consequences of emotional labor for workers has been an ongoing project among students of emotional labor. While these consequences include both economic and noneconomic costs and rewards, the latter were Hochschild's focus and receive my attention here. In particular, I discuss studies that explore the psychosocial effects of emotional labor on those who perform it. While some of these effects—such as burnout and job satisfaction—have been studied extensively by sociologists of work, they have been of special interest to students of emotional labor. Because emotional labor seems to implicate the self more directly than other types of work (Hochschild 1983), it may have distinctive psychological costs and benefits for workers. Indeed, the degree to which the psychological costs and benefits of emotional labor diverge from those associated with other types of work is an important empirical question.

WHAT IS EMOTIONAL LABOR?

Identifying and assessing what we know about the consequences of emotional labor first require an understanding of what counts as this type of work. Though there is no complete consensus on this issue, some common elements have emerged. Together, these provide what I view as a useful operational definition of emotional labor. This definition has several components.

First, most research recognizes the distinction between emotional labor and what Mumby and Putnam (1992) call "work feelings" (477). In Mumby and Putnam's view, work feelings represent the "spontaneous and emergent" consequences of social interaction at work, while emotional labor refers to the managed and, hence, more instrumental expression of emotion in the workplace (477). Along the same lines, Rosenberg (1990) distinguishes emotional labor from emotional expression, the latter referring to the unintentional demonstration of emotion. While the growing literature on the sources and consequences of work feelings acknowledges the emotional ties between social interactants in the workplace (cf. Marks 1994), the expression of these ties is not evidence per se of emotional labor.

A second, related distinction involves the separation between emotion as displayed and emotion that is internally felt. Most research on the consequences of emotional labor associates this labor with the display of emotion. For example, Hochschild's definition (1983) of emotional labor (that is, "the management of feeling to create a publicly observable facial and bodily display" [7]) acknowledges the importance of display, as does Rosenberg's (1990). In particular, Rosenberg uses the term "emotion management" to refer to the "self-regulation of emotional exhibition for the purpose of producing intended effects on others' minds" (2). Consistent with these understandings, Ashforth and Humphrey (1993) define emotional labor as "the act of displaying the appropriate emotion" (90). While sociologists of emotion such as Hochschild and Rosenberg believe that people also have the capacity to intentionally regulate their emotional experiences so as to bring forth or create internal states of arousal, research on the consequences of emotional labor has generally been concerned with the requirement that people display particular emotions on the job.

Is the expectation that workers display the appropriate emotion a formal or informal part of job requirements? Is this expectation enforced by workers themselves or by external authorities, such as managers or customers? In general, research on the consequences of emotional labor has focused on jobs where adherence to emotional display rules is considered a formal job requirement and where the guidelines for its performance are not solely controlled by workers themselves. This focus thus excludes more informal types of emotional labor, such as the mothering of others that may be implicitly expected of female workers.

Finally, most research on the consequences of emotional labor has examined it in the context of workers' interactions with "external" rather than "internal" customers (cf. Ashforth and Humphrey 1993, but see Erickson and Wharton 1997). That is, the primary focus of attention has been workers in "organization boundary roles," defined as positions that represent the organization to individuals or groups outside organizational boundaries (Miles 1980). Jobs at the boundaries of organizations are assumed to require emotional labor in part because workers in these roles must interact with people over whom they lack any formal authority. The use of affective strategies to gain compliance with organizational objectives thus becomes a substitute for reliance on more formal means of exercising authority.

Taken together, these conceptual distinctions yield the following operational definition of emotional labor: emotional labor refers to the effort involved in displaying organizationally sanctioned emotions by those whose jobs require interaction with clients or customers and for whom these interactions are an important component of their work.

ISSUES FOR RESEARCHERS

While a useful starting point for research, even a superficial application of the criteria previously described yields a long list of jobs that require emotional labor. According to Hochschild's estimates (1983), 38.1 percent of all occupations involve "substantial emotional labor" (236). Focusing attention on "nurturant work" rather than emotional labor per se, England (1992) identified 58 occupations that required "an application of social skills to activities providing a service to customers or clients" (136). In their study of hospital and bank workers, Wharton (1993) and Erickson and Wharton (1997) determined that over half of the workers employed by these two companies held jobs requiring at least some emotional labor.

While systematic efforts to identify jobs requiring emotional labor remain scarce (but see Steinberg and Figart 1996, 1997), what does seem clear is that emotional labor is a component of many occupations and that it is not completely coextensive with any other occupational, job, or organizational characteristic. For example, while many jobs in the service sector involve emotional labor, this sector also employs workers who do not interact with customers or clients. Similarly, while interaction with customers or clients is an aspect of many nonprofessional positions, several professions also include this component (for example, teaching, nursing, medical doctor). Hence, although some occupational groups may be overrepresented in a list of jobs requiring emotional labor, emotional labor—as previously defined—is found across the occupational spectrum.

This occupational diversity suggests that variations between jobs that require emotional labor call for serious attention, as this variability may be even greater than the variation between jobs requiring emotional labor and those not requiring this effort. In addition, it is important to understand the degree to which the effects of emotional labor depend on other features of the setting where it is performed or on the characteristics of the performers. The consequences of emotional labor may be highly contingent upon other characteristics of the job, the organization, or the worker. As I will show in the following pages, research on the consequences of emotional labor that fails to attend to these issues may yield misleading conclusions and has made the task of understanding these consequences more difficult.

THE PSYCHOLOGICAL CONSEQUENCES OF EMOTIONAL LABOR

Hochschild's warnings (1979, 1983) about the potentially negative consequences of emotional labor form the backdrop against which virtually all later research on this issue has been conducted. For Hochschild (1979, 1983), these negative consequences stem from the loss of control over emotion that occurs when employers begin to regulate the feelings workers display. This transforms what is typically a strictly private act—engaged in almost unconsciously—into a public act, performed according to others' guidelines and for employers' gain. Hochschild (1983) likens this loss of control over one's emotions and emotional displays to alienation and the loss of control over other aspects of work. For Hochschild, then, the management of emotion per se is not problematic. Rather, the negative consequences of emotional labor stem primarily from the fact that employers rather than workers themselves dictate the terms of emotional display.

The regulation of workers' emotional displays by employers is problematic for at least two reasons. First, workers are prevented from interacting with customers or clients in ways that are guided by and emerge from the immediate circumstances, but instead must conform to scripts drawn up by others. That is, workers' own inclinations for interaction may be suppressed and replaced by an organizationally sanctioned response. Second, employers and workers may have different interests vis-à-vis the outcome of the interaction. For employers, workers' interactions with customers and clients serve an instrumental purpose and workers' emotional displays are in the service of that objective. While workers may sometimes share those objectives (cf. Leidner 1993), they do not always do so. In these instances, workers' interests may be sacrificed.

What are the negative psychological consequences of emotional labor? For Hochschild (1983), these consequences involve an interference with workers' capacity to strike a balance between the requirements of the self and the demands of the work role. In particular, sustained performance of emotional labor may engender a fusion of self and work role, an estrangement between self and work role that comes at the expense of the self, or an estrangement between self and work role that comes at the expense of the work role. Though Hochschild views all three conditions

as potentially damaging, later researchers have tended to treat the first two conditions as psychologically harmful for workers, while seeing the third condition as a more healthy response to emotional labor.

Fusion of self and work role

When jobs involve emotional labor, the fusion of self and work role increases the risk of burnout. Burnout has been defined as the numbing of the inner signals of emotional feelings, reflected in the inability to create or feel any emotion (Maslach 1976; Maslach and Pines 1977; Maslach and Jackson 1982). In business press discussions of service workers, this condition has been referred to as "contact overload," whose symptoms include workers' becoming "robotic, detached, and unempathetic" (Albrecht and Zemke 1985, 114).

Though workers in many kinds of jobs may be at risk of job burnout, the early research on this topic focused heavily on workers in human service occupations, such as social work, policing, counseling, and child care, where personal empathy with another is an important aspect of the job (for example, Maslach and Jackson 1982; Gaines and Jermier 1983). In these jobs, then, the problem is not that workers are expected to display a concern for clients' well-being that they do not genuinely feel. Instead, human service workers—or any workers who are too identified with their work role—are at risk precisely because the feelings expressed at work are inseparable from the self. Over time, this inability to depersonalize and detach oneself increases these workers' risk of burnout.

If burnout results when workers are unable to maintain sufficient psychological distance between the emotional requirements of their job and their sense of self, it should not only be found in human service jobs but should also occur in other jobs that involve emotional labor. Jobs that facilitate or otherwise encourage workers' identification with the work role should place workers at risk. At-risk workers should also be those for whom emotional labor feels the most natural. Ironically, while employers and customers may prefer workers whose emotional displays seem genuine, workers' sincerity ultimately may increase their risk of burnout.

Estrangement between self and work role

Burnout is not the only important psychological consequence of emotional labor. Inauthenticity, or what Hochschild (1983) calls "emotive dissonance" (90), may be another byproduct. Like cognitive dissonance, emotive dissonance reflects a disjuncture between different aspects of the person. In particular, workers may experience certain emotions during their interactions with customers and clients but feel compelled to display other emotions. While occasional disjunctures between what one displays and what one feels may be psychologically inconsequential, Hochschild and others worry that the regular occurrence of emotive dissonance may be harmful. As Ashforth and Humphrey (1993) explain, "Ulti-mately, such dissonance could lead to personal and work-related maladjustment, such as poor self-esteem, depression, cynicism, and alienation from work" (96-97). These claims rest on the belief that people "are motivated to maintain and enhance their sense of self as being meaningful and authentic" and that the chronic inability to do so is damaging (Erickson and Wharton 1997, 192; see also Bulan, Erickson, and Wharton 1997; Erickson 1994).

For Hochschild (1983), however, emotive dissonance is most harmful when it comes at the expense of the self, that is, when it produces feelings of inauthenticity. Dissonance is less problematic, she argues, when it is attributed to the work role—that is, when the acting is attributed to the demands of the job rather than to the desires of the self. Though Hochschild says little about the conditions under which emotive dissonance is resolved at the expense of one or the other, recent research provides some insight into these processes.

These concerns have inspired research in several areas. First, researchers have examined the experiences of workers who perform emotional labor, seeking to identify in broad terms how workers react to these jobs. A second line of research compares workers in jobs requiring emotional labor to workers in jobs without an emotional labor component. These studies examine whether workers who perform emotional labor display more negative job-related reactions than other workers. A third area of research focuses on the dimensions of emotional labor and seeks to identify the conditions under which emotional labor may be positive or negative, and the factors that may modify its effects on workers. A fourth research area examines variations between workers that may influence their reactions to jobs requiring emotional labor. Finally, studies have explored the consequences of emotional labor at work for workers' private lives. In this view, the emotional demands of jobs represent a feature of work roles that may overburden or conflict with the emotional demands of other roles, such as those of partner or parent. Each area of research will be discussed now.

THE EXPERIENCES
OF WORKERS WHO
PERFORM EMOTIONAL LABOR

There is a growing qualitative case study literature on workers who perform emotional labor. Examples of this research include Sutton and Rafaeli's study of convenience store clerks (1988), Paules's research on waitresses (1991), Sutton's research on bill collectors (1991), Leidner's study of fast-food and insurance workers (1993), and Pierce's study of litigators and paralegals (1995). Though emotional labor and its psychological consequences are not the primary foci of these authors, this literature offers a rich source of information about these issues.

In general, while most of these researchers heed Hochschild's warnings (1983) about the psychological dangers of emotional labor, the case study literature tends to emphasize the ways that workers resist degradation and avoid feelings of inauthenticity. Paules (1991), for example, acknowledges the "hazards of personality control" but argues that the waitresses she studied successfully resisted assaults on their selves (158). In her words, "Like all social actors, the waitress monitors her projected personality and manipulates her feelings in the course of social interaction, but she does so knowingly and in her own interests. This manipulation of self does not induce self-alienation or emotional disorientation" (162). Rather than overidentifying with their jobs, the dominant response of workers in Paules's study was to maintain a healthy distance between self and work role and thus to protect the self. Along similar lines, Leidner (1993) suggests that while "individuality, authenticity, and identity" were "everyday concerns" for the interactive service workers she studied, these workers employed a variety of strategies to express themselves and protect their dignity (179).

These studies' failure to uncover any persistently negative consequences of emotional labor is significant but raises analytical issues that may be best resolved with quantitative research. For example, in order to determine whether jobs requiring emotional labor place demands on workers that are different from or more burdensome than the burdens of other jobs, it is necessary to compare performers and nonperformers of emotional labor. To assess whether the negative consequences of emotional labor fall more heavily on some workers than others requires attention to the variability between these jobs. Finally, in assessing the psychological consequences of emotional labor, it is important to control for other features of these jobs that may be also related to the outcomes of interest. In order to consider these issues, I turn to other research on emotional labor.

COMPARING PERFORMERS AND NONPERFORMERS OF EMOTIONAL LABOR

One way to examine the broader psychosocial consequences of emotional labor is to compare emotional labor performers with those whose jobs require little or no labor of this type. These studies can help address the question of whether jobs requiring emotional labor are experienced as more psychologically demanding than other forms of work. By examining the effects of emotional labor on various outcomes net of other job and worker characteristics, this research offers a systematic way to assess the consequences of emotional labor.

This line of research has yielded some unexpected results. For instance, controlling for a variety of individual and job characteristics, Wharton (1993) found that workers employed in jobs requiring substantial amounts of emotional labor were no more likely than other workers to experience job-related burnout. Use of a different measure of emotional labor yielded similar results (Wharton and Erickson 1995). In general, workers' burnout levels were better predicted by more conventional job characteristics, such as autonomy and number of hours worked, than by emotional labor. In addition, not only

were workers who performed emotional labor no more likely than others to report job burnout, but they were significantly more satisfied with their jobs than other workers (Wharton 1993). Adelman's study (1995) of emotional labor among table servers yielded similar kinds of results. As Adelman explains:

This suggests that desirable jobs, which also happen to demand higher levels of emotional labor, produce high job satisfaction. It may also be that desirable jobs produce greater job satisfaction, which in turn motivates employees to perform a high degree of emotional labor. In either case, it appears that emotional labor per se is not strongly related either positively or negatively to job reactions. (378)

In later research, Erickson and Wharton (1997) examined the effects of emotional labor on workers' feelings of inauthenticity. Recall that Hochschild (1983) viewed feelings of inauthenticity as one possible consequence of the "emotive dissonance" associated with emotional labor. Jobs that require the routine display of emotions regardless of whether or not these displays are real may undermine workers' experience of their selves as meaningful and authentic. In this view, jobs that require emotional labor place workers at greater risk of inauthenticity than jobs that do not require display of particular emotions.

Analyzing the same data as the research on burnout described earlier, Erickson and Wharton (1997) measured inauthenticity with a two-item scale assessing how often respondents felt that they could not be themselves while at work or that they had to fake how they really felt at work. Emotional labor was operationalized as three separate dimensions: contact with the public, amount of time spent working with people on the job, and the degree to which workers viewed "handling people well" as an important aspect of their job. This analysis revealed that only one dimension of emotional labor—handling people well—was positively associated with workers' feelings of inauthenticity at work. Moreover, workers in public-contact jobs were no more likely than other workers to feel inauthentic at work, while workers whose jobs required a substantial amount of interaction with people were significantly less likely than other workers to feel inauthentic. In other words, it is the requirement that workers handle people well that increases feelings of inauthenticity—not merely the amount of interaction with people at work or contact with the public.

These findings provide some new insights regarding the consequences of emotional labor. First, the analyses of burnout, job satisfaction, and inauthenticity lend implicit support to the qualitative literature discussed earlier, which revealed the ways in which workers successfully cope with the demands of emotional labor. The qualitative and quantitative results do not necessarily refute Hochschild's concerns (1983) about the potentially negative consequences of emotional labor, but they suggest that these negative consequences may occur only under limited conditions, not all of which have been identified.

Second, comparisons of performers and nonperformers of emotional labor suggest that jobs involving emotional labor may have some pleasures as well as dangers for workers, relative to other types of work. For example, jobs that provide workers with opportunities to interact with others on the job—even if these interactions are limited—seem to be more satisfying to workers than jobs allowing less social interaction. Adelman (1995, 378-79) found that workers "see a number of good reasons for performing emotional labor," among which was its tendency to increase workers' sense that they are doing their jobs well. Moreover, as the amount of time spent interacting with people at work increases, workers' feelings of inauthenticity decrease. While workers' interactions with others on the job may engender dissatisfaction and distress under some conditions, on balance, these work conditions offer more opportunities for satisfaction than other jobs. The higher levels of satisfaction found among workers who perform emotional labor may also stem from other aspects of these jobs. For example, perhaps both employer and worker selection mechanisms are more efficient in jobs requiring emotional labor; hence, the fit between job demands and worker characteristics may be higher in these jobs than in positions where emotional labor is not required. This greater fit would also contribute to higher levels of satisfaction.

The strongest evidence that emotional labor is damaging to workers derives from the finding that workers whose jobs require them to "handle people well" feel more inauthentic than others. While this job requirement was significantly more likely to be found in public-contact jobs than others, people-handling skills may be required in a broader range of jobs than those involving interaction with clients or customers. Restricting attention to the latter sort of job may limit our understanding of the multiple ways that people may be required to manage their emotions in the workplace.

UNDER WHAT CONDITIONS IS EMOTIONAL LABOR HARMFUL FOR WORKERS?

In addition to the other comparisons between performers and nonperformers of emotional labor, Wharton (1993) examined whether different factors contribute to burnout and job satisfaction among these two groups of workers. These results suggest that while performers of emotional labor do not express higher levels of burnout than other workers, the sources of burnout and the factors that help to offset it may differ somewhat for the two groups. These results thus offer some insight as to the conditions under which emotional labor may engender job burnout. For example, high levels of job involvement were associated with lower levels of burnout among nonperformers of emotional labor, while job involvement failed to reduce burnout among emotional labor performers. As Hochschild (1983) surmised, when jobs require emotional labor, high levels of job in-

volvement may be dangerous for workers. For nonperformers of emotional labor, however, job involvement does not make the same kinds of demands on the self; hence, for this group, higher levels of burnout should be associated with lower, rather than higher, levels of job involvement.

Evidence further suggests that performers and nonperformers of emotional labor differ in the role their interpersonal skills play in protecting them from or enhancing their susceptibility to burnout at work. Most notably, among performers of emotional labor, workers who score high on self-monitoring—defined as the ability to monitor and react to the social environment—are better able to avoid burnout than workers who lack these abilities. Self-monitoring skills contribute to burnout among nonperformers of emotional labor, however. These results underscore the fact that while performers and nonperformers of emotional labor may differ little in their likelihood of burnout, these groups may differ in the factors that produce this outcome.

The factors that produce job satisfaction also appear to differ for performers and nonperformers of emotional labor in a manner consistent with the findings previously discussed. In particular, job autonomy seems to have a greater effect on the satisfaction of emotional labor performers than nonperformers, while job involvement contributes more to the satisfaction levels of nonperformers of emotional labor. The results for job autonomy lend support to

Hochschild's claim (1983, 1979) that emotional labor is problematic for workers when employers control its performance. Although job autonomy is an important predictor of satisfaction among all types of workers (Kalleberg and Berg 1987; Wharton and Baron 1987, 1991), Wharton's research (1993) suggests that it is particularly important for workers whose jobs require emotional labor. Job autonomy for these workers provides them with opportunities to deflect the dangers to self that emotional labor may entail. Regarding job involvement, it seems that workers whose jobs require emotional labor do not derive as many psychosocial benefits from this involvement as nonperformers derive. While high levels of job involvement are satisfying to all types of workers, being too involved in one's job presents dangers for workers whose jobs require emotional labor because it increases the risk of burnout.

These findings further extend our understanding of emotional labor and its consequences. First, they help to account for some of the qualitative research findings. As Leidner (1993) and Paules (1991) show, emotional labor is not necessarily distressing or unsatisfying to workers. When workers retain some control over the conditions of its performance, avoid excessively high levels of job involvement, and possess some self-monitoring abilities, emotional labor does not produce burnout or low job satisfaction, on average. In fact, as noted earlier, jobs requiring emotional labor may offer some rewards, relative to other types of work.

A second contribution of this research is its suggestion that jobs requiring emotional labor may indeed be distinct in certain respects from other types of work. Self-monitoring abilities, for example, seem to be a more useful psychological resource for emotional labor performers than for workers whose jobs do not require this activity. Not only do jobs requiring emotional labor differ from others in the characteristics that produce burnout and job satisfaction, but it may be that jobs involving emotional labor engender their own, unique set of psychosocial costs and benefits for workers.

HOW DO WORKERS'
CHARACTERISTICS INFLUENCE
THEIR RESPONSES TO
EMOTIONAL LABOR?

Women workers have been the focus of much previous research on emotional labor. This is not surprising, given Hochschild's (1983) contention that jobs requiring emotional labor "form only a quarter of all jobs that men do, and over half of all jobs that women do" (171). Jobs requiring emotional labor that are filled primarily by women tend to be in the service sector, where contact with customers or clients is a regular feature of the job. Very few of these interactive service jobs require workers to display hostile or negative emotions (but see Sutton 1991), instead demanding friendliness, sociability, and cheerfulness on the part of workers. Because compliance with these demands also requires women to display deference and subservience toward customers, Hochschild

(1983) argues that women who perform emotional labor may be more at risk than men of encountering negative reactions from customers or clients. Because women have lower status in the larger society, Hochschild believes that "their feelings are accorded less weight than the feelings of men" (171).

By referring to jobs involving "an application of social skills to activities providing a service to customers or clients" as "nurturant" occupations, England (1992, 136) makes clear the gendered character of this type of emotional labor. The interactional work involved in instilling feelings of satisfaction and well-being in others bears obvious similarities to the caretaking activities typically assigned to women in families. These patterns suggest that the consequences of emotional labor may be highly contingent upon both the gender of the worker and the degree to which the work role itself is gendered.

These observations have inspired some research on gender differences in workers' reactions to emotional labor. For example, Wharton (1993) examined whether there were any gender differences in the impact of emotional labor on workers' levels of burnout and job satisfaction. She found that while women who performed emotional labor reported higher levels of satisfaction than men in these roles, this gender difference was not significantly different from that found among nonperformers of emotional labor. In other words, women report higher levels of job satisfaction than men and this holds true even among those who

perform emotional labor. There were no gender differences in the impact of emotional labor on workers' levels of burnout.

Erickson and Wharton (1997) also examined gender differences in their study of inauthenticity. They found that women were no more likely than men to feel inauthentic at work. Further research by Bulan, Erickson, and Wharton (1997) provided greater insight into these findings. For example, Bulan, Erickson, and Wharton found that both women's and men's feelings of inauthenticity were reduced as the amount of time spent interacting with others increased. In addition, both genders felt more inauthentic when their jobs required them to "handle people well." These similarities, however, mask some important gender differences in the ways that characteristics of interactive service work, such as time spent interacting with people, and the affective requirements of jobs, such as the need to handle people well, combine with other factors to shape workers' feelings about their jobs. For example, women whose jobs required little interaction with others felt most inauthentic under conditions of low job involvement, while men who interacted with people infrequently felt most inauthentic when they were highly involved in their jobs. As Bulan, Erickson, and Wharton explain:

Women who were highly involved in the performance of interactive service work wanted to be interacting with others. Given the people-oriented nature of such work, this finding indicates that women may feel that they can "be themselves" in service-sector jobs. Men, on the other hand, need frequent interaction with others to feel authentic only when they are *not* otherwise highly involved with their jobs. (718; emphasis in original)

While these findings are suggestive, the issues raised are far from being resolved. Because researchers have focused most of their attention on interactive service jobs where female workers predominate, their samples are likely to contain few male respondents. This makes it almost impossible to identify gender differences in workers' responses to emotional labor. On a broader level, the close connection between the particular emotional requirements of an occupation and the gender of its incumbents implies that these requirements are themselves gendered and that workers' responses are contingent upon their ability to negotiate these gendered expectations (Pierce 1995). In other words, understanding gender differences in the consequences of emotional labor requires attention to the complex interactions between individual gender identity and the type of emotional labor prescribed in job requirements.

As this discussion has revealed, the kinds of emotional labor women are often encouraged to perform in interactive service roles closely resemble the kinds of socioemotional work women are expected to perform in their families. In particular, researchers have asked whether women's performance of caregiving on the job, combined with its performance in families, places women at a greater risk of burnout and other negative psychosocial conditions

than women or men with fewer responsibilities for caregiving.

THE CONSEQUENCES
OF PAID AND UNPAID
EMOTIONAL LABOR

Studies of work-family relations note at least two dangers associated with the occupancy of multiple roles. Those whose work and family responsibilities result in "a greater number of prescribed activities than an individual can handle adequately or comfortably" have experienced work-family role overload (Kelly and Voydanoff 1985, 368), while work-family role conflict occurs when "the pressures associated with membership in one organization are in conflict with membership in other groups" (Kahn et al. 1964, 20). To the extent that workers' family roles are also governed by emotional expectations, performance of emotional labor on the job would seem to place workers at risk of both kinds of work-family stress.

Researchers have just begun to understand the consequences of multiple emotional roles. Most of this research has focused on workers employed in interactive service jobs that require the same kinds of emotional labor on the job that is expected of women and, to a lesser extent, men in families. For instance, Wharton (1993) examined whether married workers whose jobs required emotional labor were more likely than other workers to experience burnout. The data failed to support this hypothesis. Being married, however, may be a poor proxy for the degree to which workers perform emotion work outside the workplace. Moreover, this study did not explore possible interactions between marital status and gender.

Using a more direct measure of family work and focusing their attention on married and cohabiting women, Wharton and Erickson (1995) found that women's levels of job burnout were increased when they performed higher levels of family emotion work but that emotional labor on the job had no effect on burnout levels. Hence, women's well-being at work seems to be threatened more by their involvement in family emotion work than by performance of emotional labor on the job. Even this relationship, however, does not hold in all circumstances. Partners' performance of family emotion work weakened the association between women's family emotion work and job burnout.

An interesting finding in this study was the positive association between women's performance of some emotional labor at work and their performance of family emotion work at home. By contrast, women whose jobs required no emotional labor and those whose jobs required high levels of this activity performed significantly less family emotion work. Do women whose jobs require moderate amounts of emotional labor develop interpersonal strategies that generalize to their family relations? Alternatively, do women who perform high levels of family emotion work seek out jobs that enable them to use these skills? These questions have yet to be answered. Overall, however, the results suggest that the

relations between the type and amount of emotional labor performed on the job and the type and amount of emotion work done at home are more complex than assumed.

Qualitative researchers have also contributed to our understanding of the consequences of emotional labor for workers' lives off the job. For example, a 1989 study by Smith and Kleinman examined how male and female medical students learned the emotional style of "affective neutrality" required of medical practitioners and other professionals (see also Parsons 1951). These researchers showed that medical students of both genders developed strategies to manage the feelings often evoked in their encounters with human bodies. While useful professionally, Smith and Kleinman note that "for some students, medical training creates a problem as new meanings for the body and for body contact go home with them at night" (65). Though not the authors' explicit intent, this research reveals the ways in which the emotional labor required on the job may conflict with that involved in sustaining intimate relations in private life. In addition, this study offers a reminder that interactive service jobs are not the only settings where emotional labor is performed.

TOWARD A RESEARCH
AGENDA: WHAT ARE
THE QUESTIONS?

This discussion of the consequences of emotional labor gives rise to several observations that future research must address. First, jobs requiring emotional labor are diverse and it may be impossible to generalize about the consequences of these jobs for workers. Most important is the diversity in the components that constitute emotional labor, such as whether emotional labor is an important feature of the job, the degree to which workers' emotional displays are monitored, and the type of emotions that are to be displayed. Further, these differences in the conditions under which emotional labor is performed are undoubtedly related to other differences in job conditions and worker characteristics.

For example, the type of emotions workers are encouraged to display appears to be strongly related to the kind of authority workers have over customers and clients. Because authority in this society is conveyed through a nonemotional persona (Smith and Kleinman 1989), the kind of emotional labor displayed by professionals—whose authority over clients is expected—should be quite different from the emotional labor required of interactive service workers for whom "the customer is always right." Professional positions, such as doctor, do not require friendliness and sociability as much as they demand the muting of these emotions. This type of emotional labor and its consequences may be very different from those found in other settings where emotional labor is performed. Similarly, deference and the kinds of emotions displayed in the service of being nice are characteristics strongly associated with interactive service jobs and other predominantly female jobs that require nurturance. Emotional labor is not a gender-neutral activity, and its effects thus

are likely to reflect an interaction between the type of emotional labor performed and the characteristics of the performer. As Bulan, Erickson, and Wharton (1997) note, "We see that women are not adversely affected by service work requirements alone, but that the effects of such requirements are intertwined with other occupational conditions" (718).

Understanding this variability also requires considerable attention to issues of sampling and measurement. No studies of the consequences of emotional labor have been conducted with a representative sample of workers or jobs. Instead, research has focused either solely on jobs requiring emotional labor or on settings, such as the service sector, where a disproportionate number of workers are employed in jobs involving emotional labor. Obviously, this has contributed to our inability to identify variations between jobs and workers who perform emotional labor. In addition to the need for representative samples, there are measurement issues that require attention. The results of research to date seem to suggest that emotional labor is better conceived as a multidimensional or continuous variable than one that is categorical. Researchers' experimentation with multidimensional and continuous measures of emotional labor thus must continue.

Despite these comments about the failings of previous research, this research has yielded some tentative conclusions that can serve as the basis for future research. For example, studies previously reviewed suggest that while emotional labor may have some negative psychosocial consequences, these seem to occur only in some limited contexts, such as when workers lack control over their work. Jobs requiring emotional labor may also have positive consequences for incumbents, especially when these jobs are compared to jobs not requiring emotional labor. Opportunities for social interaction at work are generally experienced as positive and authenticating for workers, except under some conditions. Following Marks (1994), perhaps we need to spend more time examining social interaction of all kinds at work and its consequences for workers' lives on and off the job.

On a more general level, the research suggests that investigators should consider a broader range of outcomes that may be associated with emotional labor, and explore the relations between them. Because some aspects of emotional labor may have positive consequences for workers' well-being, while others may have negative consequences, it is important that researchers not restrict attention to only positive or only negative outcomes. Moreover, it may be useful to explore how the various outcomes associated with emotional labor are related to each other. For example, workers who are highly involved in their jobs may be simultaneously at greater risk of job burnout and more likely than less job-involved workers to feel authentic at work. Exclusive attention to either one of these outcomes would miss this type of association.

There is some evidence that even workers in jobs with little autonomy are able to protect themselves from some of the most inauthenticating aspects of emotional labor. More attention to these coping strategies, as well as the conditions under which they fail, is necessary. While workers' reliance on routinized scripts may be tearing away at broader social and cultural expectations for social interactions, many factors have mitigated the negative consequences of this trend for workers.

Along these lines, Erickson (forthcoming) has argued that it may be time for us to rethink the academic discourse on emotion, especially as it relates to emotion management. The end of the twentieth century seems to be a time when Americans, in particular, spend much time and money working on their emotions. Erickson draws on Schwalbe's notion of "therapeutic individualism" (1996) to capture this emergent emotional culture. Therapeutic individualism involves the belief that each person has a unique, uncorrupted, inner self that deserves expression; paradoxically, however, this "authentic self" requires intense emotion work to be revealed. The culture of therapeutic individualism thus views emotion management not as a deviant process—as it is typically viewed in the emotions literature—but, rather, as a normative process.

What are the implications of this shift from emotion management as deviant to emotion management as normative? Most important, it suggests that emotion management may be not so much a response to norm violation, as the emotions literature presumes, but an aspect of individual action or even agency. This view is much more consistent with the research (reviewed earlier) indicating that emotional labor is not always (or even necessarily) associated with negative outcomes. In a culture of therapeutic individualism, emotion management may be a taken-for-granted part of life, and people thus may be able to engage in it in ways that are not damaging to the self. In other words, emotion management per se may not be the problem we have assumed. Further, the view that implicitly privileges so-called spontaneous emotion is called into question by these arguments. If the authentic self is a product of emotion work, in what sense can we say that managed emotions are less authentic?

ties and sense of themselves, evidence suggests that these processes are taking place. In fact, because emotional labor seems to implicate the self so directly, it is likely that workers' involvement with emotional labor shapes them in ways only hinted at in current studies. In her most recent book, Hochschild (1997) argues that work is becoming a more important arena in people's lives. If so, the impact of emotional labor on and off the job is likely to grow. Understanding the consequences of emotional labor thus remains an important topic for the future. We need new frameworks to take us into the next century.

CONCLUSION

By all indicators, emotional labor is a requirement of more and more occupations. References to "soft skills," "interpersonal skills," or simply "people work" contain an admission that the job requires some kind of emotional labor. The process of conceptualizing these job requirements owes its start to Hochschild's important work (1979, 1983). The present article aimed not so much to assess whether her claims were accurate as to examine the ways in which later researchers have explored some of her ideas.

This research has revealed the degree to which jobs carry expectations for workers' emotional demeanors and some of the psychosocial consequences of these expectations. While we need to know more about how these expectations become attached to, or detached from, workers' identi-

References

Adelman, Pamela K. 1995. Emotional Labor as a Potential Source of Job Stress. In *Organizational Risk Factors for Job Stress*, ed. Steven L. Sauter and Lawrence R. Murphy. Washington, DC: American Psychological Association.

Albrecht, Karl and Ron Zemke. 1985. *Service America! Doing Business in the New Economy*. Homewood, IL: Dow Jones–Irwin.

Ashforth, Blake E. and Ronald H. Humphrey. 1993. Emotional Labor in Service Roles: The Influence of Identity. *Academy of Management Review* 18:88-115.

Bulan, Heather Ferguson, Rebecca J. Erickson, and Amy S. Wharton. 1997. Doing for Others on the Job: The Affective Requirements of Service Work, Gender, and Emotional Well-Being. *Social Problems* 44:701-23.

England, Paula. 1992. *Comparable Worth: Theories and Evidence*. New York: Aldine.

Erickson, Rebecca J. 1994. Our Society, Our Selves: Becoming Authentic in an Inauthentic World. *Advanced Development Journal* 6:27-39.

———. Forthcoming. Putting Emotions to Work (or, Coming to Terms with a Contradiction in Terms). *Social Perspectives on Emotion.*

Erickson, Rebecca J. and Amy S. Wharton. 1997. Inauthenticity and Depression: Assessing the Consequences of Interactive Service Work. *Work and Occupations* 24:188-213.

Gaines, Jeannie and John M. Jermier. 1983. Emotional Exhaustion in a High-Stress Organization. *Academy of Management Journal* 26:567-86.

Hochschild, Arlie Russell. 1979. Emotion Work, Feeling Rules, and Social Structure. *American Journal of Sociology* 85:551-75.

———. 1983. *The Managed Heart: Commercialization of Human Feeling.* Berkeley: University of California Press.

———. 1997. *The Time Bind: When Work Becomes Home and Home Becomes Work.* New York: Metropolitan Books.

Kahn, R. L., D. M. Wolfe, R. P. Quinn, and J. D. Snoek. 1964. *Organizational Stress: Studies in Role Conflict and Ambiguity.* New York: John Wiley.

Kalleberg, Arne and Ivar Berg. 1987. *Work and Industry.* New York: Plenum.

Kelly, R. F. and P. Voydanoff. 1985. Work/Family Role Strain Among Employed Parents. *Family Relations* 34:367-74.

Leidner, Robin. 1993. *Fast Food, Fast Talk: Service Work and the Routinization of Everyday Life.* Berkeley: University of California Press.

Marks, Stephen R. 1994. Intimacy in the Public Realm: The Case of Co-Workers. *Social Forces* 72:843-58.

Maslach, Christina. 1976. Burned-Out. *Human Relations* 5:16-22.

Maslach, Christina and Susan E. Jackson. 1982. The Burn-Out Syndrome in the Health Professions. In *Social Psychology of Health and Illness*, ed. G. Sanders and J. Suls. Hillsdale, NJ: Lawrence Erlbaum.

Maslach, Christina and Ayala Pines. 1977. The Burn-Out Syndrome in the Day Care Setting. *Child Care Quarterly* 6:100-113.

Miles, R. H. 1980. Organization Boundary-Roles. In *Current Concerns in Occupational Stress*, ed. C. L. Cooper and R. Payne. New York: John Wiley.

Mumby, Dennis K. and Linda L. Putnam. 1992. The Politics of Emotion: A Feminist Reading of Bounded Rationality. *Academy of Management Review* 17:465-86.

Parsons, Talcott. 1951. *The Social System.* Glencoe, IL: Free Press.

Paules, Greta Foff. 1991. *Dishing It Out: Power and Resistance Among Waitresses in a New Jersey Restaurant.* Philadelphia: Temple University Press.

Pierce, Jennifer L. 1995. *Gender Trials: Emotional Lives in Contemporary Law Firms.* Berkeley: University of California Press.

Rosenberg, Morris. 1990. Reflexivity and Emotion. *Social Psychology Quarterly* 53:3-12.

Schwalbe, Michael. 1996. *Unlocking the Iron Cage: The Men's Movement, Gender Politics, and American Culture.* New York: Oxford University Press.

Smith, Allen C., III and Sherryl Kleinman. 1989. Managing Emotions in Medical School: Students' Contacts with the Living and the Dead. *Social Psychology Quarterly* 52:56-69.

Steinberg, Ronnie J. and Deborah M. Figart. 1996. Exploring Emotional Labor. Paper presented at the summer conference of the International Association for Feminist Economics, Washington, DC.

————. 1997. The Range of Emotional Labor at the Workplace: A Job Content Analysis. Paper presented at the annual meeting of the Eastern Sociological Association, Baltimore, MD.

Sutton, Robert I. 1991. Maintaining Norms About Expressed Emotions: The Case of Bill Collectors. *Administrative Science Quarterly* 36(June): 245-68.

Sutton, Robert I. and Anat Rafaeli. 1988. Untangling the Relationship Between Displayed Emotions and Organizational Sales: The Case of Convenience Stores. *Academy of Management Journal* 31(3):461-87.

Wharton, Amy S. 1993. The Affective Consequences of Service Work: Managing Emotions on the Job. *Work and Occupations* 20(2):205-32.

Wharton, Amy S. and James N. Baron. 1987. So Happy Together? The Impact of Gender Segregation on Men at Work. *American Sociological Review* 52:574-87.

————. 1991. Satisfaction? The Psychological Impact of Gender Segregation on Women at Work. *Sociological Quarterly* 32:365-88.

Wharton, Amy S. and Rebecca J. Erickson. 1995. The Consequences of Caring: Exploring the Links Between Women's Job and Family Emotion Work. *Sociological Quarterly* 36:273-96.

ANNALS, *AAPSS*, **561**, January 1999

Emotional Demands at Work:
A Job Content Analysis

By RONNIE J. STEINBERG and DEBORAH M. FIGART

ABSTRACT: Using qualitative and quantitative evidence from studies of several occupations in the public sector, the authors evaluate dimensions of emotional labor in the content of work performed by registered nurses, police officers, and managers. Two indexes are constructed to measure a range of emotional skills and demands found in these historically female and male jobs. The authors find that the emotional labor required of police officers and registered nurses is comparable despite the cultural ideology that portrays these jobs as requiring gender-specific skills. The authors demonstrate the utility and increased accuracy of using an augmented conceptualization of emotional labor to measure what employees actually do in performing their jobs. It is proposed that those studying emotional labor abandon their reliance on preconceived stereotypes of femininity when studying emotional labor, especially in service sector jobs.

Ronnie J. Steinberg is professor of sociology and director of the Women's Studies Program at Vanderbilt University. She is the author, coauthor, or editor of three books and over 35 articles on feminist reforms, employment policies, and gender-based labor market inequality. She received the Max Weber Award from the section on Occupations, Organization and Work of the American Sociological Association for her work (with Jerry Jacobs) on compensating differentials and wage discrimination.

Deborah M. Figart is associate professor of economics at Richard Stockton College. Her previous research has been published in Review of Social Economy, Work and Occupations, Feminist Economics, Journal of Economic Issues, *and other journals and collected volumes. She is associate editor of the* Encyclopedia of Political Economy.

EMOTIONS are stereotypically associated with femininity. Accordingly, emotional labor has typically been discussed in relation to historically female jobs, especially in the service economy. Most of the job categories identified by Arlie Hochschild as requiring a high degree of emotional labor are female-dominated jobs: registered nurses, occupational therapists, social workers, teachers, counselors, and retail sales workers, to cite a few examples (Hochschild 1983, app. C). Although her own research examined both flight attendants and bill collectors, her analysis of flight attendants was much more fully developed. Ensuing case study research on emotional labor, some of which is summarized in other articles in this volume, has also focused on this gendered aspect of emotional labor.

Feminist social scientists have emphasized the importance of (typically nonpaid) nurturing, caring, and listening tasks as gendered work (see, for example, England and Farkas 1986; Hall 1993; Glazer 1993; DeVault 1991; Folbre 1995; Himmelweit 1995). The emotional demands within male-dominated fields have been undertheorized, perhaps because it is assumed that, with the exception of anger, emotions are gendered as female. In this project, we question the empirical validity of the assumptions embedded in this past research. Specifically, we use a unique data set to ascertain whether historically male jobs require similar kinds of emotional labor as historically female work. We look at the degree to which different dimensions of emotional labor are found in female

and male jobs. To do so, we endeavor to define emotional labor more broadly by examining what it is, who does it, and its scope within and across jobs. We also seek to determine if gender mediates the emotional labor content of jobs and, if so, how.

Although recognizing and defining emotional labor have expanded scholarly conceptions of work, most previous research has failed to specify or measure the skills and job demands required in the performance of emotional labor, whether the work is performed for pay in the labor market, in the home, or as volunteer work. Our research offers a first corrective to this shortcoming by measuring specific emotional skills and demands in paid employment and by comparing these content characteristics across historically female and male job classes. A data set collected in the process of developing a job evaluation system free of gender bias, the Gender Neutral Comparison System (GNCS), was our means to investigate emotional labor across jobs hierarchically and across occupational categories by gender type.

We begin this article by allowing employees to speak for themselves about what they do on the job through content analysis of several open-ended questions. We then conduct a quantitative analysis of emotional labor across jobs, through the use of an emotional labor index and an emotional demands index constructed from a series of specific closed-ended questions. On the basis of findings, we conclude that both male and female jobs can incorporate similar ranges and degrees of emotional labor. Since emotional labor has usually been associated with historically female work, these findings suggest that social scientists privilege dimensions of a job that are consistent with its sex type. As a result, our understanding of the range of job content found in historically female and male jobs may be inaccurately mediated by our commonsense understandings of the skills and effort associated with images of masculinity and femininity.

A PUBLIC EMPLOYER
PROVIDES THE SETTING

We draw our data from a portion of the responses to an 82-page job content questionnaire. The questionnaire was developed in conjunction with a legal decision that required the regional municipality of Haldimand-Norfolk in Ontario, Canada, to implement a gender-neutral job comparison system consistent with the Ontario Pay Equity Act, effective in 1988. (See Steinberg, this volume, for a fuller description of the construction and contours of this questionnaire and the political conditions under which it was developed.) Haldimand-Norfolk comprises three towns, two townships, and one city with a population of approximately 94,000 residents. Roughly 700 of the municipality's employees, working for 12 executive departments, are covered by the act. The questionnaire was implemented to resolve a conflict between the Ontario Nurses' Association and the municipality over the implementation of the Pay Equity Act. After two sets of administrative court proceed-

ings and an impasse in the implementation of the decisions, one of the present coauthors, Ronnie Steinberg, was retained by the government agency responsible for implementation of the Pay Equity Act to develop a new, gender-neutral instrument for describing and evaluating job content consistent with legal guidelines: the GNCS.

A gender-neutral system corrects for systematic gender discrimination in compensation. Because of the way traditional job evaluation systems are constructed, they have incorporated cultural assumptions that rationalize gendered wage hierarchies (Steinberg 1992). The GNCS not only removes the sources of gender bias from traditional job evaluation but also makes visible and positively values the job content associated with systematically undervalued, historically female work. The basic premise is that all jobs must be evaluated and assigned points according to a uniform set of criteria (called factors and factor weights) that recognize and positively value characteristics differentially associated with traditionally female jobs (Steinberg and Walter 1992; Steinberg and Jacobs 1994).

The new system was designed to measure the job content of a broad range of job classes found in the municipality of Haldimand-Norfolk, including job classes held by registered nurses. It was completed in 1994.[1] The data collected in developing this system provide a rich source of information from which it is possible to evaluate the content of a variety of job classes, especially those found in public sector or health sector jobs.

The GNCS is unique in its measurement of job traits left invisible in traditional job evaluation instruments, such as emotional labor.

MEASURING EMOTIONAL CONTENT WITHIN JOBS

To design the instrument measuring job content, focus groups were conducted with four different job classes of registered nurses. These classes included registered nurses working in homes for the aged, public health nurses specializing in education, home health care nurses, and clinical registered nurses. In conjunction with a related study, several focus groups were conducted with 22 registered nurses working in different specialized departments of three provincial hospitals. The job content questionnaire, pilot-tested in 1992 and completed in 1993, was divided into sections that corresponded, with a few exceptions, to four broad categories of job content identified by the Pay Equity Act: skills, effort, responsibilities, and undesirable working conditions.

The job content questionnaire was distributed to 31 anonymous incumbents in 22 additional job classes (4 female and 18 male) in the municipality (see appendix). Employees spent between four and seven hours filling out the questionnaire. After completing this version of the job content questionnaire, each incumbent who filled out the questionnaire met with the project director for follow-up interviews either as individuals or in focus groups lasting approximately four hours.

Although the job content questionnaire was not designed explicitly for investigating emotional labor as theorized by Hochschild and other sociologists, organizational psychologists, and economists, it can be used for such analysis. It is a broad-based questionnaire for the purpose of comparing the job content in male- and female-dominated jobs. The data collection instrument does contain numerous, very specific questions addressed to emotional skills, as well as a specific section capturing emotional demands. The questionnaire combines multiple-choice questions with open-ended questions; it offers scales measuring the degree to which the job content is performed; it requests respondents to provide examples drawn from actual events on their job to ground their choices on closed-ended questions. Because of this design, we can not only glean the presence or absence of emotional labor but also measure its frequency and intensity. We are also able to ground these questionnaire responses in the specific language used by the job incumbents to describe their performance of emotional labor. For instance, employees were asked how often they communicate on a face-to-face basis with people who are upset, angry, threatening, hostile, or confused. They are then asked to provide examples of situations and circumstances in which they do so.

For this analysis of emotional labor, we drew on the respondents' answers to questions from the job content questionnaire regarding three major job content factors: communication skills, human relations skills, and emotional demands. The section of the questionnaire on communication skills seeks information regarding nonverbal communication and listening skills in addition to reading and writing requirements and speaking skills. It asks questions about the context within which communication takes place. Employees were asked, for example, to ascertain the degree of listening skills in their jobs that may involve emotion management. Incumbents were asked how often they were required to interact face-to-face with citizens or clients, how frequently they had to accurately understand their needs in sensitive or conflicting circumstances, or how often it was necessary to understand people such as agitated clients whether individually or in groups. The set of questions regarding human relations skills measures the proficiency required to work with or care for others and to shape, affect, or influence their actions or decisions. Employees were asked to describe the extent of their work that involved courtesy and tact, nurturance and reassurance, compassion, empathy, rapport, building trust, persuading, mediating, advising, and counseling.

The emotional demands factor measures the intensity and frequency of effort encompassing psychological stress and risk. Usually the emotional effort results from dealing directly with people who are in emotional and physical need, temporarily or permanently psychologically impaired, or dangerous. Emotional demands can also result from working in sensitive or controversial circumstances. Questions about emotional demands asked how often incumbents of the job interacted in person or over the telephone with clients, patients, and members of the public who were uncooperative, confused, upset, angry, abusive, and so forth. These questions also probed for the frequency with which these employees were in situations that required them to be nice when they did not feel like it. It also inquired about the frequency with which and the circumstances under which they told people things they did not want to hear. While the measurement of human relations skills includes the necessary skills required in the performance of supervisory jobs, the set of questions regarding emotional demands focuses more heavily on interactions with people outside the organization and does not measure the effort involved in dealing with direct coworkers, supervisors, or subordinates.

To generate the results, we use both qualitative and quantitative evidence from the job content questionnaire to evaluate how the job content for these positions fit with prior definitions and conceptual understandings of emotional labor. We also review the focus group discussions that substantiate the themes found in the questionnaires. Our analysis examines 17 of the 70 job classes in the municipality, with an emphasis on comparing the four classes of work performed by registered nurses and the work of two classes of police officers, in part due to the obvious emotional demands of these jobs. Nearly all of these jobs deal with the public or clients. We also examine the emotional skills and demands required in 11 managerial and supervisory single-incumbent job classes. Emotional labor in these jobs is more likely to hinge on the dynamics of intra-organizational interactions.

SKILLS AND DEMANDS: QUALITATIVE EVIDENCE OF EMOTIONAL LABOR

In reviewing the responses to the open-ended questions that asked employees for examples of the human relations skills, communication skills, and emotional demands necessary to perform their jobs, we found striking similarities across job categories. The emotional labor required of police officers and registered nurses is comparable despite the cultural ideology that portrays these jobs as requiring gender-specific skills. Registered nurses, but not police officers, are viewed as empathetic and sensitive to those with whom they come in contact. Police officers are assumed to deal with hostile and threatening situations. A more complicated story emerges from the job content analysis, however.

Face-to-face contact: Reading the emotions of others

Both registered nurses and police officers need communication skills, human relations skills, and physical skills to perform their jobs, and both jobs entail considerable emotional demands. Public health nurses, for example, spend many hours on the road visiting homes, schools, and clinics, in addition to reporting to an office where they receive supervision and are assigned work. In the job content questionnaires, the nurses report stressful, frustrating, and sometimes even dangerous work. Moreover, no two days are the same when dealing with a variety of clients and situations such as the elderly, adults with diseases and illnesses, pregnant teens, angry parents, sick infants, abusive men, and physically and emotionally disabled individuals. They feel the need to be adept in diplomacy and in showing warmth and empathy.

A police sergeant faces similar conditions when "dealing with people from all walks of life [where it is] necessary to identify and communicate with, in less than desirable circumstances." Like public health nurses, police sergeants report to their precinct for work assignments and supervision but spend the major portion of their workday in frontline work.

In performing emotional labor through face-to-face or voice-to-voice contact, employees often read emotions of others through observable facial and bodily displays (Hochschild 1983). Both registered nurses and police officers must be highly proficient at these human relations skills to perform their job well. For this aspect of emotional demands, the similarities across female- and male-dominated job categories are illustrated in Table 1. Job incumbents in the nursing and law enforcement professions must continuously assess verbal and nonverbal clues in order to assess a situation involving the physical, mental, or emotional well-being of others as well as of themselves. For instance, both nurses and constables report that they may be ascertaining whether an

TABLE 1
READING THE EMOTIONS OF OTHERS

Clinical registered nurse:
"[We] must be able to recognize what is conveyed to us by what is shown by way of body language [and] must be able to give advice on what we have been told either verbally or nonverbally," all without imposing "our own ideals and morals on those we are counseling."

Police sergeant:
"You have to listen not only to what is actually being said, but also what is not being said as well as evaluating temperament and body language," while "being able to listen to people [with] whom you have nothing in common or agreement but duty requires it."

Public health nurse:
"During an assessment of an individual you must observe (sight) individual and non-verbal cues, must hear (and record) what client says, smell for alcohol on his or her breath, [discern possible] ketoacidosis (diabetic?)."

Constable:
Among the skills of the job are "how to diffuse a domestic dispute; know when a person is impaired by alcohol or drugs; know when [a person] is subject to arrest under the Mental Health Act; the skill of knowing when your life or the life of a civilian may be in danger."

havior. For registered nurses and law enforcement officials, this involves, for example, encouraging clients or citizens to take medication or to move out of a dangerous or abusive domestic situation, or to be a witness to or confess a crime. Clearly, this objective of emotional labor spans these traditionally male and female jobs. These requirements are also found at different levels of organizational authority. Managers may have less one-on-one contact with clients but more contact with coworkers and with members of the public.

Table 2 gives examples of the management of the emotions of others in order to motivate their behavior in five female- and male-dominated job classes. These range from supervisors who foster a change in work habits or procedures (the staff sergeant, the accounting supervisor, and the occupational health and safety adviser) to a public health nurse and a registered nurse in a home for the aged who promote healthful lifestyles. A recycling coordinator might be considered to be encouraging both a healthful lifestyle and a change in habits, as he reported, "I spend a good deal of time communicating with colleagues, other agencies, etc., in an effort to advance the 3Rs [reduction, reuse, recycling] efforts both locally and provincially." Of course, the recycling coordinator also works with individuals and groups residing in the municipality to motivate them to change their habits with respect to garbage maintenance and collection. Unlike public health nurses who are on the road a lot, home care case managers spend more of their work-

individual is under the influence of drugs or alcohol, is mentally or physically impaired or injured, or is physically aggressive. Such work could be a matter of routine or could be a response to a crisis or a confrontation.

Managing the emotions of others

Another objective of emotional labor is to produce, as Arlie Hochschild (1983) puts it, "the proper state of mind in others" (7), to get other employees or clients to change their be-

TABLE 2
MANAGING THE EMOTIONS OF OTHERS TO MOTIVATE BEHAVIOR

Staff sergeant:
  "My job is trying to change employee work habits and motivate them to do a better job; when this does not work, I . . . become a disciplinary person who forces change [in] work habits, etc."
Public health nurse:
  An especially trying situation occurs when "elderly who are living in an unsafe, unclean environment . . . do not want to leave their home—[it] is very emotionally demanding when you are trying to get them to make healthy changes and decisions."
Accounting supervisor:
  "[I must] convince regional staff to follow proper accounting procedures [even when the staff feels such procedures] appear to add more work than necessary."
Registered nurse in a home for the aged:
  A nurse must perform emotional labor on "residents to persuade them to have vaccination or medication that they may not want" and on "family members who cannot deal with resident status or change in resident condition."
Occupational health and safety adviser
  "I must exercise considerable tact to motivate change," nurturance in order to "gain acceptance and credibility," and persuasion to "influence change" at the workplace.

week performing typically managerial tasks at their offices, as they are responsible for overseeing all aspects of home care. Yet they, too, must conduct home visits with their clients. Another requirement of the job is to engage in public speaking to convey the advantages of home care by way of advertising services, a job demand analogous to that of sales workers' performing emotional labor to moti-

vate people to purchase products or services (see Sutton and Rafaeli 1988; Rafaeli 1989; Leidner 1991, 1993).

Although conflict and negotiation are more commonly associated with police work, registered nurses also must manage confrontations. Public health nurses have described especially trying situations involving emotional demands, as when a client's needs conflict with the needs the nurse perceives for him or her or even when the client's needs conflict with the nurse's own needs. One specific instance suggested by a public health nurse is when a physically abused client desires the security of love or the abusive relationship and, instead, the nurse believes that the security of escaping the abuse and seeking safety is paramount. Indeed, registered nurses, claims Nicky James (1989), often tell clients things they do not want to hear. Such a situation is found in the work of the AIDS/STD educator, who counsels clients about sexually transmitted diseases (STDs) and is trying to get individuals to practice safe sex.

*Employees' management
of their own emotions,
emotional displays, and acting*

The definition of emotional labor involves the emotions of the employee performing the labor as well as the emotions of those to whom these emotions are addressed. It involves efforts to understand others, perhaps having empathy with their situation (Hochschild 1979, 1983; England and Farkas 1986). These tasks require an employee to perform what has been termed surface acting and deep acting. Employees may have to suppress their own emotions while performing their work, as demonstrated in earlier research on nurses, police detectives, bill collectors, and paralegals (Smith 1988; James 1989; Stenross and Kleinman 1989; Sutton 1991; Rafaeli and Sutton 1991; Pierce 1995). Holding back one's own emotion and showing warmth, empathy, and understanding at the same time may make it difficult to turn these sentiments on and off, according to incumbents in several occupations illustrated in Table 3.

A police sergeant and an AIDS/STD educator both must be nonjudgmental while showing concern and understanding. No matter how trivial, unimportant, or difficult a situation seems to a police constable or a public health nurse, both must understand the feelings and concerns of the victim or client. Workers who communicate with an agitated or angry public often create emotional displays as part of their job. For instance, although a water or sewer superintendent does not have constant contact with the public, he or she does on occasion deal by telephone with consumers who are accusatory and angry about water quality or water main breaks. It is a requirement of this job to reassure the constituent and thus defuse the anger being expressed. Similar situations were reported by many who responded to the job content questionnaires.

TABLE 3
SUPPRESSING EMOTIONS, CREATING EMOTIONAL DISPLAYS

AIDS/STD educator:

"Clients may wish to discuss many issues involving health and/or interpersonal relationships. I must listen actively to show interest and understanding."

"I must be very 'nonjudgmental' when dealing with the AIDS/STD client population. I must establish a trusting relationship in order to counsel and support these people."

Police sergeant:

"We are required to [act] unemotional[ly] in some situations and to detach and then the defence of showing hardness is criticized or commented. It's difficult to turn it off and on."

Constable:

"During interview of a complainant, although the information may seem trivial or possibly unimportant to me, I have to put myself in [the other person's] position, and then provide an explanation or solution."

Public health nurse:

Human relations skills required include "diplomacy with angry clients . . . diplomacy with physicians when discussing alterations to treatment . . . [and] warmth, empathy, and respect to clients and coworkers." Emotional demands include "when a client's needs are conflicting with the needs you perceive for the client (e.g., love versus security and safety) [in the case of abuse]."

COMPARISONS ACROSS JOBS: CREATING AN INDEX OF EMOTIONAL LABOR

Previous studies have most often treated emotional labor as a dichotomous variable in characterizing jobs. This study is a first attempt to develop a continuous variable measuring the emotional content of various jobs. An index was constructed based on 55 questions in which employees were presented with a five-point scale for measuring the frequency with which they were required to perform specific types of emotional tasks. These questions were garnered from three sections of the job content questionnaire relating to communication skills, human relations skills, and emotional demands as previously described. The mean of employees' self-reported assessment of these dimensions of emotional labor was calculated in constructing an emotional labor index (EL index) ranging from one to five, with one indicating few emotional labor requirements. An emotional demands index (ED index) was constructed based on the mean score on a subset of 22 questions from the emotional demands section of the questionnaire. This second index scores the emotional demands of the jobs from one to five, with one indicating few emotional demands requirements.

To report the indexes, we selected three broad occupational categories from the Haldimand-Norfolk employees who filled out job content questionnaires: registered nurses, police officers, and a varied group of managers and directors. The first class encompasses historically female occupations; the second two job classes are historically male occupations. The first two categories included line supervisors such as case managers and staff sergeants; managers and directors included higher-level administrative positions. The mean score of the EL index and ED index for employees in each

TABLE 4

INDEXES OF EMOTIONAL LABOR AND EMOTIONAL DEMANDS

Occupation	EL Index	ED Index
Registered nurses	2.9382	2.9593
	(0.4638)	(0.6752)
Public health nurses	3.3081	3.0000
Clinical nurses	2.0833	2.2558
Nurses, homes for the aged	3.3727	3.6591
Home care case managers	3.2364	3.5227
Police	2.4766	2.4636
	(0.2155)	(0.2504)
Constables	2.6606	2.5758
Sergeants (police and staff)	2.1956	2.2955
Managers	1.8390	1.2403
	(0.1639)	(0.0274)

NOTE: σ^2 in parentheses.

of these three categories was calculated and statistical tests were performed to ascertain whether these broad categories differed significantly in emotional labor and emotional demands. Specifically, single-factor analysis of variance (ANOVA) tests were performed to determine whether the sample means represented different populations.

Table 4 presents the EL index and ED index for the three broad occupational categories as well as the variance within each category. Specific categories of registered nurses and police officers, the two occupations most represented in the data sample, are also depicted. Both the nursing and police positions require substantially higher degrees of emotional labor and demand than the managerial positions, according to these indexes. There is consistency between the EL index and ED index for various job categories, indicating that jobs that

TABLE 5
EMOTIONAL LABOR: ANALYSIS OF VARIANCE

	SS	df	MS	F
Nurses-police-managers				
Between groups	4.9753	2	2.4877	7.8525***
Within groups	6.0191	19	0.31GB	
Nurses-police				
Between groups	0.7102	1	0.7102	1.8330
Within groups	5.0360	13	0.3874	
Nurses-managers				
Between groups	4.9750	1	4.9750	14.4703***
Within groups	5.1571	15	0.3438	
Police-managers				
Between groups	1.1858	1	1.1858	6.4265*
Within groups	1.8452	10	0.1845	

NOTE: The mean squares (MS) is found by dividing the sum of squares (SS) by the appropriate degrees of freedom (df) and is used to calculate the F ratio.
$*p < .05. **p < .01. ***p < .005.$

require emotional skills are also emotionally demanding. The one exception to this pattern is found in the managerial/supervisory class. For these jobs, the score for emotional demands is somewhat lower than for emotional labor. These findings warrant further investigation in subsequent analyses. To assess whether the differences between job categories are statistically significant, further tests were conducted.

The F ratios in the ANOVA summary tables (Tables 5 and 6) indicate that the EL and ED indexes of the three broad job categories are statistically different at a high level of significance. The index of at least one of these occupations varies substantially from the mean of all the jobs combined. Therefore, pair-wise ANOVA tests were conducted to ferret out the source of variation. As Tables 5 and 6 indicate, the registered nurses and police officers are not statistically different at the level of their emotional labor and emotional de-

mands content. Instead, what is underlying the difference between all three groups is the lower emotional labor required in management. Managers and directors differ significantly from both registered nurses and police officers, as shown in the tables.

In Table 5, the sum of squares (SS) shows that there is more variance in emotional labor within each of the broad occupational categories than between groups in each of the four comparisons. That is, the degree of emotional labor differs between registered nurses themselves more than the nurses as a group differ from other groups. A helpful analogy is measures of human height. There is more variation between men and between women than between male and female average heights. However, this is not the case for emotional demands in Table 6, a narrower index. Between-group variance is higher than within-group variance for all the emotional de-

TABLE 6
EMOTIONAL DEMANDS: ANALYSIS OF VARIANCE

	SS	df	MS	F
Nurses-police-managers				
Between groups	12.3420	2	6.1710	16.1900***
Within groups	7.2421	19	0.3812	
Nurses-police				
Between groups	0.8189	1	0.8189	1.5041
Within groups	7.0780	13	0.5445	
Nurses-managers				
Between groups	12.1681	1	12.1680	29.2478***
Within groups	6.2405	15	0.4160	
Police-managers				
Between groups	4.3653	1	4.3653	37.4486***
Within groups	1.1657	10	0.1166	

NOTE: The mean squares (MS) is found by dividing the sum of squares (SS) by the appropriate degrees of freedom (df) and is used to calculate the F ratio.
$*p < .05. **p < .01. ***p < .005.$

mands comparisons that incorporate the managerial category. Only the nurses-police pair-wise comparison has more variance within groups than between groups. In other words, the emotional demands of managers deviate most from the other two service jobs in the study.

These indexes are constructed from self-reported data on the emotional labor content of jobs. There are drawbacks to this methodology, especially when dealing with a small sample. It is possible that we are underestimating the quantity of emotional labor required in certain jobs due to sample selection. For example, someone who is very good at dispelling or diverting client anger may not report dealing with a lot of angry people, while a typical incumbent in the job class would have to. Also, gender-identity issues surrounding the selection of such a stereotypical masculine job as police officer or such a stereotypical female job as registered nurse might affect the way incum-

bents of these jobs respond to questions about emotional skills and demands. However, if this selection bias affected the results, we would expect registered nurses to have overstated the emotional labor involved in their jobs and the police officers to have understated their emotional labor. Even if selection bias is affecting the results, it would not change our conclusions but further confirm them. Nonetheless, the conclusions drawn from this analysis should be viewed as only a first attempt at measuring the dimensions of emotional labor more precisely.

CONCLUSION

In the literature on emotional labor, we have found that most researchers seem to operationalize the unit of analysis as the job, following the approach first used by Arlie Hochschild. In other words, social scientists investigate emotional labor by selecting a job that, on its face, involves or does not involve emotional labor. Even those scholars who do go beyond this approach to base their findings on more measures of job content, however, almost always restrict their understanding of emotional labor to nurturance or to work with clients, patients, or students. While we recognize that they have utilized the best data that have as yet been collected or are available, we consider these measures limited in that they have built into them taken-for-granted gendered assumptions about what constitutes emotional work and about who is most likely to perform it. Thus these analyses of emotional labor rely upon stereotypical associations of women with emotional labor, deriving from the organization of social reproduction.

Our definition of emotional labor focuses on the management of emotions, one's own and others', in order to accomplish something that is required in the normal performance of a particular job. In some service-delivery occupations, emotional labor is part of the product itself. Service sector occupations provide the most obvious examples of jobs with emotional labor. Yet emotional labor can also be part of the work process without being embedded in the final product.

This more complicated understanding of emotional labor poses further questions for research inquiry. To what extent are the types of emotional skills, demands, and responsibilities similar or different by gender of the job? Is there more variation within female-dominated jobs or within male-dominated jobs than between male-dominated and female-dominated jobs? Which jobs involve more complex emotional demands, and why?

Our analysis focuses on the range of emotional skills and effort as expressed in specific actions and behaviors found in a small group of job classes. It also assesses variations in emotional labor across job categories. Our findings indicate that we should move beyond the simple association of femaleness with emotional labor to analyze the types of emotional labor associated with jobs gendered both female and male. As this and other research has shown, emotional labor and emotional demands are not confined primarily to female occupations.

The qualitative evidence from the job content surveys demonstrates that occupations with very different gender labels can contain similar dimensions of emotional skills and demands. The more systematic quantitative analysis of emotional skills and emotional demands strengthens the qualitative evidence. The two indexes of emotional labor involved in the work of registered nurses and police officers were not statistically different. Yet there appears to be a social class dimension to emotional labor in that, at least in our preliminary analysis, line jobs in the service sector (public service) have higher emotional labor requirements than do management jobs. By demonstrating that emotional labor can be quantified, rather than treated either as a specific job or as a dichotomous variable, this study provides a framework for future research relating the degree of emotional job requirements to other variables, such as pay, profits, productivity, and employee well-being.

Appendix:
Job Classes in Questionnaire

Public health nurse
Clinical nurse
Registered nurse (homes for the aged)
AIDS/STD educator
Home care case manager
Police sergeant
Police constable
Staff sergeant
Public health inspector
Manager of technical services
   (water and sewer operations)
Health Department inspection
   supervisor
Water or sewer superintendent
Director of economic development
Supervisor of accounting
Manager of accounting
Director of Addictions Division
Occupational health and safety
   adviser
Party chief
Policy supervisor
Project manager
Director of roads
Manager of design construction
   and waste management

Note

1. The Haldimand-Norfolk Gender Neutral Comparison System (GNCS) is built on a body of work in feminist job evaluation. There have been a number of attempts to reconstruct traditional job evaluation systems to remove gender bias. The GNCS was developed after reviewing several systems of job evaluation constructed for pay equity as well as earlier plans of the Ontario Nurses' Association (see Steinberg and Walter 1992 for a discussion).

References

DeVault, Marjorie L. 1991. *Feeding the Family: The Social Organization of Caring as Gendered Work*. Chicago: University of Chicago Press.

England, Paula and George Farkas. 1986. *Households, Employment, and Gender: A Social, Economic, and Demographic View*. New York: Aldine.

Folbre, Nancy. 1995. "Holding Hands at Midnight": The Paradox of Caring Labor. *Feminist Economics* 1(1):73-92.

Glazer, Nona Y. 1993. *Women's Paid and Unpaid Labor: The Work Transfer in Health Care and Retailing*. Philadelphia: Temple University Press.

Hall, Elaine J. 1993. Smiling, Deferring, and Flirting: Doing Gender by Giving "Good Service." *Work and Occupations* 20(4):452-71.

Himmelweit, Susan. 1995. The Discovery of "Unpaid Work": The Social Consequences of the Expansion of "Work." *Feminist Economics* 1(2):1-19.

Hochschild, Arlie Russell. 1979. Emotion Work, Feeling Rules, and Social Structure. *American Journal of Sociology* 85(3):551-75.

———. 1983. *The Managed Heart: Commercialization of Human Feeling*. Berkeley: University of California Press.

James, Nicky. 1989. Emotional Labour: Skill and Work in the Social Regulation of Feelings. *Sociological Review* 5:15-42.

Leidner, Robin. 1991. Selling Hamburgers and Selling Insurance: Gender, Work, and Identity in Interactive Service Jobs. *Gender & Society* 5(2):154-77.

———. 1993. *Fast Food, Fast Talk: Service Work and the Routinization of Everyday Life*. Berkeley: University of California Press.

Pierce, Jennifer L. 1995. *Gender Trials: Emotional Lives in Contemporary*

Law Firms. Berkeley: University of California Press.

Rafaeli, Anat. 1989. When Cashiers Meet Customers: An Analysis of the Role of Supermarket Cashiers. *Academy of Management Journal* 32(2):245-73.

Rafaeli, Anat and Robert I. Sutton. 1991. Emotional Contrast Strategies as Means of Social Influence: Lessons from Criminal Interrogators and Bill Collectors. *Academy of Management Journal* 34(4):749-75.

Smith, Pam. 1988. The Emotional Labor of Nursing. *Nursing Times* 84:50-51.

Steinberg, Ronnie J. 1992. Gendered Institutions: Cultural Lag and Gender Bias in the Hay System of Job Evaluation. *Work and Occupations* 19(4): 387-432.

Steinberg, Ronnie J. and Jerry A. Jacobs. 1994. Pay Equity in Nonprofit Organizations: Making Women's Work Visible. In *Women, Status, and Power in the Nonprofit Sector*, ed. Michael O'Neill and Terry Odendahl. New York: John Wiley.

Steinberg, Ronnie J. and W. Lawrence Walter. 1992. Making Women's Work Visible: The Case of Nursing—First Steps in the Design of a Gender-Neutral Job Comparison System. In *Exploring the Quincentenniel: The Policy Challenges of Gender, Diversity, and International Exchange*. Washington, DC: Institute for Women's Policy Research.

Stenross, Barbara and Sherryl Kleinman. 1989. The Highs and Lows of Emotional Labor: Detectives' Encounters with Criminals and Victims. *Journal of Contemporary Ethnography* 17(4):435-52.

Sutton, Robert I. 1991. Maintaining Norms About Expressed Emotions: The Case of Bill Collectors. *Administrative Science Quarterly* 36(June): 245-68.

Sutton, Robert I. and Anat Rafaeli. 1988. Untangling the Relationship Between Displayed Emotions and Organizational Sales: The Case of Convenience Stores. *Academy of Management Journal* 31(3):461-87.

Book Department

INTERNATIONAL RELATIONS AND POLITICS

BLAIS, ANDRÉ, DONALD E. BLAKE, and STÉPHANE DION. 1997. *Government, Parties, and Public Sector Employees: Canada, United States, Britain and France.* Pp. ix, 189. Pittsburgh, PA: University of Pittsburgh Press; Montreal, Quebec: McGill-Queen's University Press. $35.00. Paperbound, $17.95.

The study reported in this book asks, for the four countries of the title, whether parties and governments of the Left are more likely to implement policies that are favorable to their public sector employees than are parties and governments of the Right. Quantitative data are arrayed in a standard manner for comparative analysis, although there is less parallelism in the qualitative aspects of discussion. The book contains about 40 tables. The authors are three senior and accomplished Canadian political scientists. Since 1996 Professor Dion has been Minister Dion, holding the new ministerial portfolio for intergovernmental affairs.

Within countries, the quantitative data are arrayed for the 40 years up to the late 1980s. The authors provide thumbnail descriptions of patterns of public sector employment and of party structure in each country. The quantitative variables are the quantity of public sector employment and wages. Both quantitative and qualitative information is presented on the other factors of interest: unionization and bargaining rights, and political activism rights. The authors also look at the content of party positions. Society-centered and state-centered perspectives are offered. In the first, the idea is that leftist rulers would reward public sector employees for their voting support. The authors interpret the second perspective as insisting that parties are "not necessarily hostages to their clientele" (10).

In their conclusion, the authors report that their work involved 34 general tests of the same hypothesis. They find that governments of the Left are generally somewhat more generous on the variables assessed, with nuances: for example, leftist and center parties tend to slightly expand public sector employment but are not notably more generous in overall wage settlements. The authors interpret this to mean that expansion by leftist politicians of public sector capacity may be ideological-instrumental, as opposed to a response to voters' pressure or even a sympathetic response (the society-centered perspective) due to the heavier presence in leftist parties of former public servants. The patterns hold for both American and European cases.

The book is unfailingly clearly written and well presented. I would have, however, appreciated a more complete indication of how public sector employees are counted and arrayed in each country, particularly in the case of Canada, plus a short update at the end of each chapter for the years after data collection ended on this variable.

SHARON L. SUTHERLAND

Carleton University
Ottawa
Canada

GAMBONE, MICHAEL D. 1997. *Eisenhower, Somoza, and the Cold War in Nicaragua, 1953-1961.* Pp. xiv, 247. Westport, CT: Praeger. $65.00.

Michael D. Gambone has chosen to analyze the economic and military relations between the United States and Nicaragua during the presidency of Dwight D. Eisenhower. His study is based on archival research in the United States and in published Spanish-language sources. Gambone's purpose is to challenge those *dependencia* and world systems theorists who have suggested that the power of the United States guaranteed near absolute compliance with its interests in Latin America. Gambone argues that his examination of the Nicaraguan political milieu demonstrates that the Somoza family fashioned U.S. economic and military policies for its own purposes. Nicaragua "was more an independent actor in a bilateral relationship" than a mere client state (10). Gambone concedes, however, that the asymmetrical nature of the relationship prevented Nicaragua from being a full partner with its northern neighbor.

Unhappy over the Eisenhower administration's unwillingness to provide economic assistance, Anastasio Somoza García worked assiduously to attract European capital, diversify Nicaragua's agrobusinesses, and broaden his nation's trading relationships. By 1961, Nicaragua could no longer be tagged a "banana republic," and it had escaped the U.S. economic orbit. Increased economic activity also permitted the Somoza regime to strengthen its ties with Nicaragua's upper-income groups and add to the family fortune of over $100 million. In the area of military cooperation, the regime ignored the U.S. request to train and equip a unit for hemispheric defense. A battalion of professional military men could pose a challenge to the Guardia Nacional, the fountainhead of the family's power. Instead, the Somozas constantly stressed the threat of internal Communist subversion, correctly judging that the Eisenhower administration would respond with military assistance to Nicaragua's National Guard.

Although Gambone adeptly shows that the Somozas favored family concerns over U.S. interests, his points are neither remarkable nor unique. Eisenhower's men never expressed alarm or strident opposition to the Somozas, because the family remained firmly committed to the U.S. core values of anticommunism and international capitalism. Only extreme, radical interpretations would assert that the United States demanded that Nicaraguans adhere precisely to every U.S. policy. In any case, these themes have been thoroughly explored by other scholars, including Kyle Longley in his analyses of U.S.–Costa Rican relations. Gambone could have enriched the debate if he had studied the U.S. relationship with the Somozas over an extended period, not just the Eisenhower years. Comparing U.S. polities toward the Somozas to initiatives toward other dictators, such as Rafael Trujillo of the Dominican Republic, would have also assisted Gambone in explaining what was singular about U.S.-Nicaraguan relations.

STEPHEN G. RABE

University of Texas
Dallas

LARSON, DEBORAH WELCH. 1997. *Anatomy of Mistrust: U.S.-Soviet Relations During the Cold War.* Pp. xi, 329. Ithaca, NY: Cornell University Press. $35.00.

In this work, Deborah Larson seeks to defend one of three alternative explanations for the Cold War. One explanation is that the superpowers had deep conflicts of interest, as a result of which they rationally preferred not to take steps that would have ended their hostility. Another is that there were structural features of the two political and economic systems that led to the hostility. Larson links the first of these explanations with economics and rational choice theory and the second with political science. The third explanation, the one Larson argues for, she links with social psychology. In this explanation, the hostility was based largely on the superpowers' misperceptions of each other, leading to their being unwilling to reach agreements that could have ended the hostility. In defending this explanation, she presents a study of how the mistrust in the Cold War relationship that allowed the hostility to continue was due to misperception.

In Larson's view, there is one important feature distinguishing the third explanation from the other two, a feature that determines the mode of argument she adopts. If the Cold War had been due primarily to a deep conflict of interests or to domestic structural features, then it would have been in some sense inevitable. The leaders of the two nations could not have been expected to choose other than the way they did in their actions perpetuating the hostility. On the other hand, if the Cold War was due to misperception, then it was not inevitable. Leaders would have chosen differently, taking actions that could have substantially reduced their mutual hostility, had they not misperceived. Larson therefore seeks to demonstrate the existence of "branching points," times in the history of the Cold War where leaders would have chosen to reduce the mutual hostility but for misperception. Providing evidence for the implicit counterfactual claims involved in the assertion of branching points is Larson's main task. The bulk of her study is a careful examination of five such branching points, ranging from the failure of the superpowers to reach agreement on the unification and neutralization of Germany in the early 1950s to the failure of Reagan and Gorbachev to agree on substantial cuts in strategic arms in exchange for a limitation on strategic defenses.

STEVEN LEE

Hobart and William Smith
  Colleges
Geneva
New York

SKOCPOL, THEDA. 1996. *Boomerang: Clinton's Health Security Effort and the Turn Against Government in U.S. Politics.* Pp. xvii, 288. New York: W. W. Norton. $27.50.

Experts have written numerous journal articles, books, lectures, and seminars on the failure of the Clinton administration's health care reform venture. Many of them provide insights into the dance of the legislative process. However, none, until Theda Skocpol's book, has provided an analysis of the political, social, and historical context for the Clinton proposal. Most of the writing so far on the Clinton health care reform efforts has been either based upon interviews with the players in the administration, Congress, and the special interest groups or written by the players themselves.

Skocpol's book supplies a new way to view the failed health care reform effort. Her historical and political framework gives the reader a context for understanding the issues that laid the groundwork for Clinton's proposal and for any future proposals. Skocpol links the social policies of the past, including Social Security and Medicare, to the policy options available to Clinton and others. She also works to connect the changes in the Democratic and Republican parties to these policy options.

The book provides insights on many levels. For members of the public who wish to understand some issues in the health care debate, the book is an excellent primer. Skocpol provides excellent definitions of important terms like "play or pay" and "managed competition." For a student of government, the book shows the difficulty of promoting dynamic social change within the United States in the late twentieth century. Skocpol's objective writing illustrates the challenges of a president to shape a social program and the impact that those in Congress and elsewhere have on its fate. She also explains why a proposal, from a president who many thought was centrist, was not viable.

An author of a book like *Boomerang* is challenged to be an objective, analytical thinker. It is not until the end of the book that Skocpol states her bias toward a single-payer plan for health care. Even with this bias, Skocpol lays out the reasons why a single-pay plan could not have been enacted. Her book provides a sound and logical argument for government partnering with all sectors in the United States to achieve economic and social goals.

LOWELL ARYE

Alliance for the Betterment
   of Citizens with Disabilities
Hamilton
New Jersey

SUMIDA, JON TETSURO. 1997. *Inventing Grand Strategy and Teaching Command: The Classic Works of Alfred Thayer Mahan Reconsidered*. Pp. xix, 164. Baltimore, MD: Johns Hopkins University Press. $24.95.

Jon Sumida, a historian now doing a great deal of work in the military and naval field, has produced a beautifully written and very provocative reexamination of the ideas of Alfred T. Mahan. Captain Mahan, having won worldwide acclaim for his 1890 book, *The Influence of Sea Power upon History*, has since then been too much subjected, like Clausewitz, Jomini, and other renowned strategists, to stereotyping and oversimplification, thus being more cited than read over the years, and reduced to a benchmark of analysis, as if no nuances and no changes of mind were ever to emerge.

Sumida's reexamination of the great naval strategist is meant to be a corrective to this. The book very much succeeds, breathing life into the man, showing all the points on which he was indeed capable of changing his mind and of being complicated and subtle, rather than starkly oversimplified.

Sumida has taken the trouble to read all of Mahan's writings over several decades (this book presents a very valuable index to the themes and questions addressed in all these works), and he makes the case that Mahan was actually more in the Clausewitzian mode, rejecting once-and-for-all propositions, than in the mechanistic mode of Jomini, who was coldly mathematical in his analysis.

The presentation of Mahan's ideas is neatly interwoven with an account of his career, and the book, as a sort of intellectual biography, thus makes fascinating reading for anyone interested in the evolution of strategic thought. It is indeed difficult to denote anything that a reader would find lacking here, for the book will be indispensable to anyone wishing to grasp Mahan in the overview or wishing to teach a course on how he fits into the history of strategy.

One possible omission is the interface with Mackinder and the other later analysts of "geopolitics," who have sometimes been viewed as reacting to Mahan, stressing the centrality of land power and control over Eurasia, in contrast to his emphasis on sea power, thus in effect making Mahan the original geopolitician. One also might have liked a little more discussion of the impression that Mahan's first book made on Great Britain (where he was awarded honorary degrees at Oxford and Cambridge in the same week, perhaps the only person ever so honored) and on the German kaiser Wilhelm, who said that "he could not put the book down," and ordered it translated immediately into German. All this may simply be to complain that the book is shorter than it could have been (an unusual complaint these days, since the criticism is normally just the opposite), for Sumida tells his story well and does not lose his reader.

GEORGE H. QUESTER

University of Maryland
College Park

AFRICA, ASIA, AND
LATIN AMERICA

BOROUJERDI, MEHRZAD. 1996. *Iranian Intellectuals and the West: The Tormented Triumph of Nativism.* Pp. xix, 256. Syracuse, NY: Syracuse University Press. $45.00. Paperbound, $16.95.

In the years prior to the 1979 revolution in Iran, some Iranian intellectuals developed a nativist reaction against the political and economic development of their country. Mehrzad Boroujerdi has now written an excellent book on the work, development, and contributions of these intellectuals. Boroujerdi defines nativism "as the doctrine that calls for the resurgence, reinstatement or continuance of native or indigenous cultural customs, beliefs, and values" (14). In Iran and elsewhere in the Third World, nativism emerged in response to Western expansion and colonialism. Nativism, according to Boroujerdi, often appealed to those whose traditional, tribal, ethnic, and national identities were adversely affected and eroded by the globalization of capitalism. The entry and incorporation of new popular classes into the political scene provided nativism with adherents, benefactors, recruits, and instigators (17). Despite its appeal, nativism is criticized by Boroujerdi because of its negative consequences. In the Iranian context, he argues, nativism became a tool for middle-class intellectuals seeking hegemony amid social disruptions and normative torsion of their society.

Expanding his theoretical framework, in chapter 2, Boroujerdi discusses the structural characteristics of Iranian society. In addition to the globalization of capitalism, Boroujerdi discusses the peculiarity of the state and its development strategies, both of which contributed to popular alienation. In particular, the state development strategy led to severe disparities, social dislocation and massive migration from the countryside, and political tensions.

Faced with these developments and the expansion of the West, some Iranian intellectuals advocated an imitation of Western modernization, while others advocated a return to the glorious past. Still others attempted to formulate a middle ground. Although during the past five decades Iranian intellectuals mainly pursued this middle ground, some sought a nativistic response to the formidable ideological penetration by the West. Ultimately, this return to nativism was used brutally by the revolutionary elite to coerce and eliminate other perspectives.

In the subsequent chapters, Boroujerdi discusses the works of several specific intellectuals, their intellectual development, their interactions with each other, and their relations with Iranian society and culture, as well as with the government. In the chapter "The Clerical Subculture," Boroujerdi criticizes the modernization theorists who explain the Iranian revolution in terms of rapid change and reaction by traditional segments of the society. Instead, Boroujerdi argues, what occurred in Iran was

the development of a "religious subculture," which was more innovative, enduring, and popular than its secular counterpart. This religious subculture involved a "politicization of Islam," transforming the latter into the primary agency of political socialization and contestation. In other words, Islam became an ideology par excellence, capable of such functions as granting identity and legitimacy upon and integrating and mobilizing the masses. (77)

Boroujerdi's analysis of these intellectuals is sophisticated and provocative, and it relies on a considerable amount of primary data and sources unavailable in English. Nonetheless, his analysis of the ideological appeal of Islam can be disputed. In addition, although critical of modernization theory, Boroujerdi at times uses a very similar framework to explain Iranian political development. Though not his main focus, it is incompatible with other aspects of his analysis and has been demonstrated by some scholars to be inadequate.

These criticisms aside, *Iranian Intellectuals and the West* remains a significant and original work by a very sophisticated, highly competent scholar. This book should serve to make the work

of Iranian intellectuals more familiar to Western audiences interested in the topic.

MISAGH PARSA

Dartmouth College
Hanover
New Hampshire

JOHNSON, HOWARD. 1997. *The Bahamas from Slavery to Servitude, 1783-1933*. Pp. xvii, 218. Gainesville: University Press of Florida. $49.95.

This publication confirms the vanguard position in Bahamian scholarship occupied by Howard Johnson of the University of Delaware. Through the 1980s, Johnson authored a series of seminal articles on the region's socioeconomic history, which he published together, with some additional material, as *The Bahamas in Slavery and Freedom* (Kingston: Ian Randle Press, 1991). Subsequent expansion of his research agenda, combined with extensive revisions to the previous work, has culminated in this eminently satisfactory monograph, which displays all the hallmarks of a mature historian at the height of his craft.

Johnson examines the persistence of the control of the Bahamian white merchant elite over the colony's society and economy as slavery gave way to a freedom so partial and circumscribed as to be labeled by one contemporary commentator "a modified form of slavery" (104). The book's nine chronologically organized chapters detail the sequence of exploitative labor systems, both urban and rural, borne by the Bahamian working people: slavery was succeeded by the "slow and extended abolition" (33) of self-hire by slaves, which was in turn replaced by apprenticeship, then indentured servitude, dependent tenantry, and truck systems that subjugated through indebtedness.

Johnson also demonstrates convincingly how government legislation and coercive policing strategies complemented worker exploitation to secure mercantile social and economic hegemony. The brunt of the white elite's aspirations was borne, of course, by the Afro-Bahamian laboring population, whose actions and reactions, from domestic opposition to out-migration, Johnson not only portrays sensitively but also locates successfully within a broader circum-Caribbean context of working-class resistance both before and after slavery. In his conclusion, Johnson extends this comparative perspective, suggesting important directions for further research into "the systems of domination" (165) that survived the transition from slavery to freedom in the West Indies.

The carefully prepared and clearly presented scholarly apparatus of tables, map, notes, bibliography, and index allows easy access to Johnson's well-written text, while the book's handsome production confirms the University Press of Florida's well-earned reputation as a distinguished academic publishing house. This study should attract a wide readership, since it addresses issues of both historical and contemporary relevance in understanding all of those societies and economies throughout the Americas that experienced slavery and its baneful and enduring legacy.

RODERICK A. MCDONALD

Rider University
Lawrenceville
New Jersey

MCGUIRE, JAMES W. 1997. *Peronism Without Perón: Unions, Parties and Democracy in Argentina*. Pp. xvii, 388.

Stanford, CA: Stanford University Press. $55.00.

The so-called Argentine question—Argentina's rapid postwar decline and the high levels of political instability and civil violence that have characterized its contemporary history—continues to attract the attention of both Latin American specialists and social scientists interested in comparative economic and political development. Political scientist James McGuire's study of Peronism and specifically the Peronist trade union movement offers the most persuasive explanation to date of this curious failure of what had once been a success story in Latin America, Argentina, a country characterized between 1880 and 1930 by increased integration into the world economy and the growing legitimacy and effectiveness of political parties to mediate competing class and sectoral interests.

In the postwar period, though economic problems and poor policy decisions have established the parameters for destabilizing sectoral conflicts, Argentina's problems have essentially been political. McGuire explains the failure of democracy in Argentina with a cogent, painstaking analysis of the history of the Peronist trade union movement, highlighting characteristics of Peronist trade union politics incompatible with democracy and political institutionalization. By concentrating on two periods that crystallize the nature of the Peronist unions and their role in the political system (the period of Augusto Vandor's party-building project of a "Peronism without Perón" in the 1960s, and the role of Peronist labor in the last decade and a half of democratic restoration), McGuire exposes the real problem with Peronism in a pluralistic democratic system. McGuire eschews the facile, and popular, argument that the fundamental problem has been the power itself of the Peronist trade unions and the labor movement (which, as he argues, could have worked to strengthen democracy and the legitimacy of political institutions). The problem, rather, has been an antiparty tradition whose roots can be traced back to the very origins of Peronism and Perón's conception of his movement, one that the current Peronist president, Carlos Menem, is a faithful executor of. Peronism's self-identity as a movement rather than a political party weakened its stake in party politics. The possibilities of evolving into a viable labor party, which Vandor's project represented, were undermined both by Perón's tactical considerations to impede democratic consolidation (in order to ensure his own return to power) and by the political culture of the Peronist working class, which had exercised political influence outside the formal structures of the Peronist party and thus had little stake in a party system. The failure of a similar attempt in the 1980s by the so-called Renovadores, reform-minded Peronists, to integrate Peronism into the party system—indeed, an attempt that went beyond Vandor's project and sought to democratize Peronism from within—is brilliantly explained by McGuire and casts doubts on the ability of Peronism in its current form to continue the process of democratic consolidation. McGuire's study, compelling in its analysis and rich in historical detail, will join the list of a handful of books essential for the understanding of Argentina's crisis over the last half century.

JAMES P. BRENNAN

University of California
Riverside

SHARKANSKY, IRA. 1997. *Policy Making in Israel: Routines for Simple Problems and Coping with the Complex.* Pp. viii, 216. Pittsburgh, PA: University of Pittsburgh Press. $45.00. Paperbound, $19.95.

Ira Sharkansky's *Policy Making in Israel* is an attempt to combine three distinct elements. One is a discussion of some principles of policy analysis and policy theory, including a discussion of the logic of the failure of policies. Sharkansky is especially interested in the existence of dilemmas and conundrums in policy and the number of problems that are not amenable to solution through the usual routines of politics and governing.

A second element is a general discussion of Israeli politics and society and their relationship to public policy decisions. The role of religion in Israel, and the conflict between the extremes of orthodoxy and secularism, are central to that discussion. Also central is the role of tensions with the non-Jewish residents of Israel and especially of Jerusalem. These factors make policymaking even more difficult than in other settings, with the existence of multiple predicaments and dilemmas in Israeli policy making.

The third element comprises several case studies of policy issues in Israel and the difficulties that confront any Israeli government attempting to solve those problems. Three cases demonstrate a good deal about the nature of policy in Israel. The cases—immigration, national security, and relationships between the religious communities with respect to Jerusalem—all point to the complexity of almost any issue in the complicated and intricate politics of Israel.

Each of the three elements in the book is interesting, but, unfortunately, the linkage between them is rather weak. In particular, the initial discussion of the sources of policy failure is largely ignored later in the book. These ideas could have been very useful in providing a framework for analyzing the case studies, but they tended to be ignored until the short concluding chapter. For example, even the simple dichotomy between routines and coping behavior would have strengthened the discussion of the individual cases. Further, the focus on failure, while common in the policy literature, tends to obscure the fact that some policies do succeed and therefore also neglects the question of why some successful and some failing programs are adopted.

B. GUY PETERS

University of Pittsburgh
Pennsylvania

WIARDA, HOWARD J. 1996. *Democracy and Its Discontents: Development, Interdependence, and U.S. Policy in Latin America.* Pp. ix, 367. Lanham, MD: Rowman & Littlefield. $68.50. Paperbound, $27.95.

For nearly three decades, University of Massachusetts political scientist Howard J. Wiarda's historically grounded conceptualizations of a distinct, corporatist tradition in Latin American political culture have helped to shape our understanding of politics and national development in that volatile region. In recent years, writing from part-time bases in various Washington, D.C., think tanks and the National War College, Wiarda has become one of our most prolific interpreters of U.S. policy toward Latin America. In this timely and thought- provoking, if occasionally repetitive, anthology, he collects 17 of his recent published articles and unpublished conference papers focusing on Latin America's current development trajectory and U.S.-Latin American relations in the 1990s.

Wiarda is at once optimistic and cautionary about Latin America's prospects. On one hand, he finds the region's post–Cold War transitions from authoritarianism and statism to democracy and free-market neoliberalism "heartening," and he applauds the recent efforts of the U.S. government to advance those trends. He admits that the classic, liberal, modernization theories of W. W. Rostow, Seymour Lipset, and others— theories that posited correlations between capitalist development and democratization and that placed Latin America and the United States on a common historical trajectory of liberal development—look much better in the 1990s than they did in the 1960s and 1970s (when Wiarda was sharply critical of their "ethnocentrism").

On the other hand, he warns, the region's recent "journey toward progress" remains incomplete and reversible. The legacy of the past is still powerful. The durability of traditional patrimonialist and corporatist dynamics—in which a dominant centralized state controls its society, in a top-down manner, through semiautonomous but patronage–co-opted functional interest groups (business associations, labor, military and other bureaucratic elements, and so on)—makes the Latin American democracies of the 1990s, at best, tenuous "halfway houses" on the road from authoritarianism to democracy. The "vast web of corporate controls, privilege, and entrenched interests" has not been thoroughly dismantled, while the inability of recent elected governments to deliver sufficient goods and services to their citizens is already beginning to erode popular euphoria for democratic government. If a model exists for democracy in Latin America, Wiarda concludes, it is probably not the Lockean, Madisonian-Jeffersonian model of U.S. democracy but, rather, a French or southern European model—centralized, "organic" "Rousseauian," "neocorporatist"—in which "labor relations, social welfare programs, and many other areas of public policy are managed in ways that combine electoral democracy with an essentially corporatist system of interest groups." Unless U.S. policy comes to terms with these realities, he warns, it is built on sand.

MICHAEL GROW

Ohio University
Athens

EUROPE

BOYD, CAROLYN P. 1997. *Historia Patria: Politics, History, and National Identity in Spain, 1875-1975.* Pp. xxi, 358. Princeton, NJ: Princeton University Press. $49.50.

Historia Patria is a fine study of the use and abuse of national history in Spain, from the restoration of the Bourbon monarchy in 1975 to the death of General Francisco Franco in 1975. Examining over 200 primary and secondary school textbooks, and drawing on a wide range of other sources from teachers' manuals to parliamentary records, Boyd seeks to explain what Pierre Vilar has called Spain's "counter-experience" in the nineteenth century: the failure to develop a strong sense of Spanish identity, and the continuing vitality of local and regional attachments.

Historia Patria takes a novel approach to this old question: while much of the historical literature examines the development of regional identities in Catalonia and Euzkadi, Boyd looks at the largely unsuccessful attempts by the political elites in Madrid to shape and diffuse a popular sense of national history and identity through schools, both public and private. The vast literature on European nation building in this period has long considered how educational systems contributed significantly to the develop-

ment and diffusion of national identity by presenting a consensual understanding of the national past. In Spain, however, this did not happen, and Boyd explores a number of reasons: the lack of a "strong" state, a chronically divided political class, the continuing strength of the institutional church, the oscillation of its political regimes between Left and Right, and the rise of regionalist movements. All these prohibited the emergence of a pedagogical consensus about Spain's national past. As a result, Spanish national identity remained highly contested—and history education was a significant site where the distinct political sensibilities of ruling groups were played out.

In chronologically organized chapters, Boyd relates the succeeding attempts to create an acceptable national past. She considers the "regenerationists" after 1898 and their educational reform; the "invention" of a Spanish history by supporters of the liberal state; the "sacralization of the national past" by Catholic integrists; the constitution of a "national Catholicism" under Primo de Rivera; the failures of a republican civic culture during the early 1930s; and the "historical amnesia" of the Franco regime. Boyd tries to link systematically the content of the widely used histories of Spain to the institutional development and political crises of twentieth-century Spanish history. She effectively presents a highly readable study of Spanish educational policy, the rise of the Spanish historical profession, and the changing fashions of history textbooks, all consistently treated within a broad, comparative context. But the book says unfortunately little about the publishing history of the textbooks; it sometimes asserts rather than demonstrates the links between individual authors and historians and political platforms, and it occasionally slights the perspective from the periphery (except in the conclusion) and especially Catalonia, where the debate about regional identity presented a fundamental challenge to the development of a national political culture. Yet scholars interested in the problem of nation building, the development of the historical profession, and the role of public and private schooling in the making of national identity will find much that is valuable in this study.

PETER SAHLINS

University of California
Berkeley

TANNER, MARCUS. 1997. *Croatia: A Nation Forged in War*. Pp. xiii, 338. New Haven, CT: Yale University Press. $30.00.

JUDAH, TIM. 1997. *The Serbs: History, Myth, and the Destruction of Yugoslavia*. Pp. xvii, 350. New Haven, CT: Yale University Press. $30.00.

The tragic war in the former Yugoslavia gave birth to a whole industry of English-language books about the region. Many of them were written by journalists after some months or years of experience in covering the war. With few exceptions, most of the authors were not specialists in the Balkans. Nevertheless, their publishers often touted them as Balkan experts, and in their efforts to explain the war and its development, these authors often assumed the authority of historian and political analyst. The results were understandably uneven and often contributed to the further perpetuation of old myths about the region and its several national communities. The various myths about the Serbs and Croats colored every study of the Balkan conflict, although none of the journalists attempted to examine the long history of either people.

Now, in the course of one year and from one publisher, there is an effort to

fill that void with Tim Judah's *Serbs* and Marcus Tanner's *Croatia: A Nation Forged in War*. These are popular histories that are similar in purpose, approach, and design. Each author uses history to frame his observations about the contemporary catastrophe he witnessed as a war correspondent. The result in each work is a descriptive narrative that supports the author's major thesis while avoiding some of the more interesting historiographical complexities that accompany the history of his subject.

Tanner argues in his preface that his book is about the country of Croatia and not about Croats. He subtitles the book *A Nation Forged in War*, but "nation" and "country" are not necessarily interchangeable. Indeed, his book is a study of the Croats and their centuries-long struggle to form a state. Tanner views all events, ideas, and individuals in that long history from the perspective of that struggle. This leads him to embrace his subject somewhat uncritically and offer a view of history that suggests a rather romantic determinism. He gives us thumbnail sketches of selected events and individuals, all of which appear to be on an inevitable path toward the eventual realization of an independent Croatian state.

The narrative is quite engaging and certainly serves to introduce the uninformed to a fascinating and very complex history. The chapter on Croatia during World War II is particularly interesting. At the same time, this study could have benefited from some analysis of broader themes in Croatia's historical development and closer attention to the subtitle of the book. Clearly, the most important years for Croatia's struggle toward statehood are the decades between the creation of the first Yugoslavia in 1918 and the beginning of the recent wars in 1991, and yet much of this period is given the least critical attention in Tanner's study.

On the other hand, one should not be surprised to discover that it is Tanner's analysis of the collapse of Yugoslavia, the war, and the internal political situation in Croatia during this time that is the most interesting part of his book. This reflects his firsthand experiences as a correspondent in the Balkans from 1988 to 1994.

Tim Judah, unlike Tanner, introduces his readers to broad themes that have directed his reading of Serbian history. He subtitles his work on the Serbs *History, Myth, and the Destruction of Yugoslavia*, and he believes that centuries of struggle, sacrifice, and martyrdom have shaped Serbian national consciousness and offer some explanation for the tragic events of recent years. The publisher suggests that Judah rejects "the stereotypical image of a bloodthirsty nation . . . [and] makes the Serbs comprehensible by placing them within the context of their history and their hopes." Unfortunately, Judah, like Tanner, cannot overcome the narrow framework of his view of history and ends up accepting certain stereotypes about his subject rather uncritically.

Judah's historical narrative is actually less successful than Tanner's because Judah tries to "draw together history, modern politics and war" throughout that narrative. As a result, the reader must jump back and forth between distant centuries and contemporary perspectives. If you do not already know the history quite well, the road can be very bumpy.

The history of Yugoslavia in the twentieth century is most critical for understanding the recent demise of that multinational state, and yet Judah, like Tanner with the Croats, offers far too little analysis of the Serbs and Serbia during the seven decades of Yugoslavia's existence. On the other hand, Judah's firsthand experiences as a correspondent ensure that his treatment of the war

years is the most interesting part of the study. Ironically, his analysis of the corruption, power struggles, and sheer opportunism among Serb leaders draws into question his primary thesis, which seeks explanations for the destruction of Yugoslavia in Serbian history, myth, and national consciousness.

In spite of the obvious shortcomings of each study, these are certainly important contributions to the relatively meager number of popular works about the Serbs and Croats in English. While one may wonder how large the targeted popular audience may be, one must still appreciate the effort to expand the conversation. At the same time, it is important to note that these books, while published by a university press as "powerful history," are clearly not directed at a university audience.

THOMAS A. EMMERT

Gustavus Adolphus College
St. Peter
Minnesota

UNITED STATES

KINDER, DONALD R. and LYNN M. SANDERS. 1996. *Divided by Color: Racial Politics and Democratic Ideals.* Pp. xi, 391. Chicago: University of Chicago Press. $27.50.

In the evolution of the application of a racial paradigm to American history and social relations, social scientists explored the socioeconomic conditions of racial groups. Great racial divisions were discovered by late-nineteenth-century and early-twentieth-century sociologists. The mid-twentieth-century literature on race relations also discovered chronic racial inequalities in educational attainment; rates of crime, violence, and incarceration; and longevity, living standards, social mobility, wealth, and income. So convincing is the evidence that it is now a standard thesis that America is a racially separate and unequal society. Following this tradition of research on "blacks" and "whites," some social scientists investigate perceived racial images; they discover patterns of racial polarization and hostility: blacks perceive whites as racists, and whites see blacks as biologically and/or culturally deficient. Continuing this tradition of empirical racial research, other social scientists explore the "opinions" of the "races" on policies to ameliorate the conditions facing "blacks." They claim that here, too, there are great racial divisions and resentments. This is the argument developed by Kinder and Sanders in *Divided by Color*.

Kinder and Sanders allude to the original problem of racial socioeconomic inequalities, and they insist that American society is still deeply segregated by race. Their main purpose, however, is to "explore" racial politics by examining public opinion toward racial policies. This exploration involves designing research programs to elicit black and white beliefs about racial matters. The results indicate that the divisions persist: "In the extreme, blacks and whites look upon the social and political world in fundamentally different and mutually unintelligible ways. Black and white Americans have taken possession of distinct paradigms" (288). Whites support racially egalitarian principles but not the required policies, while blacks support both principles and programs, such as affirmative action, school desegregation, and welfare. What underlies white opinion and opposition is racial resentment, a form of racism that Kinder and Sanders describe as "symbolic." In other words, white racism maintains pervasive racial inequalities in American society as well as white opposition to their amelioration. This is the Kerner Commission all over again.

A significant contribution to the study of "racial politics" would have been made had Kinder and Sanders explored the reasons for the domination of the racial paradigm in American intellectual and political life. But they show no concern for philosophical and theoretical reflection and thereby render their conclusions most unoriginal and incomplete. Their analysis contains the untenable assumption that research on the opinions of blacks and whites on racial policies could provide an explanation of racial politics. A more likely explanation, however, is the imposition of arbitrary racial identities on citizens. More focused on empirical discovery than analytical rigor, Kinder and Sanders fail to reflect on their own racial theoretical orientation; they also ignore the creation and cultivation of "black people" and "white people" by the government (the Census Bureau), the media, and the academic bombardment of citizens with racial names and images. They endorse the racial paradigm, even in the face of a voluminous literature that refutes its anatomical categories. *Divided by Color* would have been better titled *Divided by Design*.

YEHUDI WEBSTER

California State University
Los Angeles

LANDSBERG, BRIAN K. 1997. *Enforcing Civil Rights: Race Discrimination and the Department of Justice*. Pp. xii, 276. Lawrence: University Press of Kansas. $35.00.

The Civil Rights Division of the U.S. Department of Justice occupies a special position within the government's law enforcement machinery. It is responsible for enforcing the federal laws that guarantee equal opportunities for American citizens. The division was created by Attorney General Frank Murphy in 1939 as a section within the Criminal Division. For almost 20 years the Civil Rights Section limited its activities to occasional criminal prosecutions under the authority created by the Reconstruction Civil Rights Acts. During this period, it was not particularly aggressive or effective. When Thurgood Marshall was nearly lynched following a trial in rural Tennessee in the late 1940s, there was no response to his repeated requests for an investigation.

In the late 1950s, the section was upgraded to division status and was given responsibility for enforcing, among other things, voting rights under the Civil Rights Act of 1957. This limited authority was considerably enhanced by the landmark civil rights legislation of the 1960s. These laws, which defined the division's mandate, represented the culmination of the civil rights movement of the 1950s and 1960s. During this period, the division assumed a far more activist role. Southern officials who engaged in acts of violence and intimidation against civil rights workers were successfully prosecuted. The division also aided in efforts to desegregate educational institutions during the years of "massive resistance" when elected officials attempted to thwart the implementation of *Brown* v. *Board of Education*. It was instrumental to securing the voting rights of thousands of previously disenfranchised African Americans in the deep South. This has resulted in the election of hundreds of black officials and changed, perhaps forever, the political dynamics of the southern states.

These and other activities are analyzed in Brian K. Landsberg's *Enforcing Civil Rights*. A professor of law at McGeorge College of Law, Landsberg served as an attorney in the Civil Rights Division from 1964 to 1986. His thoughtful and well-researched book combines scholarly analysis with the keen insight of an individual who was intimately involved in many of the events that are described. Landsberg delineates the organizational structure of the division and explains the manner in which it implements its responsibilities. These duties are carried out by a surprisingly small group of attorneys primarily through direct enforcement actions in federal courts as well as the submission of amicus curiae briefs for important cases.

One of the most interesting features of the book involves Landsberg's explanation of the tensions that can be caused by the shifting priorities of various presidential administrations. There were periods of intense activism under presidents Kennedy and Johnson. President Nixon attempted to curb the use of busing to achieve school desegregation, but his administration introduced many of the most controversial affirmative action programs. The Reagan administration introduced an entirely new and what was viewed by many observers as a disingenuous approach to civil rights enforcement. Throughout the 1980s, the Justice Department switched sides in litigation, intervening on behalf of white males in affirmative action cases and taking many other positions that were at odds with the views of the civil rights establishment.

Landsberg's analysis of these developments is nuanced and usually restrained. It is not entirely clear, for example, how he views the changes that were wrought during the tumultuous years of the Reagan administration. Nevertheless, *Enforcing Civil Rights* represents a valuable addition to the existing literature. It provides a detailed account of the history of the Civil Rights Division and describes the federal government's many accomplishments as principal enforcer of civil rights laws. It is beyond dispute that profound changes in race relations have occurred since 1957, when the Civil Rights Section was upgraded to division status. State-sanctioned discrimination has been eliminated, but, as Landsberg makes clear, many of the advances of the 1960s are beginning to unravel. The lingering vestiges of segregation, which continue to operate as daunting barriers to racial equality, will remain in place well into the twenty-first century.

LELAND WARE

St. Louis University
Missouri

LANE, ROGER. 1997. *Murder in America: A History.* Pp. xi, 399. Columbus: Ohio State University Press. $24.95.

In this overview of the historical record on intentional killing in America from the colonial era to the recent past, Roger Lane attempts to answer some interesting questions. How does the current murder rate compare with those in past times? Have the nature and levels of homicide changed in the last 30 years? Why has the American murder rate been the highest in the developed world? In addition to trying to answer these questions, Lane recounts some of America's most publicized murder cases. A series of photos and drawings bolster these accounts and suggest that Americans have been fascinated with murder for generations. They are all there, from Lizzie Borden to O. J. Simpson, from Jesse James to the Unabomber.

Lane treats all forms of intentional killing as murder, which means that war, riot, rebellion, execution, lynching, and assassination are included in his overview. In trying to understand these acts, Lane examines a variety of popular, anecdotal, and official explanations of changes in homicide rates. This makes it a fascinating but often puzzling book. Some of the puzzlement is caused by the absence of good crime data for most of the country's history, and some, by the changing definition of murder. Switching from homicide data for specific cities to national data and back again creates additional confusion. However, the wider availability of data on victims of murder and the absence of dependable national data on the characteristics of homicide offenders also make the project difficult. It is not clear at points whether the rate discussed is a victimization rate or an offender rate.

There are some obvious advantages to Lane's basic approach. His discussion of the death rates in the colonial era for indentured servants and their marginal status following completion of their - required service may be a clue to the high homicide rates—victim and offender—for others excluded from the economic, political, and social mainstream. His discussion of the role of notions of honor and respect as recipes for serious violence may be another important clue for changes in some types of murder rates. In the end, however, he suggests that the long-standing love of guns, the continuing gap between rich and poor, and especially the racial hostility growing out of slavery have created a legacy that virtually guarantees a continuation of the historically high murder rates in the United States.

ROLAND CHILTON

University of Massachusetts
Amherst

MARSHALL, SUSAN E. 1997. *Splintered Sisterhood: Gender and Class in the Campaign Against Woman Suffrage.* Pp. vii, 342. Madison: University of Wisconsin Press. $55.00. Paperbound, $21.95.

At the heart of this study lie three machine-readable databases: the organizational records of the Massachusetts Association Opposed to the Further Extension of Suffrage to Women (including its correspondence with other antisuffrage organizations), antisuffrage writings (on which a content analysis comparing male and female authors was done), and a collective biography based on memoirs, letters, and census listings of publicly identified opponents of suffrage, including prominent members of the various associations. Susan Marshall does a suggestive regression analysis comparing male and female voters in a Massachusetts referendum on extending the suffrage in local elections in which women were permitted to vote and their votes counted separately. Her ecological analysis undercuts beliefs that immigrants were particularly opposed to women's suffrage and shows clearly that women and men had different reasons for voting pro or con. She also analyzes state referendum votes in which only men voted, but she finds few common patterns; conditions were historically unique from state to state.

Marshall's interdisciplinary methods counter the notion that suffragists and historians alike believed that the "antis" (as they were called) were simple conservatives seeking to protect women's traditional place. She argues that women antis were not fronts for manipulative men but actors in their own gendered class interests; the founders of the Massachusetts movement were the wives and sisters of elite men who networked with similar women in other east coast cities and the South, who in turn founded antisuffrage organizations. Antis often held appointed office in state or local government social administration and wielded influence through powerful male kin. They feared that their arena of activity would be undercut by women's suffrage and the expansion of professional careers for women. These women and their organizations avoided political confrontation and indeed denied that

what they were doing was politics; this reluctance ended by undermining their effectiveness.

Drawing on social movement theory, Marshall argues that the political interaction between the suffrage and antisuffrage movements affected the strategies of the suffrage movement itself, in particular its move from a rights argument to one of expediency, and its decision to seek an amendment to the federal Constitution because of the difficulty in achieving victory state by state.

Overall, this is an exhaustively documented and persuasively argued reinterpretation of the anti-women's-suffrage movement in the United States.

LOUISE A. TILLY

New School for Social Research
New York City

ROBERTS, ROBERT N. and MARION T. DOSS, JR. 1997. *From Watergate to Whitewater: The Public Integrity War.* Pp. xxii, 210. Westport, CT: Praeger. $55.00.

Roberts and Doss have produced a very important, timely, and prescient book. Written well before President Bill Clinton was accused, in January 1998, of having sex with a young female White House intern and of encouraging her to lie about it under oath, *From Watergate to Whitewater* anticipates precisely how the public integrity industry would respond. Independent counsel Kenneth Starr, whose legal staff of 20 had little to show for the thirty million taxpayer dollars it spent during his four-years' tenure, sprang into action. Relying on surreptitiously made tapes (some of which were clearly illegal), trickery, and leaks, Starr initiated an around-the-clock media "feeding frenzy" like no other. Innuendo upon innuendo was heaped on allegation after allegation. The public integrity watchdogs, virtue-crats, pundit class, and media professori-ate filled the airwaves with ponderous analysis and speculation. Calls for the president's resignation or impeachment quickly surfaced.

Basic facts, however, were scarce. Did the president give the intern a dress or was it a large T-shirt? The tapes were de-scribed as "reportedly" indicating this and that, but the press, the president, and the intern's attorney had not actu-ally heard their full content. Did they contain a smoking gun, was Starr using them to try to jar loose additional infor-mation, or was he simply overreaching?

The president denied doing anything improper, and, much to the astonishment of those pushing the story, his popularity soared to new highs. Taking a cue from the public, commentators began attack-ing Starr's operation for its smarmy, slimy, and abusive tactics, as well as for impeding the presidency. There were calls from both the political Right and Left to do away with the independent counsel law. The press engaged in ritual hand-wringing over its deviations from professionalism in covering the story. Fi-nally, just as Roberts and Doss would have predicted, a subtext far more impor-tant for the Republic than the original story emerged: how had the quest for public integrity gotten so far off track that it threatened to weaken the govern-ment it was meant to protect?

Roberts and Doss's book not only an-swers that question but is absolutely es-sential reading for anyone who wants to understand the development, applica-tion, and politics of federal ethics law. They show how what was once a battle against late-nineteenth-century ram-pant political corruption turned into a "public integrity war" in the aftermath of Watergate—and why it subsequently de-generated into partisan guerrilla attacks and even factional street-fighting.

Like any war, the public integrity war requires organization and infrastruc-ture. Roberts and Doss explain that there is a "public integrity bureaucracy" (88) consisting of the Federal Bureau of In-vestigation, the Public Integrity Section of the Criminal Division of the Depart-ment of Justice, U.S. Attorneys, the Of-fice of Government Ethics, independent counsels appointed under the Ethics in Government Act, and inspectors general offices attached to more than two dozen federal agencies. The bureaucracy is busy. It processes reams of financial dis-closure and other forms. It chases count-less allegations and leads. In the 1980s through 1992, federal prosecutors ob-tained 11,256 corruption convictions against state, local, and federal officials and others (88).

Apparently all's fair in the public in-tegrity war, which is a major problem. Due process will continue to suffer as "movement conservatives and new pro-gressives battle for political power" (xii). The Federal Bureau of Investigation uses stings to entice if not entrap. Starr sees nothing wrong with betrayal, illegal tapes, leaks, and intimidation as the tools of investigating a sitting president. Damage to the presidency is considered collateral. "Gotcha" dominates perspec-tive. If truth is a casualty of war, the me-dia more than does its share. What can be done to reverse this quarter-century trend?

Roberts and Doss offer calm, in-formed, and sage insight:

The public integrity war is not a story of saints and sinners. It is a story of how easily the pas-sion for policies and programs can cloud one's judgement. Congress can do little to legislate an end to the public integrity war. New presi-dential directives on government ethics will only complicate the problem. The public integ-rity war will only end when we stop viewing political opponents as mortal enemies. Only then will we regain the ability to distinguish between individuals who have truly violated the public trust and those individuals simply caught up in the battles of the public integrity war. (175)

From Watergate to Whitewater is an extremely valuable book. It brilliantly analyzes the history and contemporary organization of federal ethics law and politics. It is exceptionally well researched, comprehensive, and clearheaded. It should be required reading for everyone in public life, including journalists and public integrity lawyers.

DAVID H. ROSENBLOOM

American University
Washington, D.C.

SCHWARZ, JOHN. 1997. *Illusions of Opportunity*. Pp. 237. New York: Norton. $23.95.

The central theme of *Illusions of Opportunity* is that the American dream is a myth for millions of hard-working Americans. With personal profiles and an eclectic array of statistics, John Schwarz asserts that as many as 16 million households are in economic distress, unable to attain the standard of living that the American mainstream regards as "minimally adequate" (an income of about $25,000 per year for a family of four). Worse yet, Schwarz asserts, the gap between the dream and the reality has steadily widened, even while the U.S. economy has apparently been thriving. This widening gap has spawned rising illegitimacy rates, juvenile delinquency, family dissolution, and increasing social disorder.

To recapture the American dream, the federal government must spend another $200 billion a year to create "adequate" jobs and broaden advancement opportunities for those already in the mainstream. Schwarz's policy prescription includes public jobs, a higher and in-dexed minimum wage, more generous tax credits for low-wage workers and growing businesses, child support assurance ($2500 per child per year), apprenticeship programs for youths, retraining programs for adults, and a reduction in class size in elementary schools. To finance this agenda, Schwarz proposes a new wealth tax and higher income taxes on the rich. To monitor the success of this massive restructuring, Schwarz proposes a new "distress index" that would change the availability of "adequate" jobs (paying at least $15,000 per year) and advancement opportunities.

Schwarz allows that his proposals are "meant to spur discussion, not end it." In the fiscal climate of present-day Washington, I doubt anyone will even start discussing Schwarz's diagnosis, much less his agenda. His clear and powerful writing will stir lively academic debates, however. Like his earlier *Forgotten Americans*, Schwarz's *Illusions of Opportunity* is a superb vehicle for awakening our social conscience to the economic hardships that coexist with general prosperity. No one who has examined employment statistics carefully will be persuaded by Schwarz's back-of-the-envelope calculations on the dimension of economic distress in the United States today. Even if his computations are off by a factor of two or three, however, his alarm over the incompleteness of the American dream is worthy of serious concern.

BRADLEY R. SCHILLER

American University
Washington, D.C.

SITTSER, GERALD L. 1997. *A Cautious Patriotism: The American Churches and the Second World War*. Pp. x, 317. Chapel Hill: University of North Carolina Press. $39.95.

Gerald Sittser contends that most church leaders during World War I had tarnished their claims to moral authority by vacillating from a utopian pacifism to an unbridled militarism. Having learned from this experience, most church leaders during World War II embraced a cautious patriotism that maintained a prophetic witness to higher ideals while simultaneously supporting standards of relative justice. These church leaders would have been alarmed to discover that World War II has become the paradigmatic case of a righteous America fighting the embodiment of evil.

Although Sittser draws upon official pronouncements from a comprehensive range of Christian communities, his articulation of the mainline Protestant perspectives, particularly Reinhold Niebuhr's Christian realism, are much stronger than his articulation of Roman Catholic perspectives, particularly the just war tradition. In Sittser's defense, the just war tradition was not as prominent in U.S. public policy debates during World War II as it would become during the Vietnam war, the Cold War, and the Persian Gulf war.

Sittser demonstrates that the prophetic patriotism of the church leaders set them apart from the jingoistic patriotism common on the domestic front. The churches generally avoided caricatures of the enemy, challenged American hubris, and insisted upon fostering the conditions that would sustain a just and durable peace. At a time when many Americans evaded the issue of civil liberties, church pronouncements condemned U.S. policies toward Japanese Americans, African Americans, and other minorities in U.S. society. These church leaders insisted that genuine patriotism required fearless evaluation, particularly when the principles of liberty and justice for which America proclaimed to fight were being denied to its own citizens.

Sittser's analysis is persuasive until he jumps from World War II to the present and accuses the contemporary churches of becoming uncautiously patriotic. Arguably, this may be true of most Christians in the United States, but the official pronouncements from the Roman Catholic church and the mainline Protestant churches during the Persian Gulf war were remarkably similar to their official pronouncements during World War II. The fact that these official pronouncements had little influence in the public policy debates during the Persian Gulf war and even less influence on the attitudes of the people in their own congregations might lead one to reconsider the influence of the official pronouncements of the church leaders during World War II or at least to question the contemporary implications that Sittser draws from his analysis.

ANDREW DEAN WALSH

Indiana University–Purdue
   University
Indianapolis

TARR, JOEL A. 1996. *The Search for the Ultimate Sink: Urban Pollution Control in Historical Perspective*. Pp. xlvii, 419. Akron, OH: University of Akron Press. $49.95. Paperbound, $24.95.

Joel Tarr has been conducting basic research about U.S. "urban environmental history" for more than 20 years. This book, which collects 15 of his articles from scattered books and journals, clearly and forcefully presents his contributions to the history of urban pollution control, particularly in the late nineteenth and early twentieth centuries. His primary theme is that pollution control strategies are "time and culture specific" phenomena rather than simple technological responses to obvious problems. Second, as he shows in essay after essay and captures in the title, innovations created new problems. The introduction, mainly in the 1880s, of "water carriage technology"—sewer systems that pumped human waste into rivers—contaminated water supplies for downstream cities (engineers held that "running water [purified] itself"). The introduction of tall smokestacks, chiefly in the 1950s and 1960s, diluted ground-level air pollution in the form of dense smoke but spread that pollution over larger areas and caused acid rain. More intensive use of landfills in the post–World War II era, itself a result of efforts to reduce the use of the air and water as "sinks," destroyed wetlands, attracted rats and flies, and contaminated groundwater.

These stories of failure, however, should not obscure the third major theme of Tarr's essays: there have been major successes in urban pollution control. Sewer systems were a vast improvement over privy vaults and cesspools, which were costly to empty and tended to overflow. Pittsburgh cleaned its air when a 1941 smoke control ordinance led over half its households to switch from bituminous coal to natural gas for home heating between 1945 and 1950. The hazards of automobile exhaust are placed in relief by Tarr's descriptions and photographs of city streets filled with huge piles of horse manure.

There is inevitable repetition. In several essays, Tarr recounts a nineteenth-century debate about whether sewer systems should combine storm water with waste water or pipe them separately. Yet this story richly illustrates the contingent nature of technology: changing methods of measuring financial costs, the professionalization of engineering and public health, epidemiological theories linking sewage with diseases such as typhoid, and the role of a particular personality, the pioneer sewage engineer George Waring, Jr. The power of what Tarr calls "historical analogy" in understanding environmental decision making should attract many readers interested in pollution control today.

ROBIN L. EINHORN
University of California
Berkeley

THERNSTROM, STEPHEN and ABIGAIL THERNSTROM. 1997. *America in Black and White: One Nation, Indivisible: Race in Modern America.* Pp. 704. New York: Simon & Schuster. $30.50.

Social scientists will not learn much from this book. The Thernstroms' well-publicized target is race-based affirmative action. Unfortunately, they fail to advance the debate over that controversial topic. By virtually ignoring women and other minorities (a facile discussion of immigrants and Asian Americans as a model minority argues that current racial problems are due to failures by blacks), the book's black-white focus retards the full discussion of race and opportunity that this nation deserves.

The argument is two-pronged and familiar: the authors believe affirmative action is a divisive practice that impedes the nation's march toward fully harmonious race relations and is ineffectual since "the serious inequality (black-white) that remains is less a function of white racism than of the racial gap in levels of educational attainment, the structure of the black family, and the rise in black crime."

This conclusion is advanced on the basis of a journalistic discussion of masses of data on education, employment, poverty, crime, residential segregation, family structure, and so on. While other conservatives have forced serious scholars to address the role of behavior in perpetuating inequality, the Thernstroms' intended rebuttal of arguments claiming that discrimination is a significant cause of their listed black-white inequalities is restricted to attacking straw men: they write that liberals believe "poverty causes crime"; metaphorical statements by public persons saying that race relations have changed little since slavery are treated as if they were meant to be taken literally. In this regard, it is disappointing that after a 180-page discussion of Jim Crow racism from 1900 to 1965, there is no serious analysis of possible legacies of past racism to today's black poor. The overview of past racism and the discussion of contemporary conditions are analytically disconnected. The historical overview's primary function is to highlight great positive change from a remote baseline. The actual terrain of the contemporary debate, however, addresses what has been happening since 1970.

The book's strongest section is its hardheaded discussion of education and low standards and work effort in predominantly black schools. But here, as throughout the book, the Thernstroms offer no analysis and no constructive policies that might rejuvenate this intellectually, if not politically, stale debate. Their one-sided perspective, which invariably locates contemporary race problems with black failures, is less an argued analysis of a complicated social problem than the considered opinions of intelligent moderate conservatives.

GERALD D. JAYNES

Yale University
New Haven
Connecticut

WIETHOFF, WILLIAM. 1996. *A Peculiar Humanism: The Judicial Advocacy of Slavery in High Courts of the Old South, 1820-1850.* Pp. xi, 247. Athens: University of Georgia. $37.00.

William Wiethoff's *Peculiar Humanism* sets out with the ambitious goal of recovering an understanding of pro-slavery legal thought. It contributes in important ways to the recent impressive body of scholarship that takes seriously the ideas of antebellum Southerners. Wiethoff helps us gain an appreciation for how judges decided cases, for the diversity of opinions held by members of the Southern judiciary, and for how public attitudes toward slavery correlated with judicial opinions. An important book, it speaks to scholars in law, history, and rhetoric.

Wiethoff identifies nearly 70 Southern jurists who occupied state benches from 1820 to 1850 and whose opinions contained pro-slavery oratory. He traces the influence of civic humanism's emphasis on public virtue and eloquence to the antebellum judiciary. The humanist tradition led judges to use opinions as a way of explaining and supporting their decisions with appeals to policy, expediency, and morality, even as they ignored important elements of the Renaissance and Enlightenment humanist agenda, which was antislavery. Wiethoff effectively mines those opinions for the evidence they provide of the beliefs and values of the ruling class.

His data—more than 160 appellate opinions and numerous speeches delivered by judges off the bench—yield several important insights. First, they demonstrate a close connection between law and letters—in this case, classical writings. Second, they show the judges' concern with the preservation of Southern society. Moreover, they reveal the struggle that judges faced in reconciling their decisions to the slaves' humanity.

Judges frequently told their audiences that the decisions they made were for the benefit of the slave society and, thus, were in keeping with the interests of humanity. It is the (sometimes) tension between those two themes—the humanist interest in preservation of society and the judges' recognition of the slave's humanity—that leads to the intriguing title, *A Peculiar Humanism*. Despite the consensus on the importance of humanism, there was great diversity about what constituted humanism and on how to weight the relative importance of the preservation of slave society and the humane treatment of the slaves.

A Peculiar Humanism fits well with studies that look to rhetoric to understand antebellum political thought, such as David Zarefsky's *Lincoln, Douglas and Slavery* (University of Chicago, 1990), as well as books like Drew Faust's *Sacred Circle* (Johns Hopkins, 1977), which recover the nuances of Southern intellectual thought. Moreover, it contributes to the findings of legal historians like Morton Horwitz and Perry Miller that antebellum judges drew many of their ideas from their culture. Its greatest contribution may be in demonstrating how pro-slavery rhetoric drawn from popular culture correlated with judges' discourse, thus linking culture and law.

ALFRED L. BROPHY

Oklahoma City University

SOCIOLOGY

BOYTE, HARRY C. and NANCY N. KARI. 1996. *Building America: The Democratic Promise of Public Work.* Pp. xvi, 255. Philadelphia: Temple University Press. $54.95. Paperbound, $18.95.

Remarking upon the efflorescence of democracy in the nineteenth century, Alexis de Tocqueville observed that in only one country in the world did citizens make use of an unlimited freedom of association, and use it continually, as a part of their everyday life. By these means,

Tocqueville asserted, Americans had come to enjoy all the advantages civilization can offer.

Boyte and Kari are concerned with responding to what they think is the steady erosion of associative citizenship in the United States and the subsequent "disengagement of ordinary people from productive involvement in public affairs." To revitalize public life, they have written a book that is both theoretical in its conceptualization of public work and practical in its documentation of examples of public work that may help to "bring democracy to life again" in America.

In theorizing public work, Boyte and Kari forge an emancipatory concept grounded in the reality of ordinary people's collective actions in civic life. Public work combines the value of productive labor (Karl Marx's central category) with the power of public action (Hannah Arendt's central category) in a way that thematizes citizenship as simultaneously plural, participatory, productive, practical, and attuned to problems. With this concept, Boyte and Kari offer an important alternative to many current studies of democratic rejuvenation that tend either to undermine work by reducing democracy to talk, or to commodify public life by elevating categories like social capital to the status of action.

Boyte and Kari reasonably surmise that effective citizenship depends not only upon people's thinking of themselves as productive workers but also upon their having a passion and an eagerness for public work. Hence a great deal of their book is devoted to illuminating (through field research and interviews) actually existing associations that offer "a repertoire of images" and "tools and programs" for democratic change. As Boyte and Kari show, public work takes place in a variety of departments of life, from churches, schools, and neighborhood councils, to labor unions, farm cooperatives, and small businesses. They identify organizations both famous and familiar—such as Hull House, the Civilian Conservation Corps, and the National Association for the Advancement of Colored People—as well as lesser-known associations that are nonetheless integral to liberty, such as BUILD in Baltimore, Neighborhood House in St. Paul, the Nehemiah Project in East Brooklyn, the Common Ground Association in St. Louis, and the Floating Homes Association in Seattle. Amid this abundance of riches, Boyte and Kari call upon Americans to draw on their capacity for public work and learn some habits of acting together in the affairs of daily life. At stake is not only liberty but also power, for, to paraphrase Tocqueville, what government could ever carry on the vast multitude of lesser undertakings that associations daily enable American citizens to control, if only they would continue to associate?

MARY DIETZ

University of Minnesota
Minneapolis

CALAVITA, KITTY, HENRY N. PONTELL, and ROBERT H. TILLMAN. 1997. *Big Money Crime: Fraud and Politics in the Savings and Loan Crisis.* Pp. xvii, 263. Berkeley: University of California Press. $27.50.

This book will vex any impartial reader. Consider the claim that "savings and loan crime . . . brought the American financial system to the brink of disaster." In 1992 inflation-adjusted dollars, the cost of resolving failed federally insured savings and loans from 1980 through 1996 was $173 billion. As 2.8 percent of 1992 gross domestic product, this total cost, let alone the portion due to crimes, was hardly enough to bring the American financial system to the brink of disaster.

The book also tells us that in the early 1980s with "virtually all restrictions on thrift investment powers removed . . . deregulators had combined in one package the opportunity for lucrative fraud." In fact, expanded activities allowed federally chartered institutions roughly coincided with existing commercial bank activities; wider activities allowed some state-chartered institutions were subsequently curtailed.

The expansion was in reaction to the effects of earlier regulations requiring savings and loans to make fixed-rate, long-term mortgages. As the authors themselves state, as a result of these regulations and rising interest rates, "by 1982 the industry was insolvent by $150 billion."

Thus the authors' own discussion of this regulatory chain of events contradicts the theme of criminal centrality.

Not to be deterred, the book recycles criminal referral statistics and discusses some of the most heralded cases. This is part of an attempt to establish the false impression that previous examiners of the crisis downplayed crime. To the contrary, a congressional commission cited in the book estimated that 10 to 15 percent of the cost of the crisis (between $17 billion and $26 billion in 1992 dollars) was due to fraud.

The authors focus more broadly "on insider abuse for personal gain" using "terms insider abuse, wrongdoing, fraud, and crime interchangeably" because "this makes . . . scientific and legal sense."

Ultimately, the authors conclude only that "total losses due to fraud must be several times higher" than the $8 billion involved in cases in 1992 that led to indictments and convictions. If this means three, four, or five times higher, the estimated cost due to crime is $24, $32, or $40 billion, leaving $149, $141, or $133 billion in costs to be explained by other causes.

Big Money Crime has a lot of explaining to do.

JAMES R. BARTH

R. DAN BRUMBAUGH

Auburn University

Alabama

KATZ, STEPHEN. 1996. *Disciplining Old Age: The Formation of Gerontological Knowledge*. Pp. x, 209. Charlottesville: University Press of Virginia. Paperbound, $18.50.

In *Disciplining Old Age*, Stephen Katz looks at gerontology as a disciplinary phenomenon in order to examine what it does. Drawing on theories from Foucault, Althusser, and Bourdieu, Katz explores how the knowledge of old age has emerged as a discipline and how it has problematized old age. He looks at four domains within which old age has become an object of knowledge: medicine (the aged body), demography (the elderly population), textual formations of gerontology, and the field of gerontology. The overarching theme that runs through these four domains is the disciplining of old age.

Focusing on the medical sciences of the nineteenth and early twentieth centuries, Katz delineates how the aged body has been transformed into a pathological subject. Treating populations as historical, political phenomena, he illustrates how the elderly population has been differentiated into a homogeneous group, and how the institutionalization or bureaucratization of the life course has brought old age (the elderly population) into the domain of power/knowledge relations. Using clinical, popular, and mixed-genre multidisciplinary texts, Katz examines the relationship between the imaginary and disparate characteristics of old age and the scientific and professional rhetorics of gerontology to show how the discursive exercise of gerontology has been a struggle in which authors, subjects, rhetorics, and institutions made old age a knowable feature and in the process made old age a problem of knowledge. Applying what he calls the "gerontological web," Katz analyzes the parameters (funding organizations, university centers, large-scale studies, and the schools of thought) of gerontology as a field and illustrates how gerontology has disciplined knowledge with the examples of the problematization of individual adjustment and the problematization of population aging.

In the final chapter, Katz offers his insight into where gerontology might be going. He suggests that the prospects of gerontology have less to do with its disciplinary vision than with the "undisciplining" forces: debates on heterogeneity in old age; the recognition that age and generational relations are crosscut by gender, class, ethnic diversions, religious affiliations, and regional differences; conceptions of time; the breaking of spaces; and a redistribution of life-course definitions and experiences. By successfully accomplishing what he argues for—to contribute to current "critical gerontology" and to strengthen the connection between gerontology and contemporary theories of disciplinarity, subjectivity, and discourse—Katz's work is a valuable contribution to the field of gerontology as well as disciplinary studies.

CHANG-MING HSIEH

University of Pennsylvania

Philadelphia

KAWASH, SAMIRA. 1997. *Dislocating the Color Line: Identity, Hybridity, and Singularity in African American Literature*. Pp. ix, 266. Stanford, CA: Stanford University Press. Paperbound, $15.95.

Dislocating the Color Line enters the contemporary discussion of identity politics with an intellectually challenging, though occasionally overtheorized, analysis of the definition and regulation of racial identities and boundaries. Political power is foremost "the power of subjectification," the power to "assign, regulate, distribute, and control" racial, as well as other, identities. Historically, Kawash argues, the color line has functioned not to designate a "natural" division of peoples but, rather, to produce those classifications that define racial difference. Recent liberal attempts at correctives to racial division such as notions of diversity, hybridity, or multiculturalism are nevertheless always already infected by essentialist assumptions of a color line.

The cultural functioning of the color line is demonstrated through discussions of familiar narratives such as the antebellum slave autobiographies of Frederick Douglass and Harriet Jacobs, "passing" novels of the Harlem Renaissance, and Douglas Sirk's 1959 film version of Fanny Hurst's *Imitation of Life*. Although most of these narratives have been subjected to extensive analysis in recent years by literary scholars and critical race theorists, Kawash offers some provocative new theoretical perspectives. For example, she explores the relationship between racial difference and geography, between subjectivity and self-ownership, between fugitivity and freedom, between justice and "just-ness." This last idea is one of Kawash's original contributions to the discourse of identity politics. In Zora Nearle Hurston's novel *Their Eyes Were Watching God*, Kawash suggests, Hurston is "searching for the possibility of community beyond the boundaries of self and other, and beyond the selfish, violent, destructive hand of justice." "Just-ness" is offered as a neolo-gism to describe the desired alternative, "a togetherness that cannot be aligned with the orders of identity, race, and nation and that evades the attendant forms of violence that sustain and preserve such orders."

Kawash's most original contributions are contained in a densely theorized final chapter that presses the analysis toward some proposed correctives for the politics of the color line. The concept of singularity is offered as an alternative to hybridity as a way of displacing socially or politically predetermined identities. Though such a notion may leave us without the assurance of known entities, it "demands the suspension of the standards of right and authority by which any particular position becomes unassailable, self-evident, or commonsensical" and thus demands the taking of responsibility for all of our actions, at all times, in all relationships. Such universal behavior would indeed "dislocate the color line."

ELAINE K. GINSBERG

West Virginia University
Morgantown

LYNN, RICHARD. 1996. *Dysgenics: Genetic Deterioration in Modern Populations.* Pp. ix, 239. Westport, CT: Praeger. $59.95.

Are the gene pools of modern Western nations deteriorating because individuals high on socially desirable traits such as intelligence and good character are being outreproduced by individuals low on such traits? Francis Galton and the other nineteenth-century eugenicists certainly thought so. Yet during the past half-century, "eugenics" has become a dirty word among the intellectually elite. Adolf Hitler undoubtedly had a hand in this, as does the fact that scores on intelligence tests seem to be rising, not falling as predicted.

Richard Lynn thinks that it is time to take a second look. In this short but scholarly book, he reviews the considerable demographic evidence that the less intelligent and responsible members of modern societies continue to have more children than their more intelligent and responsible peers. He also surveys the evidence from twin and adoption studies that individual differences in intelligence and conscientiousness are partly heritable. He concludes that dysgenic trends are still present in most Western societies; that they may be even more severe in societies just making the transition to modernism; and that they must always be viewed in a context of other simultaneously acting trends, such as improvement in nutrition or education, which may temporarily mask their very real effects.

Perhaps wisely, Lynn does not propose specific political solutions to the problems presented by dysgenic trends, deferring this topic to another book. He does, however, acknowledge and comment on many of the arguments and objections that have been raised on both sides.

In summary, this is a useful and readable book. Lynn presents lots of empirical evidence, brings in some interesting historical material, and argues his views effectively. He can sometimes overstate the quantitative strength of his case and can ignore a tortuous but logically possible counterargument here or there. But people who are concerned by the possibility of dysgenic trends should read it. Many people who do not put much stock in such trends should also take a look.

JOHN C. LOEHLIN

University of Texas
Austin

PETERSON DEL MAR, DAVID. 1996. *What Trouble I Have Seen: A History of Violence Against Wives.* Pp. xi, 244. Cambridge, MA: Harvard University Press. $39.95.

This study of wife abuse in Oregon, from the earliest white settlements in the mid-nineteenth century to the present, unites two of David Peterson del Mar's interests, first as volunteer counselor to battered women and second as historian. Oregon has a progressive reputation, its divorce laws having been liberalized well before women won the vote, its rate of violence low, its wife beaters always denounced by its establishment—indeed, briefly condemned, early in this century, to the whipping post. But Peterson del Mar uses this very reputation to underline his thesis. Husbands are led to assault wives, he argues, neither by social class position nor, in any simple sense, by biology. The culprit rather is culture, an American culture that embraces all of us, the apparently gentle as well as the overtly violent, so that "this book is a history of all Oregon men," indeed of all American men.

Many reasons for wife beating are apparently as timeless as jealousy or a generally angry disposition. But there are historical differences. In the early years, Oregon's frontiersmen used violence to defend patriarchy itself. The practice declined, Peterson del Mar believes, later in the nineteenth century, as Victorian ideals both encouraged the repression of anger and recognized a separate and theoretically equal women's sphere. However, beginning in the 1920s and certainly since the 1960s, an emphasis on consumerism, self-expression, marriage as fun, and rampant individualism generally has led to ever increasing violence.

Peterson del Mar uses a variety of cultural sources: novels, sermons, even the daily comics. For statistical evidence he relies on some 3500 divorce petitions, sources that provide much vivid detail but are, he admits, of less use in establishing real trends. The escalation in wife beating that he alleges over the past three generations runs counter to several national swings in spousal homicide, which has declined dramatically over the past 25 years. In addition, while Peterson del Mar presents his feminist case with *brio*, arguing that we need to reexamine some of the ideals of the 1960s, which once promised freedom but have led instead to a selfish flight from commitment, he is also prone to strong but dubious statements. A historian, faced with a line about "modern men's general lack of interest in child rearing," wants to know, compared to when? Finally, given the author's own long list of social, economic, and psychological factors that keep battered women from leaving home, it seems oversimple to suggest that fear of more violence is the biggest of them. *What Trouble I Have Seen* is, in short, a provocative addition to a new field, but it is hardly the last word.

ROGER LANE

Haverford College
Pennsylvania

QUINN, D. MICHAEL. 1996. *Same-Sex Dynamics Among Nineteenth-Century Americans: A Mormon Example.* Pp. x, 477. Champaign: University of Illinois Press. $29.95.

Social histories of modern homosexuality have centered on large cities—London, Paris, New York, San Francisco. For this reason, D. Michael Quinn's study of same-sex relationships in the hinterlands—specifically, in Mormon cultural regions such as Utah—is especially welcome. Quinn uses archival sources, census data, and interviews to show that social networks based on eroticism were present among Mormons early in the history of the Church of Jesus Christ of Latter-day Saints.

By the late nineteenth century, the Salt Lake Bohemian Club offered gay men and lesbians, many of them Mormons, opportunities for socializing, and it continued to do so for 50 years. The very first sociological study of American homosexuals, conducted early in this century, was of this community.

In nineteenth-century America, it was acceptable for two men or two women to hug and kiss in public, to live together, and even to share beds; these activities were not seen as sexual. Quinn argues that these relaxed gender norms, which the Mormons shared, allowed intimate sexual relationships to flourish unobtrusively. Even newspaper publicity failed to generate much outrage.

In recent decades, the Mormon hierarchy has strongly condemned homosexual relations, yet Quinn shows that in the nineteenth century, it was remarkably tolerant, treating masturbation, adultery, incest, and premarital heterosexual sex as much more serious. Even the homosexual rape of minors was treated with remarkable leniency. Only in the 1950s did the church toughen its stance toward homosexual relationships. Quinn speculates that in an atmosphere of virtual indifference, much homosexual activity took place without being recorded, because it was thought to be so ordinary and unremarkable.

Quinn's book is lengthened unnecessarily by a long introductory defense of the normalcy of homosexuality. Discussion of topics unrelated to nineteenth-century Mormonism, such as New Guinea initiation rituals and marriages between women among certain African peoples, could have been dropped without loss.

At times, Quinn might have been more skeptical of other scholars. He reports John Boswell's claims that the early

Christian Church performed same-sex marriages, seemingly unaware of the serious criticism this claim has drawn. In writing that "the concept of homosexuality as a state of being or personal identity did not even exist in European-American culture until the late nineteenth century," he overstates Foucault's contention and ignores recent scholarship that calls the claim into question. Notwithstanding these quibbles, *Same-Sex Dynamics* should be heralded as a major contribution to the history of same-sex eroticism.

DAVID F. GREENBERG

New York University
New York City

RANSOM, JOHN S. 1997. *Foucault's Discipline: The Politics of Subjectivity.* Pp. xi, 225. Durham, NC: Duke University Press. $49.95. Paperbound, $16.95.

John Ransom's book is rooted firmly in the school of Foucault scholarship, which holds that the French thinker had something to say that deserves serious consideration. The writers in this school are not all apologists for Foucault; and whether they see his writings as a contribution to be accepted or as a challenge to be overcome, the dialogue between them serves as a contribution to clarifying his thought.

As a part of this dialogue, Ransom's work accomplishes the two things offered within the framework of that ongoing dialogue: helping the reader to a better understanding of Foucault and advancing the dialogue about the value of his work for contemporary social and political thought.

The present book's greatest strength is in the fact that it does both simultaneously and without becoming so technical as to lose the novice or oversimplified in a way that would lose those more familiar with the terrain of Foucault scholarship. Ransom effectively takes on the most serious of the critics, such as Charles Taylor and Thomas McCarthy, by being faithful to Foucault's whole corpus, by keeping key principles of Foucault's work in the forefront of his writing. What Ransom never forgets, what he never lets his interlocutors forget, is Foucault's insistence on certain principles such as the productive capacity of power as opposed to the generally assumed oppressive or coercive nature of power. As Foucault did, he insists on the relational nature of power and knowledge as opposed to their identity. He is brilliant in situating Foucault within the traditions of enlightenment critique and classical liberalism and the latter's subsequent development; he is equally adept at identifying points of departure.

There is a trick to reading and understanding Foucault that Ransom uses well and that is essential to avoiding the traps that have lured many commentators and have dissuaded many potential readers. Ransom largely ignores some of Foucault's earlier, albeit major works. *The Archaeology of Knowledge* and *The Order of Things*, which have been read as structuralist in their sympathies if not their actual content, play no significant role here. While this could be read as a sympathetic move to render Foucault in a more positive light, it is just as consistent with Foucault's own subsequent statements about those works as all of Ransom's writing is consistent with Foucault's own words.

DAVID J. McMENAMIN

Boston College
Chestnut Hill
Massachusetts

ROSE, PETER I. 1997. *Tempest-Tost: Race, Immigration, and the Dilemmas of Diversity*. Pp. xiv, 257. New York: Oxford University Press. $30.00.

In *Tempest-Tost*, Peter Rose distills 40 years of teaching and research on race, ethnicity, and international migration. Few readers will finish this book without feeling humbled by the breadth of Rose's expertise. He is as adept at analyzing the provision of social services to Southeast Asian refugees as he is in explaining the origins of contemporary nativism.

Yet *Tempest-Tost* is anything but overwhelming. Rose has a unique writing style that gives a reader the impression of being part of a conversation. In some chapters, the reader is participating in a public forum on a controversial topic like relations between blacks and Jews. In others, one is a traveling companion during fieldwork in a Southeast Asian refugee camp. Still other chapters treat the reader as a personal friend to whom the author reveals how his family life shaped his views of diversity. Thus, while the book is a collection of previously published articles, book chapters, and book reviews, the variety of readings make it more accessible than many a monotone monograph.

Rose's understanding of diversity is rooted in Simmel's work on the stranger and Park's concept of marginality. These ideas have never been as central to sociology as have the concepts alienation (Marx) and anomie (Durkheim). But Rose skillfully weaves the themes of exile and ambivalent identity throughout the book to spotlight the dilemmas of diversity.

The primary dilemma for Rose is a sense of marginality by almost all racial and ethnic groups, albeit to varying degrees. This paradox is both old and new. Unlike the nation-states of Western Europe, the United States has a continuously evolving civic culture in which the positions and identities of racial and ethnic groups change over time. Contempo-

rary public policy on race and ethnicity has only compounded the multiple meanings of American pluralism. The result is a diversity Rorschach test: members of any group can present themselves as outsiders in some context, while others perceive them as insiders in a different context.

This dilemma is painfully evident in President Clinton's current forums on race relations. Most participants can identify something that makes them feel marginal: the existence of affirmative action, the retreat from affirmative action, or a black-white discussion of affirmative action that excludes Asians and Hispanics. All of these voices can be found in *Tempest-Tost*.

JEREMY HEIN

University of Wisconsin
Eau Claire

ECONOMICS

BERK, GERALD. 1997. *Alternative Tracks: The Constitution of American Industrial Order, 1865-1917*. Pp. xi, 243. Baltimore, MD: Johns Hopkins University Press. $15.95.

This is a very intelligent and important book about an uncommon subject: an alternative mode of corporate organization (regional and diversified rather than national and specialized) that existed and, in a limited sphere, flourished in the late nineteenth century but failed in the early twentieth. It failed, Gerald Berk argues, not because of "natural" (market-driven) economic processes but largely for political reasons. Despite strong ideological roots in nineteenth-century republicanism, a few congressional advocates, and some early support from the Interstate Commerce Commission, it fell victim to more powerful political institutions (the federal judiciary) that nurtured national railroad organization and to finance capital, its own position a political artifact in no small measure and its principles intimately bound up in the national market project of the judiciary.

This is a fascinating story, and it goes against the grain of Alfred Chandler's inexorable (and virtually politics-free) national corporate triumph. It even differs from recent labor and social movement history and the new institutionalism. The latter is often in thrall to modernization theory and the former tantalizes us with what-ifs (What if the Knights of Labor had lasted, the Populists had won?) but usually sees the ultimate triumph of national corporate capitalism as a foregone conclusion. Berk sees more contingency, and even believes that the 1990s present us with a new "constitutive moment" when corporate liberalism (read: nationally organized, hierarchical, monopolistic, or oligopolistic managerial capitalism) is vulnerable and might again be challenged by a new "moral order" featuring regional self-sufficiency and vitality, more competition, and smaller-scale corporate organization. Berk clearly sees more contingency in the current political era than seems plausible, but his point is that the form of corporate organization that prevailed in the late nineteenth century was politically constituted and can be politically reconstituted. It was about as natural as Polanyi's market economy.

Berk's approach resonates with much of contemporary political economy and new institutional work but is critical of both. The political economists (this reviewer included) come in for particularly harsh criticism for relying too much on economic interests. Like intellectual historians, Berk feels strongly that ideas matter and that they are largely autonomous from economic interests. People who championed the "regional republican" alternative come in for a good deal of attention. Who were these men of ideas?

A. B. Stickney, president of the Chicago Great Western Railway; Senator James Wilson of Iowa; and Thomas M. Cooley, first chairman of the Interstate Commerce Commission. This is a very short list for a presumably viable alternative. The political economist might point out that all three were midwesterners and that the Midwest was probably the only region that could sustain and would be expected to argue for a decentralized, diverse, small-to-medium-sized-firm-centered economy and regulatory apparatus. The other advocates of federal railroad regulation in the gilded age, and for decades thereafter, had different economic interests. Westerners benefited from the low long-haul rates of the "corporate-liberal" system, as well as from the Republican tariff, which kept them quieter than one would expect on issues of corporate regulation. The South, quite unlike the Midwest, had very little industry and was probably resigned to its agrarian status. For these two regions (which together furnished the large majority of regulation advocates), a national regulatory framework that could keep bulk freight rates low and (thereby) effect some regional redistribution from northeastern corporate coffers back to primary producers was the best that could be hoped for.

While regional decentralization, therefore, may have been a plausible alternative, it lacked precisely the resource that Berk considers determinate: a political constituency. Moreover, while the alternative is labeled "republican," it should be noted that its construction and maintenance relied on a far-seeing, highly discretionary, expert bureaucracy—an institution whose support was largely limited to the Midwest and a few intellectuals. Most agrarian champions of railroad regulation were hostile to bureaucracy; their regulatory proposals relied on virtually self-enforcing, punitive statutes. The ideal bureaucracy may have existed for a few years under Cooley, but southern and western agrarians were highly skeptical that an agency independent of northeastern railroads and finance capital could be maintained for any length of time, especially if Republican presidents were making the appointments.

It was, after all, those same Republican presidents, beginning with nationalist (and railroad lawyer) Abe Lincoln, who appointed the federal judges who, in an audacious doctrinal coup, began to use the receivership process to reconstruct national railroad systems just at the moment when "natural" economic processes were throwing them into bankruptcy and probably dismemberment. (This account is the most intriguing section of Berk's book.)

How do we explain the emerging pro-corporate capitalist ideology of the federal judiciary in the gilded age? We so-called reductionist political economists would probably point to the appointment process, the life term, the elite recruitment pool, the link to presidents and parties, and their links to advanced northeastern capital. These interests and institutions were hard to beat. They had judicial review, the Senate, and the presidency. Against them, a handful of regional Republicans, themselves isolated even in Congress, did not have much of a chance. Berk's story would be more interesting if he had spent more time on the conflict of these ideological positions inside and between institutions and on probing where the alternative ideas came from and how their partisans built their supporting coalitions in government and society. Such an exploration could well have replaced some of the wishful thinking in the last two chapters.

ELIZABETH SANDERS

Cornell University
Ithaca
New York

OTHER BOOKS

ABOUD, FRANCES E. 1998. *Health Psychology in Global Perspective.* Pp. xiii, 326. Thousand Oaks, CA: Sage. $29.50.

AGAMBEN, GIORGIO. 1998. *Homo Sacer: Sovereign Power and Bare Life.* Pp. viii, 199. Stanford, CA: Stanford University Press. $45.00. Paperbound, $16.95.

AKERMAN, NORDAL. 1998. *The Necessity of Friction.* Pp. viii, 320. Boulder, CO: Westview Press. Paperbound, $24.00.

ALLOTT, MARGARET and MARTIN ROBB, eds. 1998. *Understanding Health and Social Care.* Pp. ix, 318. Thousand Oaks, CA: Sage. $68.00. Paperbound, $27.50.

ALVAREZ, SONIA E., EVELINA DAGNINO, and ARTURO ESCOBAR, eds. 1998. *Cultures of Politics / Politics of Cultures: Revisioning Latin American Social Movements.* Pp. xiii, 459. Boulder, CO: Westview Press. $70.00. Paperbound, $25.00.

BARBERA, HENRY. 1998. *The Military Factor in Social Change: From Provincial to Political Society.* Pp. x, 246. New Brunswick, NJ: Transaction. No price.

BARRY, JOHN M. 1998. *Rising Tide: The Great Mississippi Flood of 1927 and How It Changed America.* Pp. 524. New York: Touchstone Books. Paperbound, $15.00.

BAYER, BETTY M. and JOHN SHOTTER, eds. 1997. *Reconstructing the Psychological Subject: Bodies, Practices and Technologies.* Pp. viii, 234. Thousand Oaks, CA: Sage. $75.00. Paperbound, $32.00.

BOX, RICHARD C. 1998. *Citizen Governance: Leading American Communities into the 21st Century.* Pp. xiv, 186. Thousand Oaks, CA: Sage. $44.00. Paperbound, $21.95.

BROUWER, STEVE. 1998. *Sharing the Pie: A Citizen's Guide to Wealth and Power in America.* Pp. vi, 180. New York: Owl Books. Paperbound, $12.95.

BUCHANAN, BRUCE. 1996. *Renewing Presidential Politics: Campaigns, Media, and the Public Interest.* Pp. xxi, 207. Lanham, MD: Rowman & Littlefield. Paperbound, no price.

BURNETT, STANTON H. and LUCA MANTOVANI. 1998. *The Italian Guillotine: Operation Clean Hands and the Overthrow of Italy's First Republic.* Pp. xii, 331. Lanham, MD: Rowman & Littlefield. $62.00. Paperbound, $22.95.

CHANG, MARIA HSIA. 1998. *The Labors of Sisyphus: The Economic Development of Communist China.* Pp. x, 259. New Brunswick, NJ: Transaction. $39.95.

CHRISTOPHER, WARREN. 1998. *In the Stream of History: Shaping Foreign Policy for a New Era.* Pp. xvii, 586. Stanford, CA: Stanford University Press. $60.00. Paperbound, $22.95.

CLARK, ARTHUR J. 1998. *Defense Mechanisms in the Counseling Process.* Pp. xvi, 254. Thousand Oaks, CA: Sage. Paperbound, $23.50.

CLAWSON, PATRICK L. and RENSSELAER W. LEE III. 1998. *The Andean Cocaine Industry.* Pp. xii, 292. New York: St. Martin's Press. Paperbound, $16.95.

COHEN, JODI R. 1998. *Communication Criticism: Developing Your Critical Powers.* Pp. xiv, 220. Thousand Oaks, CA: Sage. Paperbound, $24.50.

COLAMERY, S. N. 1998. *Affirmative Action: Catalyst or Albatross?.* Pp. 331. Commack, NY: Nova Science. $59.00.

COLLIER, KENNETH E. 1997. *Between the Branches: The White House Office of Legislative Affairs.* Pp. xii, 330. Pittsburgh, PA: University of Pittsburgh Press. $50.00. Paperbound, $22.95.

COOMBS, ROBERT HOLMAN. 1998. *Surviving Medical School.* Pp. ix, 196. Thousand Oaks, CA: Sage. Paperbound, $23.50.

COPPENRATH, ROBERT A. M. 1997. *The Leadership Luxation: Anointed Scorpions, Spiders, and Rats.* Pp. 186. Pittsburgh, PA: Dorrance. $17.00.

CORRIGAN, PETER. 1997. *The Sociology of Consumption.* Pp. viii, 197. Thousand Oaks, CA: Sage. Paperbound, $24.95.

CORTRIGHT, DAVID, ed. 1997. *The Price of Peace: Incentives and International Conflict Prevention.* Pp. xiv, 347. Lanham, MD: Rowman & Littlefield. $65.00. Paperbound, $24.95.

CROLY, HERBERT. 1998. *Progressive Democracy.* Pp. li, 438. New Brunswick, NJ: Transaction. Paperbound, $29.95.

DAVIS, DAVID HOWARD. 1998. *American Environmental Politics.* Pp. xiii, 256. Chicago: Nelson-Hall. Paperbound, $28.95.

DAYNES, BYRON W., WILLIAM D. PEDERSON, and MICHAEL P. RICCARDS, eds. 1998. *The New Deal and Public Policy.* Pp. x, 293. New York: St. Martin's Press. $49.95.

DENNIS, EVERETT E. and ROBERT W. SNYDER, eds. 1998. *Media and Democracy.* Pp. xix, 202. New Brunswick, NJ: Transaction. Paperbound, 24.95.

DIANU, TIBERIU. 1997. *Non-Custodial Sanctions: Alternative Models for Post-Communist Societies.* Pp. xviii, 195. Commack, NY: Nova Science. $49.00.

DOORNBOS, MARTIN and SUDIPTA KAVIRAJ, eds. 1997. *Dynamics of State Formation: India and Europe Compared.* Pp. 441. New Delhi: Sage India. $36.00.

DRAKE, PAUL W. and MATHEW D. McCUBBINS, eds. 1998. *The Origins of Liberty: Political and Economic Liberalization in the Modern World.* Pp. xi, 205. Princeton, NJ: Princeton University Press. $55.00. Paperbound, $17.95.

DUCK, STEVE. 1998. *Human Relationships.* 3d ed. Pp. xi, 250. Thousand Oaks, CA: Sage. Paperbound, $24.95.

ELAINE, SHARON. 1997. *The Book of Affirmations.* Pp. xxiii, 252. Commack, NY: Kroshka Books. Paperbound, $18.95.

FRIED, AMY. 1997. *Muffled Echoes: Oliver North and the Politics of Public Opinion.* Pp. xii, 308. New York: Columbia University Press. $49.50. Paperbound, $19.50.

GILBERT, PAUL. 1998. *The Philosophy of Nationalism.* Pp. vii, 205. Boulder, CO: Westview Press. $59.00. Paperbound, $19.50.

HARRE, ROM. 1998. *The Singular Self: An Introduction to the Psychology of Personhood.* Pp. x, 192. Thousand Oaks, CA: Sage. Paperbound, $24.95.

HARRINGTON, WALT. 1997. *Intimate Journalism: The Art and Craft of Reporting Everyday Life.* Pp. xlvi, 325. Thousand Oaks, CA: Sage. $56.00. Paperbound, $26.95.

HASLAM, S. ALEXANDER and CRAIG McGARTY. 1998. *Doing Psychology: An Introduction to Research Methodology and Statistics.* Pp. xiii, 297. Thousand Oaks, CA: Sage. Paperbound, $28.50.

HASSARD, JOHN and RUTH HOLLIDAY, eds. 1998. *Organization Representation: Work and Organizations in Popular Culture.* Pp. x, 271. Thousand Oaks, CA: Sage. Paperbound, $26.50.

HAZARIKA, ANJALI. 1997. *Daring to Dream: Cultivating Corporate Creativity Through Dreamwork.* Pp. 207. New Delhi: Sage India. Paperbound, $17.95.

HILLSTROM, KEVIN and LAURIE COLLIER HILLSTROM. 1998. *The Vietnam Experience: A Concise Encyclopedia of American Literature, Songs, and Films.* Pp. xiii, 322. Westport, CT: Greenwood Press. $65.00.

HUANG, YASHENG. 1996. *Inflation and Investment Controls in China: The Political Economy of Central-Local Relations During the Reform Era.* Pp. xviii, 371. New York: Cambridge University Press. $59.95.

HUBAND, MARK. 1998. *Warriors of the Prophet: The Struggle for Islam.* Pp. xix, 188. Boulder, CO: Westview Press. $25.00.

HUTCHINSON, EARL OFARI. 1996. *Betrayed: A History of Presidential Failure to Protect Black Lives.* Pp. x, 262. Boulder, CO: Westview Press. No price.

HYDE, ALAN. 1997. *Bodies of Law.* Pp. xii, 278. Princeton, NJ: Princeton University Press. $49.95. Paperbound, $16.95.

KAMERMAN, SHEILA B. and ALFRED J. KAHN, eds. 1998. *Family Change and Family Policies in Great Britain, Canada, New Zealand and the United States.* Pp. xi, 463. New York: Oxford University Press. $95.00.

KANET, ROGER E., ed. 1998. *Resolving Regional Conflicts.* Pp. x, 257. Champaign: University of Illinois Press. $39.95. Paperbound, $21.95.

KAPUR, MALAVIKA. 1997. *Mental Health in Indian Schools.* Pp. 168. New Delhi: Sage India. $26.00.

KELLY, PHILIP, ed. 1998. *Assessing Democracy in Latin America.* Pp. xii, 329. Boulder, CO: Westview Press. No price.

KELSEY, SEAN. 1997. *Inventing a Republic: The Political Culture of the English Commonwealth, 1649-1653.* Pp. x, 254. Stanford, CA: Stanford University Press. $49.50.

KISHLANSKY, MARK. 1996. *A Monarchy Transformed: Britain 1603-1714.* Pp. xiii, 386. New York: Penguin. $29.95.

KLEIN, DANIEL B. 1998. *Three Libertarian Essays.* Pp. v, 89. Irvington-on-Hudson, NY: Foundation for Economic Education. Paperbound, $8.50.

KREML, WILLIAM P. 1997. *America's Middle Class: From Subsidy to Abandonment.* Pp. xviii, 225. Durham, NC: Carolina Academic Press. Paperbound, $22.50.

KRISLOV, SAMUEL. 1997. *How Nations Choose Product Standards and Standards Change Nations.* Pp. viii, 264. Pittsburgh, PA: University of Pittsburgh Press. $45.00. Paperbound, $19.95.

KUIK, O. J., M. V. NADKARNI, F. H. OOSTERHUIS, G. S. SASTRY, and A. E. AKKERMAN. 1997. *Pollution Control in the South and North: A Comparative Assessment of Environmental Policy Approaches in India and the Netherlands.* Pp. 253. New Delhi: Sage India. $38.00.

LEVIN, BRUCE LUBOTSKY, ANDREA K. BLANCH, and ANN JENNINGS, eds. 1998. *Women's Mental Health Services: A Public Health Perspective.* Pp. xix, 428. Thousand Oaks, CA: Sage. Paperbound, no price.

LINOWES, DAVID F. 1998. *Creating Public Policy: The Chairman's Memoirs of Four Presidential Commissions.* Pp. x, 232. Westport, CT: Praeger. $59.95.

LYNTON, ROLF P. 1998. *Social Science in Actual Practice: Themes on My Blue Guitar.* Pp. 314. Thousand Oaks, CA: Sage. $38.00. Paperbound, $17.95.

MABEY, CHRISTOPHER, DENISE SKINNER, and TIMOTHY CLARK, eds. 1998. *Experiencing Human Resource Management.* Pp. xiv, 256. Thousand Oaks, CA: Sage. Paperbound, $27.95.

MARES, DAVID R., ed. 1998. *Civil-Military Relations: Building Democracy and Regional Security in Latin America, Southern Asia, and Central Europe.* Pp. xiii, 274. Boulder, CO: Westview Press. $69.00.

McCARTHY, E. DOYLE. 1997. *Knowledge as Culture: The New Sociology of Knowledge.* Pp. vii, 130. New York:

Routledge. $65.00. Paperbound, $16.95.

MELZER, ARTHUR M., JERRY WEINBERGER, and M. RICHARD ZINMAN, eds. 1998. *Multiculturalism and American Democracy.* Pp. viii, 237. Lawrence: University Press of Kansas. $40.00. Paperbound, $17.95.

METTENHEIM, KURT VON. 1995. *The Brazilian Voter: Mass Politics in Democratic Transition, 1974-1986.* Pp. xii, 295. Pittsburgh, PA: University of Pittsburgh Press. $49.95.

MEYER, DAVID S. and SIDNEY TARROW, eds. 1997. *The Social Movement Society: Contentious Politics for a New Century.* Pp. ix, 282. Lanham, MD: Rowman & Littlefield. $65.00. Paperbound, $22.95.

MICHALOS, ALEX C. 1995. *A Pragmatic Approach to Business Ethics.* Pp. 282. Thousand Oaks, CA: Sage. Paperbound, $19.95.

MONTGOMERY, JOHN D., ed. 1997. *Values in Education: Social Capital Formation in Asia and the Pacific.* Pp. x, 199. Hollis, NH: Hollis. $29.95.

MORIAKI, TSUCHIYA and KONOMI YOSHINOBU. 1997. *Shaping the Future of Japanese Management: New Leadership to Overcome the Impending Crisis.* Pp. xiv, 247. Tokyo: LTCB International Library Foundation. No price.

MOSS, JEREMY, ed. 1998. *The Later Foucault.* Pp. x, 201. Thousand Oaks, CA: Sage. $66.00. Paperbound, $22.95.

OCHIAI, EMIKO. 1997. *The Japanese Family System in Transition: A Sociological Analysis of Family Change in Postwar Japan.* Pp. xii, 197. Tokyo: LTCB International Library Foundation. No price.

PARK, GEORGE. 1998. *The Marke of Power: Helgeland and the Politics of Omnipotence.* Pp. 336. St. John's, Newfoundland: Institute of Social and Economic Research. Paperbound, no price.

PARSE, ROSEMARIE RIZZO. 1998. *The Human Becoming School of Thought: A Perspective for Nurses and Other Health Professionals.* Pp. xiv, 130. Thousand Oaks, CA: Sage. Paperbound, $24.50.

PEREZ-LOPEZ, JORGE F., ed. 1998. *Cuban Studies.* Vol. 27. Pp. viii, 350. Pittsburgh, PA: University of Pittsburgh Press. $40.00.

POLLOCK, JOYCELYN M. 1998. *Counseling Women in Prison.* Pp. ix, 217. Thousand Oaks, CA: Sage. Paperbound, $21.00.

POWER, J. GERARD and THERESA BYRD. 1998. *U.S.-Mexico Border Health: Issues for Regional and Migrant Populations.* Pp. xviii, 278. Thousand Oaks, CA: Sage. $23.50.

RAJAN, NALINI. 1998. *Secularism, Democracy, Justice: Implications of Rawlsian Principles in India.* Pp. 220. New Delhi: Sage India. $28.00.

RIKER, WILLIAM H. 1996. *The Strategy of Rhetoric: Campaigning for the American Constitution.* Pp. xv, 283. New Haven, CT: Yale University Press. No price.

ROBINSON, EVA CHEUNG. 1998. *Greening at the Grassroots: Alternative Forestry Strategies in India.* Pp. 144. New Delhi: Sage India. $26.50.

SABERWAL, SATISH and HEIKO SIEVERS, eds. 1998. *Rules, Laws, Constitutions.* Pp. 289. New Delhi: Sage India. $35.00.

SCHULZ, DONALD E., ed. 1998. *Conference Report: The Role of the Armed Forces in the Americas: Civil-Military Relations for the 21st Century.* Pp. xvii, 187. Carlisle Barracks, PA: Strategic Studies Institute. Paperbound, no price.

SEKHAR, R. C. 1997. *Ethical Choices in Business.* Pp. 265. New Delhi: Sage India. $39.95.

SHUKLA, SURESHCHANDRA and REKHA KAUL, eds. 1998. *Education, Development and Underdevelopment.* Pp. 308. New Delhi: Sage India. $39.95.

SICKLES, WILLIAM R. 1997. *Natural History of the Mind: New Views on the Relatedness of Life.* Pp. 354. Commack, NY: Nova Science. $34.00.

SIMON, JULIAN L., ed. 1998. *The Economics of Population: Classic Writings.* Pp. xxiii, 235. New Brunswick, NJ: Transaction. $34.95.

SINGH, RAJENDRA, ed. 1998. *The Native Speaker: Multilingual Perspectives.* Pp. 226. New Delhi: Sage India. $34.95.

SOLOMON, GERALD B. 1998. *The NATO Enlargement Debate, 1990-1997: Blessings of Liberty.* Pp. x, 189. Westport, CT: Praeger. Paperbound, no price.

SPARKS, COLIN. 1998. *Communism, Capitalism and the Mass Media.* Pp. xix, 214. Thousand Oaks, CA: Sage. Paperbound, $26.50.

STARR, RICHARD F., ed. 1998. *Transition to Democracy in Poland.* 2d ed. Pp. xxi, 298. New York: St. Martin's Press. $49.95.

SUE, DERALD WING, ROBERT T. CARTER, J. MANUEL CASAS, NADYA A. FOUAD, ALLEN E. IVEY, MARGARET JENSEN, TERESA LaFROMBOISE, JEANNE E. MANESE, JOSEPH G. PONTEROTTO, and ENA VAZQUEZ-NUTALL. 1998. *Multicultural Counseling Competencies: Individual and Organizational Development.* Pp. xiv, 161. Thousand Oaks, CA: Sage. Paperbound, no price.

SUGRUE, THOMAS J. 1997. *The Origins of the Urban Crisis: Race and Inequality in Postwar Detroit.* Pp. xviii, 375. Princeton, NJ: Princeton University Press. $35.00.

TAMBIAH, STANLEY J. 1996. *Leveling Crowds: Ethnonationalist Conflicts and Collective Violence in South Asia.* Pp. x, 395. Berkeley: University of California Press. Paperbound, no price.

TIAN, XIAOWEN. 1998. *Dynamics of Development in an Opening Economy: China Since 1978.* Pp. xiv, 298. Commack, NY: Nova Science. $69.00.

TREFOUSSE, HANS L. 1997. *Thaddeus Stevens: Nineteenth-Century Egalitarian.* Pp. xiii, 312. Chapel Hill: University of North Carolina Press. $39.95.

VAN KLEY, DALE K. 1996. *The Religious Origins of the French Revolution: From Calvin to the Civil Constitution, 1560-1791.* Pp. x, 390. New Haven, CT: Yale University Press. No price.

VOGEL, EZRA F., ed. 1997. *Living with China: United States–China Relations in the Twenty-First Century.* Pp. 336. New York: Norton. Paperbound, $18.00.

WEINER, EUGENE, ed. 1998. *The Handbook of Interethnic Coexistence.* Pp. 653. New York: Continuum. No price.

WILSON, BRADFORD P. and KEN MASUGI, eds. 1997. *The Supreme Court and American Constitutionalism.* Pp. viii, 298. Lanham, MD: Rowman & Littlefield. $68.00. Paperbound, $23.95.

WODAK, RUTH, ed. 1997. *Gender and Discourse.* Pp. ix, 303. Thousand Oaks, CA: Sage. Paperbound, $27.95.

ZHANG, XING QUAN. 1998. *Privatisation: A Study of Housing Policy in Urban China.* Pp. xiv, 188. Commack, NY: Nova Science. $49.00.

ZUCKERT, MICHAEL P. 1994. *Natural Rights and the New Republicanism.* Pp. xx, 397. Princeton, NJ: Princeton University Press. Paperbound, $18.95.

ZURBRUGG, NICHOLAS, ed. 1997. *Jean Baudrillard, Art and Artefact*. Pp. viii, 184. Thousand Oaks, CA: Sage. Paperbound, $26.50.

INDEX

STATEMENT OF OWNERSHIP, MANAGEMENT, AND CIRCULATION
P.S. Form 3526 Facsimile

1. TITLE: THE ANNALS OF THE AMERICAN ACADEMY OF POLITICAL AND SOCIAL SCIENCE
2. USPS PUB. #: 026-060

3. DATE OF FILING: October 1, 1998

4. FREQUENCY OF ISSUE: Bi-Monthly
5. NO. OF ISSUES ANNUALLY: 6
6. ANNUAL SUBSCRIPTION PRICE: Paper-Bound Institution $292; Cloth-Bound Institution $332; Paper-Bound Individual $59; Cloth-Bound Individual $86

7. PUBLISHER ADDRESS: 2455 Teller Road, Thousand Oaks, CA 91320
CONTACT PERSON: Geane Dvorak, Circulation
TELEPHONE: (805) 499-0721

8. HEADQUARTERS ADDRESS: 2455 Teller Road, Thousand Oaks, CA 91320

9. PUBLISHER: Sara Miller McCune, 2979 Eucalyptus Hill Road, Montecito, CA 93108
EDITOR: Dr. Alan W. Heston, The American Academy of Political and Social Science, 3937 Chestnut Street, Philadelphia, PA 19104
MANAGING EDITOR: Erica Ginsburg, The American Academy of Political and Social Science, 3937 Chestnut Street, Philadelphia, PA 19104

10. OWNER: The American Academy of Political and Social Science, 3937 Chestnut Street, Philadelphia, PA 19104

11. KNOWN BONDHOLDERS, ETC.
None

12. NONPROFIT PURPOSE, FUNCTION, STATUS:
Has Not Changed During Preceding 12 Months

13. PUBLICATION NAME: THE ANNALS OF THE AMERICAN ACADEMY OF POLITICAL AND SOCIAL SCIENCE

14. ISSUE FOR CIRCULATION DATA BELOW: JULY 1998

15. EXTENT & NATURE OF CIRCULATION:

	AVG. NO. COPIES EACH ISSUE DURING PRECEDING 12 MONTHS	ACT. NO. COPIES OF SINGLE ISSUE PUB. NEAREST TO FILING DATE
A. TOTAL NO. COPIES	4458	4300
B. PAID CIRCULATION		
1. SALES THROUGH DEALERS, ETC.	720	534
2. MAIL SUBSCRIPTION	2466	2922
C. TOTAL PAID CIRCULATION	3186	3456
D. FREE DISTRIBUTION BY MAIL	178	177
E. FREE DISTRIBUTION OTHER	0	0
F. TOTAL FREE DISTRIBUTION	178	177
G. TOTAL DISTRIBUTION	3364	3633
H. COPIES NOT DISTRIBUTED		
1. OFFICE USE, ETC.	1095	667
2. RETURN FROM NEWS AGENTS	0	0
I. TOTAL	4459	4300
PERCENT PAID CIRCULATION	95%	95%

16. NOT REQUIRED TO PUBLISH.

17. I CERTIFY THAT ALL INFORMATION FURNISHED ON THIS FORM IS TRUE AND COMPLETE. I UNDERSTAND THAT ANYONE WHO FURNISHES FALSE OR MISLEADING INFORMATION ON THIS FORM OR WHO OMITS MATERIAL OR INFORMATION REQUESTED ON THE FORM MAY BE SUBJECT TO CRIMINAL SANCTIONS (INCLUDING FINES AND IMPRISONMENT) AND/OR CIVIL SANCTIONS (INCLUDING MULTIPLE DAMAGES AND CIVIL PENALTIES).

Geane Dvorak   10-1-98

Geane Dvorak   Date
Circulation Manager
Sage Publications, Inc.

American Behavioral Scientist

CHANGING FORMS OF PAYMENT

Guest Editor: Viviana Zelizer, *Princeton University*

Popular views of monetization raise three questions impelling social science research. Are there forms of social relations which are incompatible with money exchange? Does monetization inevitably transform the quality of social life? What are the causes and consequences of different types of monetary transfers?

The August 1998 issue of **American Behavioral Scientist**, *Changing Forms of Payment*, examines and answers these questions while raising others about the social role of money in contemporary life. Guest editor Viviana Zelizer of Princeton University has skillfully compiled the interdisciplinary perspectives of the five scholars featured in this volume, contributing to the analysis of payments and to the rethinking of the economic process.

In "Money, Meaning, and Morality," Carruthers and Espeland discuss the variable cultural meanings of money, proposing a research agenda to uncover those meanings by identifying a grid of monetary transactions.

At a time when multiple European currencies may soon merge into the nationless euro, Eric Helleiner's "National Currencies and National Identities," provides us with a compelling historical demonstration of how national currencies have served as vital markers and creators of national identity, from powerful symbolic nationalist imagery to a means of shared communication.

Reva Siegel's "Valuing Housework: Nineteenth-Century Anxieties About the Commodification of Household Labor" takes us into the contested economies of nineteenth-century households; focusing on public and legal debates over household labor.

The final two pieces, commentaries by Christopher Tomlins and Julie A. Nelson, further advance the debates presented in this issue.

Changing Forms of Payment is a must for every scholar interested in modern monetization and its evolving effect on social behavior.

Contents: Introduction: How People Talk About Money / Money, Meaning, and Morality / National Currencies and National Identities / Valuing Housework: Nineteenth-Century Anxieties About the Commodifidaition of Domestic Labor / Loose Change: Making Money Through History / One Sphere or Two?

Order Today!
Phone: 805-499-9774 ■ Fax: 805-499-0871
E-mail: order@sagepub.com

American Behavioral Scientist
Volume 41, Number 10 / August 1998
Individual: $11.00 / Institution: $50.00

SAGE PUBLICATIONS, INC.
2455 Teller Road
Thousand Oaks, CA 91320

SAGE PUBLICATIONS LTD
6 Bonhill Street
London EC2A 4PU, England

SAGE PUBLICATIONS INDIA PVT. LTD
M-32 Market, Greater Kailash I
New Delhi 110 048, India

WOMEN IN LATIN AMERICA

Editor: Sheryl L. Lutjens, *Northern Arizona University*

It is clear that the increased recognition and inclusion in the developmental and humanitarian work of international organizations has not translated into economic, political, or social equality for women. The recent International Conference on Population and Development held in Cairo provided a backdrop for acknowledging how multiple feminist perspectives have defined and redefined the problems of women in general, and Third World and Latin American women in particular.

Feminists argue that the methodology used to study women must change. Traditionally the role of women has been defined by social and political theory, enforced by the historically and culturally rooted conceptions of the proper places of women and men in social life, and constrained by the structural dynamics of global and domestic economies. Women's issues are an integral part of theoretical and practical issues of Latin American politics and development.

Contemporary realities underscore the perils of ignoring women. In this Special Issue, case studies and essays explore general patterns in the experiences of Latin American women in the 1980's and 1990's, and show the structural shifts in the global economy, women's responses, and the enduring issues of women and power in Latin America.

Contents:
Part 1: The Urban Family and Poverty in Latin America / Economic Restructuring and Gender Subordination / Planned Developemnt and Women's Relative Power: Steel and Forestry in Venezuela / Gender, Class, and Water: Women and the Politics of Water Sevice in Monterrey, Mexico / Reading Between the Lines: Women, the State, and Rectification in Cuba

Part 2: Women in Argentina During the 1960's / After the Revolution: Neoliberal Policy and Gender in Nicaragua / The Disruptions of Adjustment: Women in Nicaragua / The Mother of the Nicaraguans: Doña Violeta and the UNO's Gender Agenda / The Sociodemographic and Reproductive Characteristics of Cuban Women / The Color of Love: Young Interracial Couples in Cuba / Modernization, Adjustment, and Peasant Production: A Gender Analysis / Constructing and Negotiating Gender in Women's Police Stations in Brazil

Latin American Perspectives
Part 1:Volume 22, Number 2 / Spring 1995
Part 2: Volume 23, Number 1 / Winter 1996
Individual $11 / Institution $51

Order Today!
Phonee: 805-499-9774 • Fax: 805-499-0871
E-mail: order@sagepub.com

SAGE PUBLICATIONS, INC.
2455 Teller Road
Thousand Oaks, CA 91320

SAGE PUBLICATIONS LTD
6 Bonhill Street
London EC2A 4PU, England

SAGE PUBLICATIONS INDIA PVT. LTD
M-32 Market, Greater Kailash I
New Delhi 110 048, India

A Special Issue of
Gender & Society

GENDER AND SOCIAL MOVEMENTS, Part I

Editor
Verta Taylor, *Smith College* and
Nancy E. Whittier, *Ohio State University*

Contents

Gender & Society
Volume 12, Number 6 /
December 1998
Single issue: Individual $13 /
Institution $43